The Gardener's Guide to Growing
IVIES

The Gardener's Guide to Growing
IVIES

Peter Q. Rose

TIMBER PRESS
Portland, Oregon

To Olive, my wife, 1915–1993.

NOTE Throughout the book the time of year is given as a season to make the reference applicable to readers all over the world. In the northern hemisphere the seasons may be translated into months as follows:

Early winter	December	*Early spring*	March	*Early summer*	June	*Early autumn*	September
Midwinter	January	*Mid-spring*	April	*Midsummer*	July	*Mid-autumn*	October
Late winter	February	*Late spring*	May	*Late summer*	August	*Late autumn*	November

A catalog record for this book is available from the Library of Congress.

ISBN 0-88192-364-8

Typeset by ACE
and printed in Italy by Lego SpA

Published in North America by
Timber Press, Inc.
133 SW Second Avenue, Suite 450
Portland, Oregon 97204, USA

CONTENTS

FOREWORD

During the last twenty years or so there has been a notable upsurge of interest in this horticulturally versatile genus and the impact of fresh introductions of *Hedera* species and their variants, some previously not cultivated, has been considerable. The introduction of selected cultivars for both garden and greenhouse use, boosted by the increasing American regard for the genus, has also contributed to an awakening of enthusiasm for this plant.

Since the publication of his book *Ivies* (1981) which became a standard work on ivies for gardeners and filled an important gap in horticultural literature, Peter Rose has continued diligently to research all aspects of the genus and in this new book has greatly expanded not only his coverage of species and cultivars but also his historical survey of the genus. In addition he includes a detailed account of variegation in ivies whilst also providing careful assessments of recent taxonomic work on *Hedera* particularly in relation to some of the vexed nomenclatural issues that beset ivy species from the Azores, the Canary Isles and North Africa.

Those whose interest in ivies is mainly in its decorative capacity in the garden or house or its potential as a ground-cover or landscape plant will find that Peter Rose is very much a practical gardener who grows and knows the plants he describes and can give detailed information on the cultivation and placement of ivies from his experience over many years.

I have no doubt that the author's blend of personal experience and knowledge of both the theoretical and practical aspects of the genus will make this excellent book the standard work on *Hedera* for many years to come.

CHRIS BRICKELL
Chairman, International Commission for the Nomenclature of Cultivated Plants

Opposite: top left *Hedera helix* Glymii, winter colouration, below in summer; top right *Hedera helix* 'Atropurpurea' in winter, below in summer. From a painting by Victoria Gordon-Friis

INTRODUCTION

This book aims to give a comprehensive view of ivy in all its aspects; in that sense it attempts to be "All things to all men" but in respect of ivy that quotation from Paul's letter to the Corinthians must be hastily amended to "women and men" for, throughout history, ivy has been regarded as the female plant, its Christmas companion the holly being the macho male.

Indigenous to Europe, North Africa and Asia, ivy was an early introduction into America but happily the canard that it is parasitic and will damage trees and walls did not travel with it. In America the plant has been enthused over and treasured. The historical section of this book gives details of that misconception which persists even to this day, encouraged perhaps by the occasional sight of ivy climbing over dead and dying trees. Healthy trees will comfortably sustain ivy which provides pleasant winter greenery and cover for roosting birds; it is only when the tree fails to leaf, either from disease or from old age, that ivy takes over. Having said that I would not encourage ivy into rare or specimen trees. If you do have to destroy ivy, do not just cut the stem and leave it for you will be left with an unsightly mass of adhering stems and persistent dead leaves. The only way to do the job is to cut and disentangle the plant from the top downward, removing it piece by piece and then digging out the root.

"Of making books there is no end and much study is wearisome of the flesh". The preacher Ecclesiastes could equally have been speaking of ivy varieties for they are indeed numerous. In this book I describe most of those in cultivation, 279 kinds, and enumerate with explanations a further 261 names that are often misapplied. Chapters on the plant's fascinating history, its botany and nomenclature lead on to cultivation and the very many uses of ivy in house, garden and landscape. As to the latter part of Ecclesiastes' comment I can say only that I have not found the book's construction "wearisome of the flesh" and I hope likewise that the reader will not find it unduly burdensome.

Acknowledgements

Writers of books are indebted to others in various ways. The foremost debt that I owe is to my late wife; to her perception and ability in so often steering me away from rather turgid scientific prose towards something more readable. Before she died she was able to check the earlier chapters; if they have readability the credit rests with her.

Anyone examining any genus of plants will owe much to the writings of those who have gone before. To unlock that wisdom we rely on libraries and librarians. I have enjoyed the cooperation of libraries in Britain and the USA but particularly that of Dr Brent Elliot and the staff of the 'Lindley', the world's leading horticultural library, now I trust assured of its rightful home in London.

Whilst acknowledging the past there are my many contemporaries, including members of the British and American Ivy Societies, who have readily given me help and information. Among so many I am particularly indebted to Susyn Andrews, Chris Brickell, Garry Gruber, Ingobert Heieck OSB (recently deceased), Hazel Key, Roy Lancaster, Harry van de Laar, Professor Stearn and, whilst alphabetically last by no means least, Stephen Taffler and Ron Whitehouse. All have given me considerable help and advice but at the end of the day the responsibility for considering and incorporating it in this book is mine and mine alone.

Hedera helix 'Ralph'

THE HISTORY OF IVY

THE EARLY DAYS

The history of ivy and its association with mankind is largely confined to Europe, for while the genus has representatives in Asia, North Africa and Macaronesia, it has a particularly prominent place in the flora of Europe. Nowhere is this more so than in Britain, whose moist and insular climate is so much to the plant's liking. Whilst scarce on moorland and high mountain areas, it is ever present in hedgerow and woodland.

In prehistoric times when woodland covered much of Britain, ivy would have been a dominant and very available plant. This availability helps to explain the discoveries made by archaeologists who, examining sites of Stone Age Neolithic and Mesolithic occupation, have found concentrations of ivy pollen greatly in excess of that of other plant species. Pollen grains are extraordinarily durable and their presence gives information as to the plant life in that particular period.

In the excavation of a Mesolithic site at Oakhanger in Hampshire, UK, ivy pollen was found to form 87 percent of the pollen-grain total. The preponderance of ivy pollen in this and other similar sites in Europe suggests that the flower-bearing ivy had been gathered and brought to the site for some purpose. Some archaeologists have suggested that it was winter fodder used to feed penned, semi-domestic animals, possibly red deer. In this connection there is anecdotal evidence of shepherds in 19th-century Britain feeding sheep with bush ivy when snow had covered all grass and low-growing green stuff. Others suggest that it was brought to the site for some ritualistic purpose.

Carbon dating of material from the Oakhanger site placed it at around 5,600 BC, the earliest evidence so far of man's connection with ivy.

Originally from Los Angeles as long ago as 1943, *Hedera helix* 'Glacier' is widely grown as a house-plant ivy

Ivy flowers and fruits successfully only when the mean temperature of the warmest month is greater than 13°C (47°F) and of the coldest month greater than -1.5°C (24°F). This limitation has provided useful evidence as to the prevailing climate of various prehistoric periods. At the present time ivy grows no further north than the southern tip of Norway and Sweden.

The first written references to ivy are those of Theophrastus (c 370–287 BC). Many of his writings have been lost but happily his *Historia Plantarum* (c 314 BC) survives and in this he describes ivy as follows:

> There are many varieties of ivy; one creeps along the ground, another grows high and of the latter there are several varieties, the white one, and the one which has the name *helix*. In the white variety the colour is seen either on the fruits or also on the leaves. All varieties have many roots which are woody and thick but do not go deep. If ivy grows up on trees, then it does damage to them by sucking on them. Occasionally it grows to tree-like dimensions but rarely grows up by itself; but rather grows on another trunk or on walls for which by its nature puts out roots between its leaves by means of which it clings. If it is then chopped off below it can yet continue to live by means of the roots clinging to a tree or wall.

There is more information, including the first description of a variegated plant, in the writings of Pliny the Elder (23–79 AD). In his *Natural History* he tells that Alexander's army came back from India wearing wreaths of ivy because of its rarity. This would have been the Himalayan ivy (*H. nepalensis*) whose orange berries might well have reminded them of the orange-berried poet's ivy used to crown those victorious in sports as well as art. Pliny repeats Theophrastus' erroneous remarks regarding the injurious habits of ivy but goes on to give a fair description of the plant and its varieties.

It is the *helix* which has most varieties of all as it differs greatly in leaf; three are most noticeable, the grass-green *helix* which is the commonest, a second kind with a white leaf and a third with a variegated leaf.

This must be the first description of a variegated ivy but we know that an ivy with a 'white leaf' would not survive because of the lack of chlorophyll and must assume that he referred to a totally white shoot growing from a variegated plant, a situation that often occurs. He mentions also a stiff ivy that will stand without a prop. This refers I suggest to the tree ivy (see page 150) which indicates that the practice of raising tree ivies by taking cuttings of adult shoots was known even at this time.

His interest in ivy is not surprising when we read accounts of the 'younger Pliny', so called to distinguish him from his uncle. The younger Pliny was an active member of the Roman bar, particularly the Chancery Court; he was a landowner and typical senator of the late half of the first century. In describing his own Tuscan property he wrote

It is planted round with ivy-clad plane trees,
green with their leaves above, and below with the
ivy which climbs over trunk and branch and links
tree to tree as it spreads across them.

This is possibly the first recorded description of ivy as a landscape plant. He recorded too that his uncle the Elder Pliny, 'my father by adoption' as he puts it, was a historian of scrupulous accuracy and that he wrote a *Natural History*, "A learned and comprehensive work as full of variety as nature itself." He even wrote in his bath and had himself carried so that he could write as he was transported about town.

While Theophrastus and Pliny are the first recorded writers on ivy, myth and legend involving the plant go back far beyond the written word. The Greek god Dionysus, more commonly known as Bacchus, was said to have come to Greece from Thrace, the modern Bulgaria. Several myths explain why ivy was sacred to Dionysus. One has it that his mortal mother entreated her lover, the god Zeus, to come before her in his divine splendour. When he did so his radiance consumed the woman, but an ivy suddenly grew up and spread to protect the baby Dionysus from his father's Olympian fire. Henceforth Dionysus was depicted crowned with ivy and carrying a thyrsus entwined with ivy.

Mythology also linked Dionysus with the Egyptian God Osiris, builder of cities, law-maker and benefactor of mankind. He too carried an ivy-wreathed thyrsus, which was originally an emblem of virtue. Early worship of Dionysus and Bacchus was wild and orgiastic. Female devotees, Bacchantes, wore ivy garlands and were reputed to attain a

That the plant was held in high esteem, indeed almost venerated, in early history is shown by this superb gold ivy wreath now housed in the Benaki Museum, Athens. It is of Macedonian origin from the 4th century BC and displays very accurately the leaves and berries of ivy

religious frenzy by chewing ivy leaves. This must have been largely a mental state for there is no evidence today that the practice would induce anything more than stomach-ache! Term 'Bacchanalian' has passed into the language as a term for intemperate drinking and orgiastic behaviour.

In later times the plant attained a more sober image. Being evergreen, ivy was held to be an emblem of eternity of fame. In Sparta it crowned victorious athletes and the orange-berried variety crowned winners of poetry contests, a use enshrined in the botanic name of the poet's ivy, *H. helix* f. *poetarum*. It was presumably the victor's ivy crown that St Paul had in mind when he wrote,

And every man that striveth in the games, they
do it to receive a corruptible crown; but we an
incorruptible. (*Corinthians* 1.9.25.)

THE MIDDLE AGES

Despite these more lofty connections it was the legend of wine and drinking that persisted. From the Romans came the custom of hanging on a pole a 'bush' of ivy, a clump of the bushy adult growth, to indicate that the premises sold wine or ale. The custom spread throughout Europe, the sign being called an 'alepole' or 'alestake'. In *The Canterbury Tales* (c 1387–8) Chaucer introduces the Sompnour (Summoner): "A garland hadde he sette upon his hede, As gret as t were for an alestake". The connection lingers in the aphorism 'Good wine needs no bush'. The phrase was current in Roman times as *Vinum vendible hedera non est opus* and exists to this day in several European languages. It signifies of course that a worthy product needs no advertisement – anathema surely to the modern advertising industry!

The bush became the accepted sign for premises selling ale: a Court Roll of 1687 lists the fees that the Lord of the Manor of Castle Cary in Somerset, UK, received at markets and fairs. Among the assortment of trades and crafts, cutlers, bakers, peddlers, butchers, weavers and so on, every beer seller 'who exposed ivy' had to pay 2d. In Frome, another Somerset town, such stalls were known as 'bush houses'.

From Roman times until the 16th century references to ivy are scant. There are of course occasional references to it, as to other plants and trees, in daily life. For example, in 739 AD an ivy grove is quoted as forming one of the boundary marks in a transfer of land between Aethelheard, King of the West Saxons and Forthere, Bishop of Shelbourne. Much later we learn from the accounts of the Church of St Martin, Outwich, London, that in 1524 the churchwardens paid "for holy and ivy at Chrystmas 2½d".

Prior to the Reformation churches were extensively decorated with flowers and greenery and many Churches had gardens attached to them specifically to supply flowers for the great functions and festivals, including the garlands and wreaths, *coronae sacerdotales*, worn by priests. Ivy was unlikely to have been planted at St Martins, indeed that account included items for rose garlands, so it may be that the church had no garden of its own.

The Reformation swept away all these colourful practices and it was many years before churches enjoyed the decoration we associate today with the great festivals, decoration in which ivy often plays an important part.

The lack of reference to ivy in early Christianity has been explained in some detail by a Benedictine monk, the late Brother Ingobert Heieck (1936–93). In *The Significance of Ivy in the Mythology of Antiquity and in the Christian Era* (1981) he points out that Christian customs, symbols and rites are partially of pagan and partially of Jewish origin. The esteem which ivy enjoyed in the myths of antiquity was not echoed in Christianity. The reason is clear when we read of its reputation in Judaism. The Jews hated ivy and ivy wreaths on account of the cult of Bacchus which was forced upon them. According to the books of the Maccabees Jews were forced to attend at the feasts of Dionysus and, adorned with ivy wreaths, to take part in the processions. At the behest of Ptolemy, all Greek cities were instructed to ensure that Jews participated and that those who would not accommodate themselves to the Greek way of life should be executed (The Apocrypha to the Bible, 2nd Maccabees 6, 7–9). A dislike for the plant lingered but this seems to have disappeared, certainly in Britain, for there is no evidence of Christian hostility to ivy which was, by the 16th century, commonly used in church decoration.

The early herbals concentrated on plants as sources of medicaments and made only passing reference to their garden value. In his *Histories of Plantes* of 1597 Gerard depicts ivy thus:

> The greater ivie climbeth on trees, old buildings, and walls... the leaves are smooth, shining especially on the upper side, ... The floures are very small and mossie... the berries are ripe after the winter solstice.

Gerard describes its virtues to "help sore and smarting waterish eis" but says nothing to indicate that it might be planted or grown in gardens. His reference to the climbing ivy being 'the greater ivy' refers to the theory held for many years that there were two kinds of ivy, the creeping and the climbing.

1 *Hedera corymbosa.*
Clymbing or berried Ivie.

A woodcut from Gerard's *Histories of Plantes*, 1597

The illustration (see page 13) in Gerard's herbal is not a particularly good example, indeed it was suggested that his woodcuts were "a job lot from the Continent".

Sixty years after Gerard's depiction a slightly extended summary of the kinds of ivy available appeared in Cole's *Adam in Eden or Nature's Paradise* (1657, London). The author quotes six kinds, "The climbing and the barren ivy, white berried, yellow berried, trefoil ivy of Virginia and five leaved ivy of Virginia." The last two are obviously *parthenocissus* sp., while the "white berried" refers to the plant recorded by Theophrastus, a reference repeated by Dioscorides, Pliny and others. It has never been seen since those early times and it seems likely that it was a single plant mutation that was soon lost. Unless it was propagated vegetatively it is doubtful whether seed reproduction would maintain the white character.

Gerard's distinction of two ivies, the climbing and the creeping, is repeated by John Ray in his *Catalogus Plantarum Anglie* (1627). It is also repeated in the *Catalogus Horti Botanici* (1658) compiled by Jacob Bobart. Appointed Superintendent of the Oxford Physic Garden in 1641 Bobart was a somewhat eccentric figure with a long black beard which he decorated with silver on Holy Days. He was followed around the garden by his tame goat – an indulgence which, considering the dietary habits of goats, might seem somewhat risky in a botanic garden!

Bobart listed *H. arborea* as the common climbing ivy and *H. helix* as the barren (or creeping) ivy.

IN THE GARDEN

What may truly be termed horticultural references to ivy do not appear until some 70 years later. It was in 1727 that nurseryman Robert Furber (c1674–1756) published his catalogue *English and Foreign Trees*. This listed among "striped" ie variegated trees and shrubs, "Ivy the broad leaved kind; ivy the small creeping kind." The "broad leaved kind" was most probably the Irish ivy now defined as a distinct species, *H. hibernica*. In 1755 the catalogue of nurseryman Christopher Gray of Fulham, Middlesex, UK, listed three kinds: the common ivy, silver striped ivy and yellow blotched ivy.

A more detailed account was given in 1770 by Richard Weston in his *Universal Botanist and Nurseryman* which set out ivies as follows:

1 *helix*
2 *argenteo variegata* – the silver striped ivy
3 *aureo variegata* – the gold striped ivy
4 *poetica baccis luteis* – yellow-berried archipelagian ivy
5 *canadensis scandens* – Virginia creeper

The last was still being classified as an ivy by botanists; in fact of course it belongs to a different genus, *Parthenocissus*.

The catalogues of Furber, Gray and Weston were followed by other late-18th-century lists. In 1774 the celebrated firm of Kennedy and Lee, whose Hammersmith nursery occupied the site of the present Olympia Exhibition Halls, listed two ivies *H. helix* and *quinquefolia,* which I assume to have been the Virginia creeper. The 1775 catalogue of John and George Telford of York listed "Ivy striped" at 6d per plant while the Early Red Honeysuckle was listed at 2d per plant (6d = 5p present UK currency). Considering the then value of money, sixpence was a high price to pay for the variegated ivy which was probably a clone we know as 'Cavendishii'. Another leading nurseryman of the day, Loddiges of Hackney, London, listed three in 1777 as *Fol. aureo, Fol. argenteo* and *quinquerol*, again presumably the Virginia creeper. By 1826 however the same firm listed seven: *H. helix* 'Arborescens' ('tree' ivy), 'Digitata', *Fol. argentea*, *Fol. aurea*, 'Fructu-alba', 'Maculata' and 'Poetica'. 'Fructu-alba' would presumably be the white-berried ivy mentioned by various earlier writers but always at second-hand; no one appears to have seen it or grown it. Either Loddiges listed it from hearsay or possibly material purporting to be that clone was acquired but its identity could not have been proven until it reached the adult berrying stage.

Interest in ivies slowly increased and by 1846 Peter Lawson and Son of Edinburgh were listing 12 varieties. In 1859

Hedera colchica, the true bullock's heart ivy, is less vigorous than its larger-leaved clone 'Dentata'

Fast he stealeth on, though he wears no wings,
And a staunch old heart has he.
How closely he twineth, how tight he clings,
To his friend the huge Oak Tree!
And slily he traileth along the ground,
And his leaves he gently waves,
As he joyously hugs and crawleth round
The rich mould of dead men's graves.
Creeping where grim death has been,
A rare old plant is the Ivy green.

An extract from Shirley Hibberd's book *The Ivy* (1872) in which he quotes a passage from Euripedes' *Hecuba* to illustrate how often the close union of ivy with its supporting tree is invoked in literature

W G Henderson of St John's Wood, London, listed 16 and by 1865 that number had increased to 39. In Germany in 1868 the nursery firm of Haage and Schmidt who were building up an international plant trade issued a catalogue listing 23 varieties and in 1867 William Paul, a noted London nurseryman, listed his collection "of more than 40 sorts" in the September issue of the *Gardener's Chronicle*. His names were published in Germany by the botanist Karl Koch and provided a basis for the names of cultivated ivies.

A new species, *H. colchica* had reached Britain in the 1840s from the Odessa Botanic Garden. It was introduced as *H. roegneriana* to commemorate M Roegner, the Director of the Botanic Garden at that time, but that name was never properly published and in 1859 Koch, realizing that the same plant had been found much earlier by the botanist Kaempfer and later by Wallich and by Koch himself, described it as *H. colchica*.

The Canary Island ivy, *H. canariensis* and the Himalayan ivy, *H. nepalensis* were introduced about the same time; the former (much confused with the Irish ivy *H. hibernica*) from North Africa. This confusion coupled with rather brief descriptions makes the identification of some of the early ivy varieties difficult. The introduction of new species helped to increase Victorian interest in the garden uses and cultivation of ivies, interest which is epitomized in Shirley Hibberd's book, *The Ivy*, (1872, second edition 1893). The book, now a collector's item, exudes the quiet charm of that Victorian era. Hibberd, the son of a sea captain who had sailed under Nelson, was intended by his parents to become a doctor; he turned however to journalism, concentrating on horticulture and home decoration. He edited a periodical, *The Floral World* from 1858 until 1875 and in addition to *The Ivy* wrote such books as *Brambles and Bayleaves* and *Rustic Adornments for Homes of Taste*, books which convey the comfortable, well ordered, quietly industrious life of the Victorian middle classes. Reading *The Ivy* one is struck by the wide sweep of the author's trawl. There can be no quotation that he has not included: Euripedes, Virgil, Cato, Horace, Dickens, Keats, Tennyson and many more are there. All the myth, magic and tradition of ivy he unearthed and presented, delicately and in a manner evocative of the age: the book is a charming piece of Victoriana.

The period following the publication of his book saw a proliferation of ivy varieties or clones as most were, with firms such as William Clibran and Son of Altrincham, Cheshire, and Dicksons of Chester, listing as many as 50 or 60 varieties. The Royal Horticultural Society maintained an ivy collection at its Chiswick garden in London (the forerunner of its Wisley, Surrey garden) and in 1889 conducted a Trial comprising 46 varieties. These were described in a report on the Trial by Hibberd in the Society's journal and given awards according to their garden value. Interest in the cultivation of ivies rose to a peak in this period which ended, as did so many things, on August 4th 1914.

After World War I and during the 1920s interest in ivies declined; anything associated with the Victorian and Edwardian eras was out of fashion and nurserymen listed fewer and fewer varieties. A notable exception was the firm of L R Russell of Richmond which, to their everlasting credit, maintained stocks of many of the Victorian kinds.

THE AMERICAN CONNECTION

There are no species of *Hedera* native to America but ivy was doubtless one of the first plants imported by the settlers. The earliest instance that I have been able to ascertain is that of ivy planted against the walls of a mill erected in 1727. Thomas Willcox, born in Ivybridge, a village some eight miles from Plymouth, Devonshire, emigrated to the USA in 1725. In 1727 he built a house and paper mill on Pole Cat Road, Wawa, Pennsylvania. He planted ivy from his native

Hedera helix 'Merion Beauty' originated in Philadelphia as a mutation from 'Pittsburgh'. It is a compact plant useful for container cultivation and topiary work

Devonshire against the mill which became known as Ivy Mill and the road as Ivy Mills Road. The mill was the second paper mill established in the USA and the first to use vellum or weave moulds; paper for Dr Franklin's newspaper came from the Willcox mill. The mill wall still stands with an adherent small-leaved ivy, which appears to be identical to the smaller ivy still occasionally found in Devonshire. Material from it is presently marketed by a leading USA ivy nursery. The Ivy Mill property, owned by Mark Willcox Jnr, is still in Willcox hands.

Ivy was certainly present in the USA by 1731: it was listed as one of the plants contained in the garden established by John Bartrum beside the Schuykill river near Philadelphia. This became America's first botanic garden. John Bartrum, from Derbyshire, sailed from Britain in 1682, the year in which Philadelphia was founded. His grandson, John, (born 1699) became a farmer. Self-taught, he became an eminent botanist and was appointed King's Botanist to George III and awarded an annual stipend of £50. Bartrum maintained a considerable correspondence with botanists and growers in many countries, indeed Linnaeus (1707–78) described him as "the greatest field botanist in the world".

A further indication of early American interest in ivy is revealed by a letter from William Hamilton who had inherited an estate near Philadelphia. The letter, now in the care of the Historical Society of Pennsylvania, was written from England presumably to a relative or perhaps to an employee and is dated 1785. It reads,

I have been frequently pleased with the effects of ivy in certain situations especially when growing over buildings and arches. Suppose you were to plant half a dozen young ones on the east side of the new bridge over the mill creek? I dare say no objection would be made by the owner of the ground.

Ivy's popularity in Victorian Britain as a parlour plant was followed or even exceeded in America. According to *Vick's Illustrated Magazine*, a popular 19th-century American periodical for indoor decoration,

We have nothing to equal ivy. It will endure more hardship, flourish under more unfavourable circumstances and endure darkness, gas and dust better than any plant we think of at present.

The trend of the period, in America as in Britain, is summed up by the following extract from the 1876 book *Floral*

Decorations by Annie Hassard. Ivy was
> employed for trailing around couches and rustic
> picture frames... and if the frame contains the
> portrait of some departed friend, ivy is perhaps
> the most appropriate of all plants for the purpose
> here suggested.

This incidentally was achieved by having the plant in a
wedge-shaped zinc container hung on the wall behind the
picture.

Moving away from the American parlours, the phrase
'The Ivy League' was coined in the 1930s to describe the
eight colleges of eastern USA that had common interests in
high standards of scholarship and athletics. Some had
planted ivy against the buildings, possibly to emulate the
appearance of ivy-clad college buildings in Britain and
Europe. At Princeton University the planting of an ivy at
the walls of Nassau Hall became part of the graduation cele-
brations, which also included the singing of an ivy song and
an ivy oration. This practice continued from 1866 until
1942. Plaques denoting the graduation class and planting
date were inserted in the walls. Not all the 'Ivy League' colleges boast ivy; one at least (Harvard), has planted Boston
ivy (*Parthenocissus tricuspidaria*, or Virginia creeper).

A development that occurred in America had a marked
effect on the future of cultivated ivies and created the multi-
million dollar – and pound – industry of the house-plant ivy.
In 1921, Paul Randolph of Verona, Pennsylvania, noted a
mutation in a plant among a batch of common ivy. The
mutation differed in having smaller, thinner leaves and a
very branching habit: it tended to produce sideshoots at
almost every node. Randolph put this plant into commerce
as 'Pittsburgh'. A new race of ivies had emerged.

Through the 1930s, further mutations from this variety
occurred and by 1940 Alfred Bates, writing in the American
National Horticultural Magazine, could describe 11 new
clones. In the course of trade these spread to Europe (Holland and Germany in particular) slowly gaining favour until
World War II checked frivolities of this kind.

IN EUROPE

The increased interest in ivies in 19th-century Britain was
echoed in Europe, particularly in Germany where the catalogues of the Haage and Schmidt nursery company of the
1860s listed numerous *helix* varieties as well as the then
newly discovered dentate-leaved form of the Persian ivy, *H.
colchica* 'Dentata'. These catalogues were issued in French
as well as German. As in Britain this ivy interest persisted
but primarily in those kinds which were able to survive
continental winters.

After World War II, ivy became a popular house-plant following the introduction from America of the short-jointed
but more tender kinds. Several German nurseries specialized in these and introduced many new clones as the list in
this book (see pages 153–6) shows.

In 1979 Brother Ingobert Heieck, the monk in charge of
the plant nursery at the Benedictine monastery at Neuburg
Abbey near Heidelberg, Germany, started to grow large
quantities of ivies for sale. With an unerring eye for the
slightest mutation and patient selection over the years, he
introduced some outstanding clones. He also accumulated
an extremely wide knowledge of the plant. He won world-
wide recognition and his death at only 57 years of age was a
great loss to what may be termed Hederaology. His example
led to the founding of the German Ivy Society in 1993, the
year of his death.

Holland, always regarded as Europe's nursery, grew and
exported popular ivies in considerable quantities from the
1920s onwards. As part of the country's trade policy, which
was to select the best clones of all genera of trees and shrubs
to grow commercially, the horticulturist Harry van de Laar
amassed a considerable ivy collection. The Dutch botanist
Dr Nannenga-Bremekamp based her 1970 account of ivy
clones on this collection.

In France interest in ivies has been spasmodic but it was a
French nurseryman, M Tantonnet of Hyères who, seeing the
virtues of the North African *canariensis* ivies, grew and
exported the Algerian variation in 1853. Thus he laid the
foundations for their popularity in the gardens of southern
France and as a house-plant in Britain.

In keeping with their tradition of producing topiary, Belgian nurseries became a standard source of 'standard' ivies
(see page 150).

Switzerland has retained an affection for the plant, indeed
from the 1964 *Year Book of the Zurich Botanic Garden* came
the very detailed descriptions of garden ivies by Professor
Mathias Jenny. The redoubtable and hardy *H. helix*
'Woeneri' we owe to a Swiss nurseryman.

More recently, the nursery trade in Denmark has seized on
the popularity of the plant and built up a considerable
export trade in house-plant ivies. Production on a vast scale
inevitably increases the potential for the appearance of
mutations and indeed the nursery of Frode Maegaard of
Ringe in Denmark has produced the brilliant, almost garish,
yellow variegated 'Midas Touch'.

IN MODERN TIMES

Following the end of World War II, contacts with Europe
introduced to British homes the fashion for house plants.

PLATE I

All plants are shown at approximately ¼ size

H. helix 'Olive Rose'

H. helix 'Fluffy Ruffles'

H. nepalensis 'Suzanne'

H. helix 'Erecta'

H. helix 'Walthamensis'

H. helix f. poetarum

H. helix 'Arborescens'

H. helix 'Spetchley'

H. nepalensis var. sinensis

H. helix 'Congesta'

H. helix 'Minor Marmorata'

This development was pioneered in Britain by Thomas Rochford Ltd, who turned their vast tomato-producing nurseries over to pot-plant production. The most suitable of all house plants, ivies, were produced by the million. Numerous nurseries followed this trend, obtaining their stock plants from many sources. If they did not know the name of the variety they were propagating they gave it what seemed an appropriate name and so confusion arose.

Another and more frequent source of confusion arose from the fact that ivies are prone to variation and a form with a particular colour or leaf shape will often throw shoots that vary, perhaps with larger leaves or less colour than the original. If cuttings are taken haphazardly, variation in the stock can arise and gradually that nursery's stock of a variety can acquire a markedly different character. This has happened noticeably in 'Glacier', 'Pittsburgh' and 'Königer', clones that have been propagated in vast numbers in many different nurseries and indeed in different countries.

Impetus to define and adopt correct names has been given by the establishment of two ivy societies. The first, the American Ivy Society, was founded in 1973 by Mrs Suzanne Warner Pierot who became the society's President Emerita. From small beginnings it developed into a vigorous organization and, from 1976, was entrusted by the International Commission for the Nomenclature of Cultivated Plants as the registration authority for ivy varietal names and a Registrar, Dr Sabina Sulgrove, appointed. The system requires that any new name given to an ivy clone should be registered with and accepted by the Registrar who can reject names already given to another clone, names which could be confused with others or of course names that do not comply with the international rules of plant nomenclature. Unhappily, as is the case with all plants, there is no compulsion on introducers of a new clone to register the name. The rules can work only by consensus but inevitably it is in everyone's interest to ensure that a specific clone or variety has one name and one name only.

Inspired by the American development, a British ivy enthusiast Mr Stephen Taffler proposed in the Journal of the RHS a meeting to discuss the formation of a British ivy society. A well attended meeting was held under the aegis of the RHS on November 19th 1974 and the society was founded. It has had immense influence in creating interest in the genus and in the correct naming of ivy clones.

There has been considerable cross fertilization between the two societies and the journals of both, published since their founding, contain considerable information on the genus. This burgeoning interest in ivies prompted the RHS in 1979/80 to conduct an Ivy Trial; interestingly it was exactly 90 years after the first Trial. It attracted considerable interest and 200 stocks were entered. As well as offering the opportunity of seeing so many clones growing side by side it revealed the wide variation in different nursery stocks of identical clones or varieties.

IN POETRY AND ARCHITECTURE

Ivy, the poet Byron's 'Garland of Eternity', features in the sign of flowers, that floral shorthand so popular in Victorian times. Almost any message could be passed by a tongue-tied suitor to his beloved by the gift of, or reference to, a specific flower or plant. Booklets and publications listed these in some detail. Popular brooches of the period depicted ivy growing around a fallen tree with the motto 'Nothing can detach me from it'. A sprig of ivy with its rootlets attached meant a wish to please. While ivy indicated fidelity and marriage, an age-old reference to its climbing and evergreen characteristics, an ardent swain might have been well advised to consider carefully before giving a *Calceolaria*, whose implied meaning was 'I offer you my fortune'!

Among evergreens, holly has always had the reputation of being the macho male representative, ivy the clinging female. Thus Titania in *A Midsummer-Night's Dream* addresses Bottom, "The female ivy so enrings the barky fingers of the elm, O how I love thee; How I dote on thee!"

Although not recommended for ground cover, *Hedera helix* 'Buttercup' is one of the best climbing ivies. In a reasonably sunny situation the lime-green leaves change to clear yellow

Ivy's tenacity and longevity has inspired poets through the ages but few more eloquent than Charles Dickens who in his charming poem, *The Ivy Green* wrote:

The brave old plant in its lonely days

Shall fatten upon the past,

For the stateliest building man can raise,

Is the ivy's food at last.

Creeping on where time has been,

A rare old plant is the ivy green.

Another poet writing on ancient and crumbling buildings mused that ivy's mission was "To gild destruction with a smile and beautify decay."

Certainly ivy can attain great age. Records of a plant growing at Ginac near Montpellier in France showed it to be 400 years old. Unhappily this venerable specimen was sacrificed to a road-widening scheme in the 1970s. The poet's assertion that "...the stateliest building man can raise Is the ivy's food at last" is not so accurate. It brings to mind the controversy that has spasmodically enlivened gardening papers for the last 150 years, the question as to whether or not ivy harms the trees or walls upon which it climbs.

Ivy is NOT a parasitic plant; the small rootlets put out by the climbing shoots help the plant to adhere to its support but they have no penetrative powers. With regard to trees, though ivy clings to its host it does not feed on it. While the

tree is in good health the ivy will be a secondary plant, its ascension of the trunk and into the branches doing no harm. However, should the tree decline for any reason or fail to leaf, the ivy will take over, as is often seen on elm trees killed by Dutch Elm Disease.

It is possible, on very old walls where the mortar is weak, for ivy shoots to take root in the gaps between the bricks but on sound walls ivy is harmless as the rootlets have no penetrative power. Indeed ivy can be have the beneficial effects of keeping walls dry in winter and cool in summer. It can however harbour flies and insects and to offset this should be clipped over in late summer. This improves the ivy and maintains a neat and effective wall covering. Very weak walls can be in danger of falling if ivy has been allowed to bush out at the top and then becomes heavy with snow or rain and susceptible to the pull of strong winds; clipping obviates this possibility.

One might add that the coverage given by ivy to walls and masonry, far from being destructive, can help to preserve them. Stonework which has been ivy covered over a long period will be seen, when the ivy is removed, to be fresh and unscathed if compared with adjacent areas that have been exposed to the elements. Additionally the roots at the base of the wall or building, in their search for moisture, keep the area dry.

In this latter connection R T Gunter in his *Oxford Gardens* (1912) tells an amusing true story. Early in this century the Great Tower of Magdalen College, Oxford, was ivy clad. Various authorities suggested that it was harming the tower and in 1892, the then Bursar proposed that it be cut down but was outvoted, as he was again in 1904. At last in November 1908, the Waynflete Professors of Physiology and Botany persuaded the College to have it removed, winning their case by 15 votes to 11.

Why did it take so long to come to this decision? The college was doubtless mindful of the attractiveness of their ivy-clad tower but perhaps their decision was influenced by the discovery that roots of the ivy had penetrated the vaults of the adjoining wine cellar. Branching about among the sawdust in which the bottles were stored, a root had penetrated the cork of one bottle, filled it with its roots and thereby drunk its contents!

It was obviously an ivy with tastes appropriate to the Senior Common Room and High Table but it would appear that its own action heralded its demise.

IVY IN MEDICINE

Our ancestors, prey to many of the same ailments that beset us today, turned to remedies based for the most part upon plants. Ivy, perhaps partly because of its mythological links, featured in many of these supposed remedies.

The first recorded medical use of ivy is attributed to Hippocrates, the 'father' of medicine, who around 460 BC recommended the leaves of ivy for making a fomentation. But not until the first century AD do references to the medical uses of ivy appear in detail. Among various potions described by Pliny the Elder was one of ivy leaves, bruised with vinegar and oil of roses, as a remedy for headache. In his *De Medicina* (37 AD) Celsus advises the same remedy against insomnia.

The berries of the golden-fruited kind were recommended by Pliny to be taken for dropsy "to remove accumulated water". He also quoted also the statement of Cato that ivy was efficacious for testing wine. "A vessel made of its wood will let wine pass through it, where if there has been any water mixed with it, this will remain behind." Adulteration of wine has occurred from time to time through the ages and this erroneous theory was occasionally repeated, certainly until 1696 when the botanist John Ray cast serious doubt on it, saying that it was believed only by "the common people".

Prominent among the first-century writers was Dioscorides whose works, copied and recopied, influenced medicine well into the Middle Ages. He wrote that ivy is acrid and astringent and attacks the nerves; that a solution of the flowers in wine, drunk twice a day, was useful for those suffering from dysentery while the leaves boiled in wine would heal ulcers and blemishes of the skin. He recommended the berries, bruised and applied as a pessary for women to "bring on the menses", a connection repeated by various other writers. He also recommended the 'gum' of ivy as a depilatory and to kill lice.

This gum was liquid resin which hardened as it exuded from cut stems. It was obtained in quantity in India, Italy, Provence and Languedoc. In his *Histoire Générale des Drogues* (Paris 1694) Pomet records some obtained from an ivy tree at Montpellier in 1680 and it is interesting to speculate that this might have been from the Montpellier ivy recorded in recent times to have attained the age of 400 years (see page 21).

The exudation of sufficient sap to harden into gum would probably occur only in warm climes. It was not mentioned by British writers and personally I have not witnessed it here or abroad.

Apuleius (c 163 AD) wrote that seven or 11 powdered ivy berries drunk in water would break up bladder stones, a remedy repeated in detail in the 10th-century Anglo-Saxon writings translated by the Rev O Cockayne (Saxon Leechdoms' 1864).

> In case the stone wax in the bladder take seven
> or eleven berries rubbed small in water, give
> them to drink; wonderfully it gathereth the
> calculi [stones] in the bladder and breaketh them
> to pieces and tuggeth them out by means of
> the urine.

It is remarkable that the passage of some nine centuries had not altered the actual number of berries recommended by Apuleius!

Culpeper in his *Physical Directory or Translation of the Dispensatory made by the College of Physititians of London* (1650) described an involved method of making oil of ivy berries. Needing some 50lbs (22kg) of berries he recommended it for 'cold disease' of the joints and stated that three or four drops in some convenient liquor "provokes the terms in women", a repetition of Dioscorides' statement of 15 centuries earlier. Despite these medical recommendations there seems little evidence in recorded history that this supposed abortifacient was generally used.

A remedy of cosmetic interest is that given by Anton Mizald in his *Memorabilium Utilum* of 1566 where he wrote:

> An ivy garland placed on pendulous and flaccid breasts or *Hedera* bruised and applied, will restore their elasticity and raise them to their proper position.

On a more serious note, Boyle, in *Some Considerations Touching the Usefulness of Experimental Natural Philosophy* (1664) endorses against the plague "a good dose of fully ripe ivy berries which work powerfully by sweat". One can ponder and sympathize with our ancestors who, faced with this ghastly pestilence, knew neither the cause nor any real means of a cure.

The use of ivy leaves, berries and gum were 'official' in the *Pharmacopoeia* of the London Royal College of Physicians until 1677 and as late as 1774 with the Royal College of Physicians of Edinburgh. From that date, however, though country folk resorted to its use from time to time, the medical profession discarded virtually all reference to ivy.

It may have been this declining interest that led Frances James Henderson Coutts to submit for his MD at Manchester University in 1898 *An Experimental Study of the Pharmacology of* Hedera helix – Common Ivy. Dr Coutts isolated the active properties of ivy as Hederic acid, Hederaglucoside and the Hederasaponins a and b. Injecting rabbits, cats and other animals with varying strengths of these preparations he found that at low concentrations they increased vigour in "feeble, irregular hearts", a beneficial effect that continued even after the drug had been washed out. Higher concentrations brought the heart to a standstill. He took small quantities of the preparations himself "without any ill effects" and proposed further experimentation.

Since Dr Coutt's thesis there has been little medical interest in ivy until recently. As part of a trawl of plants by researchers seeking beneficial properties, ivy among other plants has been extensively examined as regards its anti-mutagenic (tumour-reducing) propensities. It has also been considered as a potential antidote in attacks by the parasite *Leishmania* sp.. In tropical and sub-tropical areas this minute organism reputedly causes 400,000 cases a year of an uncomfortable and occasionally fatal condition, leishmaniasis.

Like many plants, ivy contains substances which, in certain concentrations, can induce unpleasant symptoms or even death. In addition to the properties noted by Dr Coutts, polyacetylene falcarinol has been isolated. This is an irritant which, in the small proportion of the population allergic to it, can produce temporary dermatitis. The fact that millions of ivy plants are handled daily by nurserymen without incident or complaint is testimony to the low percentage of the population prone to this allergy. Only one case of poisoning is on record, Block in the German *Archiv der Pharmacie* states that a child was poisoned by eating ivy berries, including the seeds, whilst a companion who ate only the fleshy part escaped. This suggests a similarity with Yew (*Taxus* sp.) where the seed is poisonous but the fleshy aril surrounding it is harmless. The ancients linked yew and ivy, indeed the names may have common origins (see page 34). One can speculate that in far off times it may have been this common characteristic that led to the unlikely linkage.

A few cases of contact dermatitis have been recorded. In the USA these appear to involve mainly *H. canariensis*. One instance is that of workmen cutting prostrate ivy with a rotary mower. The cutting of this lush species produced considerable sap which caused a severe but temporary rash on arms and legs. In this case the presumed cause is the irritant substance falcaronil contained in the leaves, but I suspect that some reported cases of dermatitis may well be caused by the minute hairs (see page 26) that the plant sheds. At the Royal Botanic Gardens, Kew, students clipping the Ivy Hedge around the Palm House and the collection on the Ivy Wall were wont to complain of coughing and respiratory problems. It is likely that the clipping released millions of desiccated ivy hairs.

Regarding the effects of ivy on animals there seems to be some ambiguity of opinion. There are many records of sheep surviving by eating ivy when all grass was deeply covered by snow and shepherds have been known to give ivy as a tonic.

The British Ministry of Agriculture's bulletin *Poisonous Plants in Britain* affirms that in small quantities the plant is not considered harmful to livestock and is said by some to be beneficial. It goes on however to say that ivy poisoning has been reported in cattle, deer, sheep and dogs with symptoms of vomiting, diarrhoea, muscular paralysis and dilation of blood vessels. It quotes a case of two cows who, after consuming quantities of ivy leaves and berries when pasture was scarce, staggered, became excitable and bellowed in pain. A strong odour of crushed ivy leaves in the breath and milk persisted for three days, after which recovery was complete and uneventful. This suggests that it is not the active principles in ivy that matter but the concentrations in which they are absorbed.

Manufacturers interested in the potential of ivy leaves in cosmetics have examined the plant chemically and creams having ivy as a constituent have been marketed quite widely. The advertising suggests it to be soothing, stress-relieving and elasticizing. The fact that elements of the plant have been incorporated in massage creams purported

to relieve adipose and cellulitic conditions has distinct hints of Anton Mizald's more outspoken figure-control remedy!

More factually, extracts of the plant are used homeopathically for the treatment of catarrh, coughs and asthma, diseases of the thyroid glands, arthritis and rheumatism. They can be applied to abscesses, burns, bruises and skin rashes.

In 1994 the British Horticultural Trade Association noted the growing tendency of people to sue for damages in the event of any mishap attributable to products sold. With the RHS it conceived a committee of experts to examine the potential dangers of a wide range of nursery-grown plants including ivy. As a result the Association advised its

Hedera canariensis var. *algeriensis* 'Gloire de Marengo', the variegated form of the African or Canary Island ivy, is extensively grown in Europe as a house plant

members to attach to each ivy plant sold a notice proclaiming "Harmful if eaten – may cause skin allergy". As indicated above the proportion of people with an allergic reaction to the plant is minuscule and one would have to eat vast quantities of leaves to suffer harm. There seems little justification for the inclusion of ivy in a list of poisonous plants. Inevitably the ruling raised considerable discussion and many nurseries ignore the Association's advice.

THE BOTANY OF IVY

DISTRIBUTION

The *Hedera* genus is confined to the Northern hemisphere, which it spans from Japan in the east to the Azores in the west. The small-leaved *H. rhombea* of Japan is replaced in China and northern India by the longer-leaved *H. nepalensis*, whose orange berries reminded Alexander's conquering armies of the poet's ivy of their homeland. In southern Russia and northern Iran it appears as *H. pastuchovii* while north to the Caucasus it becomes *H. colchica*. The islands of the Mediterranean and the countries of Europe embrace *H. helix* as far north as southern Sweden and westward to Ireland, where the the slightly different *H. hibernica* appears. Meanwhile south of the Mediterranean it ventures into Africa: in Morocco as *H. maroccana* and in Algeria as *H. canariensis*, which is also present in the Canary Islands and Madeira. To the north in the Azores as *H. azorica* it resembles a slightly more hairy *helix*.

That is its natural distribution, but sentimental regard for the plant led to its importation by the American settlers, certainly by the early 18th century, and the plant soon became popular in American gardens. Not naturally present in Australasia it is now nurtured by gardeners there as it is also in South Africa.

BOTANICAL FEATURES

Two noticeable characteristics of ivy are its evergreen nature and the fact that it develops two kinds of leaf growth, juvenile and adult. The juvenile leaves, those borne by the plant in its creeping or early climbing stages, are usually three- to five-lobed as in the common English ivy (*H. helix*) but in some species the leaf is only slightly lobed (*H. nepalensis*) or indeed unlobed (*H. colchica*).

When the plant has climbed and achieved a degree of height and access to light the leaves lose any lobing they possess and take on a narrow, elliptic shape. The stem produces branches initially at the top of the plant, but subsequently they can appear over the whole plant, sometimes to the extent that all growth is of this adult or arborescent kind. This change in leaf character is termed dimorphism.

The reasons for this leaf change are not fully understood but it seems reasonable to assume that a lobed leaf may be more efficient in catching the sunlight necessary for photosynthesis. This would be a useful adaptation for a plant which crept along the forest floor until it could ascend to find the sunlight and air necessary to flower. The long and complex course of evolution may have decreed that, having achieved sun and air, a narrow and unlobed leaf is better adapted to survive wind exposure than a wide-lobed leaf. The reduction in leaf size also allows the flower heads more exposure to the attentions of fertilizing flies and late-autumn wasps than would be the case were they still surrounded by the more lush leaves of the juvenile state.

The actual way in which the change is triggered is as yet unknown. Experimental work, particularly that carried out by the late Dr W J Robbins of the Department of Botany at Columbia University (American Journal of Botany, Vols 44 & 47, 1960) suggests that giberillic acid, which has shown capabilities to induce reversion from the adult to the juvenile state, may be involved. Experiments suggested that it may not be an 'all or nothing' phenomenon: certainly stages between juvenile and adult states are evident, particularly where normally short-jointed clones such as 'Glacier' are climbing against walls. Some shoots will achieve adult status but there will be many with varying leaf shapes in between the adult stage and the juvenile stage which is evident at the base. From the time of Theophrastus until well into the 18th century botanists assumed the adult and juvenile forms to be distinct and separate species.

Cuttings taken from adult growth provide plants that retain the adult type of growth and can develop into free-standing shrubs of some 1.3m (4ft) high. Often called 'tree ivies', these were in favour during the Victorian era with some nurseries listing as many as a dozen kinds. While cuttings of juvenile growth root easily, those of adult growth are more difficult. Rooting percentages vary according to variety but one of the easiest and possibly one of the showiest is *H. helix* 'Angularis Aurea' whose arborescent form is now correctly known as 'Mary Eggins'.

ROOTLETS

Ivy climbs by means of small adventitious rootlets that attach the stem to rocks, trees, walls or fences. These rootlets arise from the cambium layer of the stem and at first are soft and white, then with age become brown and woody. Encountering a rigid surface, the tip of the rootlet thickens slightly to form a minute adhesive pad. The strength of this adhesion and the number of rootlets produced mean that established ivy is often difficult to remove. Some clones, *H. helix* 'Persian Carpet' for example and some of the ramulose types, produce few or relatively weak rootlets.

The rootlets occur only on the side of the stem away from the light and will readily seek dark interstices in a wall or tree bark. Their length can vary from 1mm (⅕in) to 2 or 3cm (1in) according to age and situation.

The emission of rootlets appears to be governed by the young shoot touching a rigid surface. That they are produced only on young growth becomes very evident when planting an ivy against a wall. However close to the wall the plant is placed the existing growth will not emit rootlets and if it already has rootlets these will not cling. It is only when the young shoot touches the support that rootlets emerge and climbing begins.

When ivy is growing on the ground rootlets are produced at leaf nodes and if the node is in close contact with soil and moisture the rootlets develop into true roots. In this way an ivy shoot will grow across soil, rooting at the nodes. When it encounters a wall or suitable support and the shoot grows vertically, rootlets emerge, usually some 5– 10cm (2–4in) behind the growing point, emerging not only at nodes but along the stem between the nodes.

While the production of rootlets is governed by vertical growth it is interesting to note their absence on young shoots of the small group of erect ivies, *H. helix* 'Congesta', 'Erecta' and 'Russelliana'. In the first year small brown scars are seen but it is only in the second year that rootlets emerge, often in considerable profusion, and rapidly become rather bristly outgrowths. In this group of ivies, even when planted against a wall so that the stem is in touch and has a 'dark' side, rootlets will not emerge on the young shoot.

Rootlets have no ability to absorb food or water. Theories that ivy is parasitic and can absorb nutriment via the rootlets from trees or walls can be disproved by severing all stems that have ground contact. The plant will die above the cut point as soon as any reserves in the stems are exhausted. A covering of ivy will keep a wall dry and it used to be thought that the rootlets 'drew' water from the wall, but this is not so. The wall will be dry because the ivy leaves act as a shield, throwing off rainwater to the ground below.

FLOWERS

Ivies are seldom grown for their flowers although these are by no means without beauty. When the plant has achieved arborescence they are produced on globose umbels, sometimes solitary but usually in compound panicles, each umbel carrying 10–15 flowers, their stalks or pedicells bearing hairs stellate or scale-like according to the species.

The flower bud is enveloped by a five-sepalled, yellow-green calyx, As the flower opens the sepals fold back adhering to the side of the four- to five-celled ovary which is rather like the berry in miniature. Its top is a conical disc and has five stamens inserted around the rim; the yellow anthers which each bears give the flower a certain attraction. At the centre of the disc is the stigma whose supporting styles are fused into a single column. The surface of the disc is slightly sticky and sweet and readily attracts flies and the few autumnal wasps and bees whose busy scrambling fertilizes the flowers, after which the sepals and stamens fall away.

Hedera colchica 'Sulphur Heart', a dramatic large-scale evergreen climber suitable for walls, fences or ground cover

The expanding 'berry', 4–7mm (¼–⅜in) across and botanically a drupe retains the columnar style which hardens and remains like a pointel to the berry which, first green, colours to black except in the case of the poet's ivy, *Hedera helix* f. *poetarum* and *Hedera nepalensis*, where it attains a dull orange.

HAIRS OR TRICHOMES

At first sight one might assume ivy to be a hairless plant but, as with many plants, hairs are present to a lesser or greater degree at various stages of its growth. They were first recorded by the Kew-trained German botanist, Dr Berthold Seeman who, in his review of the genus published in the Journal of Botany in 1864, pointed out that their shape, colour, and the number of rays differed among species and served as one of the means of identification.

The hairs are present on the young shoots and leaf petioles and to a more limited extent on the upper and lower surfaces of the leaves, particularly along the veins on the under surface. As the leaf matures the hairs tend to disappear but those on the petioles are often retained, albeit in reduced numbers, and may persist even to leaf fall.

They are small, having an overall dimension of around 0.05mm (50 microns). Easily examined under a ten-times lens, higher magnification shows that they form a multicellular extension of one or more of the surface or epidermal cells. From this 'stalk', as one might term it, radiate a number of 'rays' each consisting of a single cell.

In some species the rays are few, from three to eight in number, and the stalk comparatively high, elevating them to be more visible. Indeed in *H. azorica* they are so visible and so numerous as to appear like wool. These rays lie in a star-like fashion hence they are termed 'stellate' hairs.

In other species the stalk is so short as to adpress the hair to the surface like a scale, hence they are termed 'scale-like' or more properly squamiform. The scale-like effect is enhanced by the rays being short and more numerous, 12–20 in number, and their being joined for most of their length. The species *azorica*, *helix*, *hibernica* and *maroccana* have between three and eight white rays, the number of rays and their divergence (manner of spread) varying with species. In *colchica*, *canariensis*, *nepalensis*, *pastuchovii* and *rhombea* there are 12–20 scale-like rays. On young growth the rays are white but rapidly age to brown or light orange giving the stems of some species, particularly *nepalensis*, a rusty tint. Varieties and clones follow the species hair type.

Plant hairs normally serve either to shield the stomata, the breathing pores, from undue transpiration or as a deterrent to browsing animals or insects. They can also, as in the case of certain high alpine plants, act as a shield against intense light. None of these factors seems to apply to ivy at present so the hairs are presumably vestigial evidence of evolutionary change. Possibly *H. azorica*, with its almost felted hairs, is a relict of ivy growing in a dryer or possibly more light-intense environment, a high mountainous situation perhaps.

Hairs are scarce on *canariensis* and *pastuchovii*; in *hibernica* the rays tend to lie in parallel fashion, particularly on the older growth. This can be a useful taxonomic guide to that species and its clones, whose primary difference from *helix* is greater vigour, a characteristic that can be masked by situation or cultural treatment.

The hairs are not readily detached from young growth except by physical action. On older leaves they are dead and tend to slough off although in sheltered situations they can remain as dust, causing problems to those of an asthmatic tendency when clipping ivy on walls or hedges. This was a complaint of generations of Kew students when clipping the Ivy Hedge around the Palm House (see page 23) but I suspect much of the blame could be laid on London air pollution.

Whilst the hairs are useful to botanists as an aid to species identification, those of *H. helix* did on one occasion serve a more dramatic purpose. On August 12th 1988 in Blandford, Dorset, UK, a nine-year-old girl was lured to an ivy-covered waste area, sexually assaulted and murdered. Her body was hidden by a mass of pulled-up ivy. The subsequent search of a suspect revealed a crumpled ivy leaf in his trouser pocket. My help was sought in linking this leaf to those used to cover the body but I rapidly found that such a leaf could have come from elsewhere, even from the suspect's own garden. In the course of the investigation I alerted the detective to the existence of ivy hairs and their possible transference to clothing. The crime was committed in August when the hairs would be young and could be transferred to clothing only by close physical contact.

Sticky tapes used to pick up hairs and fibre from the suspect's clothes revealed ivy hairs – even from clothes he had washed to remove blood stains. Fibres from the child's clothing were also present but could have been explained by casual friendly contact since the suspect was a local man known to the child.

At the trial the defence suggested that the police had 'planted' the ivy leaf in the suspect's pocket, but in fact the presence of the leaf was irrelevant, it was the ivy hairs on the child's clothing and on those of the suspect that linked them both to the scene, silent witnesses to the crime for which the murderer received a life sentence.

SPECIES	CHROMOSOME NUMBER		HAIR TYPE
H. azorica	2n=48	Diploid	Stellate
H. canariensis	2n=96	Tetraploid	Scale-like
var. algeriensis	2n=96	Tetraploid	Scale-like
var. maderensis	2n=144	Hexaploid	Scale-like
H. colchica	2n=192	Octaploid	Scale-like
H. helix	2n=48	Diploid	Stellate
H. hibernica	2n=96	Tetraploid	Stellate
H. maroccana	2n=48	Diploid	Scale-like
H. nepalensis	2n=48	Diploid	Scale-like
H. pastuchovii	2n=144	Hexaploid	Scale-like
var. cypria	2n=144	Hexaploid	Scale-like
H. rhombea	2n=48	Diploid	Scale-like

CHROMOSOME NUMBERS

Morphologically there is little to distinguish between the various ivy species. In spite of the differences in the shape of juvenile leaves, the flower structure and adult leaf shape are all remarkably similar. Differences in the minute hairs on the young stems and leaves show two main groupings: those with stellate hairs and those with scale-like hairs, a factor of considerable help in species identification (see page 27). References are occasionally made to chromosome numbers, but whilst these are essential for the plant hybridist they have little bearing on species differentiation. Several ivy species have the same number and even a different number is no guarantee of species separation, indeed were it to be so, many of our accepted vegetable and flower cultivars would qualify as distinct species.

Chromosomes are thread-like particles within the plant cell that carry genes determining the plant's structure and development. There is a consistent number in every cell: in ivy there are 48. In those cells devoted to reproduction the number becomes halved at the time of fertilization. Thus while the usual number for ivy is expressed as 2n=48, the 'double' (2n) or diploid number, those in the sexual cells carry half only, expressed as x=24, this is the haploid or 'single' number. In fertilization the male and female haploids unite giving the embryonic plant its diploid number, the blue-print for its growth and development.

This division can sometimes go wrong, however. It is possible for the chromosomes of one side to fail to divide and thus a diploid number may become joined to a haploid, so becoming a triploid, usually resulting in a sterile plant. A diploid joined to a diploid results in a chromosome number four times the 'x' number as in H. hibernica; this is termed a tetraploid. In nature this can be disadvantageous since the plant may be partially sterile and little or no seed produced. This is of less account in plants that spread readily by vegetative propagation as do ivies.

The table above shows the chromosome numbers for the recognized species and botanical varieties together with their specific hair type. It suggests that scale-type hairs predominate in the genus but that the hair type has no link with chromosome numbers; the copiously stellate-haired azorica having the same number of chromosomes as the scale-haired nepalensis.

HARDINESS

The common ivy H. helix is native to Britain and Europe where it extends from Ireland in the west, approximately longitude 10, to Riga, roughly longitude 25 in the east. It extends from southern Sweden latitude 60 in the north to 35 in the south, encompassing Crete, which is probably its most southerly point.

Within this area it is hardy with some variation, in that clones from the north such as H. helix 'Baltica' exhibit increased hardiness although hardiness can depend very much on the situation and its microclimate. There are instances, particularly during the 19th century, of ivy in Britain being killed in severe winters. Sometimes this can be death by drought when the soil is frozen so deep down and for so long that roots are unable to absorb even the minimal moisture requirements of winter. While in Britain H. helix and its clones can be regarded as hardy this is not so with the thinner-leaved house-plant kinds. If planted outside these may well survive but are often far from happy.

Of the remaining species H. azorica is as hardy as helix; canariensis and its varieties considerably less so. They will survive in southern Britain and there are some venerable specimens of 'Gloire de Marengo' to prove it, but a severe winter can leave them the worse for wear although they usually recover. *H. colchica* and *H. pastuchovii* are possibly a little hardier than *helix*; *H. nepalensis* and *H. rhombea* a little less so.

The varying temperature extremes that obtain across the Unites States have led the American Ivy Society to instigate numerous hardiness trials as reported in their journals. Here again results can be deceptive, for local conditions can make important differences.

THE IVY PARASITE

Parasitic plants, those that live upon other plants and, lacking the green life-producing chlorophyll, derive their nourishment from others, have a curious fascination.

Whilst it can be readily shown and cannot be over-emphasized that ivy is not in any way parasitic, the fact that it is occasionally parasitized by another plant is less commonly known. The plant that can do this is one of the broomrapes, *Orobancheae hederae*. The family *Orobancheacea* has seven species indigenous to the UK, most of them parasitic on one particular host, in this instance upon ivy. Having no green tissue of their own they depend for sustenance upon their hosts.

Where the ivy broomrape becomes established it appears from the ground near the base of the ivy as a dull-purple upright stem, 22–38cm (9–15in) high, bearing oval, slightly pointed, light-brown leaves and hooded, five-lobed, dingy-yellow flowers. Following fertilization the egg-shaped seed capsule sheds a vast quantity of minute seed. The erect stems persist, dead and brown through the winter.

Recorded as fairly frequent in the south of England, Ireland and on the continent, a colony, if that be the term, has sat at the foot of a venerable *H. hibernica* 'Deltoidea' at Kew Gardens, London, for as many years as I can recall. It is also present extensively in the Oxford Botanic Garden, having originally been introduced for botanical teaching purposes. There it has spread among several species and clones suggesting that it has no specific preferences.

Where the ivy parasite is present I have not seen visual damage or deterioration in the ivy; certainly vigorous growing species and clones can shrug it off, but I would hesitate to introduce it to less vigorous kinds. It is possible to purchase the seed which should be introduced around the young roots of a mature ivy in a reasonably moist situation. The parasitic plant will appear some 12 or 18 months later.

Another parasitic plant fairly common in Britain is the lesser dodder, *Cuscuta epithymum*, but there are no records of it nor the rarer greater dodder, *Cuscuta europea*, parasitizing

Orobanchae hederae, the ivy broomrape, can parasitize ivy but appears to do no harm to vigorous growing species

ivy. In 1902 however an instance of Indian dodder, *Cuscuta reflexa*, growing on ivy in a cool greenhouse at the Trinity College gardens, Dublin was reported in the Royal Horticultural Society Journal. Hooker in his *Himalayan Journals* (1847–51) says this dodder covered even tall trees with a golden web. Recent plant explorations in the Himalayas have not, so far as I am aware, reported plants attacked in this way although *H. nepalensis* has been found in various forms. It may be that in Dublin, under greenhouse conditions, it was an 'opportunist' infestation.

VARIEGATION

Variegation in plants has always held a fascination for mankind. In the first century AD it was noted by the Roman naturalist Pliny who, in his description of variegated ivy, gave the first written record of a variegated plant.

Plants are normally green for it is only within green leaves that photosynthesis, the process which manufactures plant material, takes place; it is the process upon which all life depends. It follows that variegation, the absence of the green matter chlorophyll from a leaf or part of a leaf, is a retrograde step.

When variegation occurs in nature it is, due to the lack of chlorophyll, the weaker growth and is rapidly overtaken by the more robust green. This is why gardeners cut out green growths that appear on variegated plants: failure so to do can result in the whole plant reverting in time to its green state. Mankind with insatiable curiosity for the unusual and decorative has noted and retained these malfunctioned plants so that variegated forms exist of almost every type of plant grown. In respect of ivies, 279 kinds are listed in this book of which 103 are variegated.

CAUSES OF VARIEGATION

A typical ivy leaf (see fig 1) is 240–60 microns thick, that is about a quarter of a millimetre. The upper and lower surfaces comprise epidermal cells, strengthened and rendered impermeable by a substance called cutin. Immediately below the upper surface cells are the somewhat vertical 'pallisade' cells, below them, rounded or roughly hexagonal, 'parenchymatous' cells. Within the cells are minute granular bodies, leucoplasts, some 50 to 100 per cell. These are usually heavily concentrated in the pallisade cells where, in proximity to the surface, they can absorb more light. Initially they are colourless but upon exposure to light they develop chlorophyll and are termed chloroplasts. The chlorophyll pigment can be of two types, chlorophyll (a) is bluish green, chlorophyll (b) yellowish green, differences which account for the slightly different greens seen in various ivy clones. Variegation is caused by any interruption of this greening process.

Genetic variegation

Sometimes it is a genetic or inherited mutation that inhibits the production of chlorophyll. This is the cause of variegation where white tissue occurs sporadically during the development of otherwise normal green foliage. *H. hibernica* 'Variegata' is an example. In such variegation, cuttings taken from green tissue will produce green plants but at some time in their growth variegation will occur. The white and green marbled leaves of the attractive little nasturtium, *Tropaeolum majus* 'Alaska', which comes true from seed, is a genetic variegation. The striking yellow of *H. helix* 'Buttercup' is probably a genetic mutation since it too comes true from seed.

Chimaeric variegation

Chimaeric variegation is caused by mutant chloroplasts. It is the result of one or more cells losing the ability to produce chlorophyll. The plastids then remain as colourless leucoplasts producing white leaf areas or degrees of yellow if and when yellow plastids are also present. By cell division and multiplication they may eventually dominate layers of the multi-layered shoot apex.

Periclinal chimaeras are those in which such a complete layer of cells overlays a contrasting core. Thus where a 'white' layer overlays a green core (fig 2) the leaves will develop with a white or yellow edge, as for example in *H.*

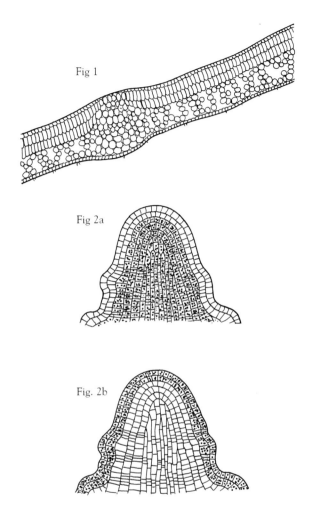

Fig 1

Fig 2a

Fig. 2b

Fig 1 Transverse section of an ivy leaf
Fig 2a An outer layer of white cells and inner core of green cells produce white-edged leaves
Fig 2b An outer layer of green cells and inner core of white cells give rise to white-centred leaves

helix 'Chester'. If the outer layer is green and the inner core yellow (fig 3) the leaves will appear yellow centred and green edged as in *H. helix* 'Goldheart'

If the mutant cells do not comprise a complete 'layer' but only a portion, the chimaera is said to be sectorial and then the variegation is random as in *H. helix* 'Cavendishii' or *H. colchica* 'Dentata Variegata'. Some sectorial chimaeras affect concentrations of chloroplasts so that the leaf has areas of different greens or grey-greens. The grey-green areas are often where the concentration of chloroplasts is in the parenchymatous cells which, being recessed in the leaf, are less prominent. Examples of these mixed greens are found in *H. helix* 'Bruder Ingobert' and *H. helix* 'Minty'.

Virus variegation

It is sometimes thought that the more unusual kinds of ivy variegation are invariably caused by virus infection. This is not so. While it is probable that the suffused type of variegation seen in *H. helix* 'Angularis Aurea' and 'Caenwoodiana Aurea' are virus induced (see page 150) very many other clones have been tested for virus and proved negative. Cases have been reported of ivies having the bright yellow 'vein clearing' type of variegation seen in *Lonicera japonica* 'Aureo-reticulata'. The most notable was that of *H. helix* 'Tessellata' (see page 119). It created a stir in the horticultural world and received an RHS Award of Merit in 1893 but after two years all variegation had disappeared. It is possible that ivies can be affected temporarily by viruses and that these may be soil borne and transmitted by nematodes. This may have happened in the case of 'Tessellata'. Many clones have clear white veins but there is no indication that this is a result of anything other than varietal differences. The pale areas seen around the veins of *H. pastuchovii* var. *cypria* appear to be low concentrations of chlorophyll b.

Coloured variegation

Yellow plastids called carotenoides are present in most leaves. They come to our notice in autumn when, following the deterioration of the chloroplasts, they remain, often combining with anthocyanins to give us the lovely leaf colours of autumn.

Carotenoides absorb light at the violet end of the spectrum and it is thought that they may contribute to photosynthetic activity. This may explain why the yellow-leaved 'Buttercup' grows quite vigorously and clones such as 'Goldchild' that have considerable areas of yellow grow perfectly well. The carotenoid in ivy is known as xanthophy; when it is missing the leaf, or a portion of it, is white and it is noticeable that in such clones, *H. helix* 'White Knight' for example, growth is less vigorous. Very rarely, variegation can combine yellow and white. This is seen in the beautiful lacecap hydrangea 'Quadricolour' but to my knowledge in only one ivy, *H. helix* 'Golden Snow'.

A pigment sometimes present in the cell sap, anthocyanin, gives the red, blue and purple colouration to most flowers and leaves. It is present in most ivies, seen in the usually purple petioles, but is totally absent in some clones, *H. helix* 'Persian Carpet' for example. The leaves of certain clones such as *H. helix* 'Atropurpurea' and *H. helix* 'Glymii'

The yellow-edged *Hedera helix* 'Chester' (top) and yellow-centred *Hedera helix* 'Goldheart' (above) are examples of two different forms of periclinal chimaera

colour deep purple in cold weather and have some horticultural value accordingly. The exact causes are not known: anthocyanins develop more strongly in acidic conditions, but it is possible that the reaction is set off by lower light and temperature levels. The same purple or red colouration can occur in ivies under stress; plants kept dry and pot-bound can appear to have 'red' leaves and indeed have been passed on to the unwary as 'red ivies'. On a happier note the purple edge to the wavy leaves of *H. helix* 'Melanie' (see page 95) is due to a band of anthocyanin-enriched cells that serve to make it one of the most attractive house-plant ivies introduced in recent years.

PLATE II

All plants are shown at approximately ³/₄ size

H. pastuchovii var. *cypria*

H. colchica

H. helix 'Angularis Aurea'

H. canariensis var. *algeriensis*

H. helix 'Goldheart'

H. colchica 'Sulphur Heart'

H. canariensis var. *algeriensis* 'Gloire de Marengo'

H. colchica 'Dentata Variegata'

H. helix 'Atropurpurea'

H. canariensis

H. azorica 'Pico'

H. colchica 'Dendroides'

H. rhombea

4
NOMENCLATURE

Botanically the world's plant life is divided into divisions, classes and orders and then into families, within which are genera. The family Araliaceae to which ivy belongs contains 57 genera, mostly tropical and varying from small trees of 12m (36ft) high to the familiar woodland ivy. The members within a genus are termed species; all ivies are of the genus *Hedera* but each species has its own distinctive name, thus we have *H. helix* the common ivy, *H. colchica* the Persian ivy and so on.

There is sometimes variation within species; the classification allows for this by sub-division into categories, subspecies (ssp.), varietas (var.) and forma (f.). A sub-species is usually a distinct variation within a species but not such as to justify species status. Variation in leaf size and character is very general and is not a basis for definition as a sub-species.

The term varietas is used to describe consistent but fairly slight differences often caused by geographic separation. Forma denotes a slight but consistent difference, for example the yellow-berried poet's ivy (see page 108) differs only in the colour of its berries and slightly lighter green leaves.

ORIGIN OF THE NAME

Ivy nomenclature has always been somewhat confused, indeed as the *Hedera* entry in *Flora Europaea* points out:

> There is little agreement among authors on the taxonomic treatment of this genus, the number of European species varying from one to six.

Theophrastus in 314 BC and Pliny the Elder (23–79 AD) recognized various ivy varieties but did not put distinct names to them. The dimorphic nature of the plant gave rise to the idea that there were two kinds, the creeping and the climbing, a delusion that persisted until the 18th century. The early 19th century saw the definition of the North African ivy by Willdenow, and as the century proceeded, the introduction and naming of the Persian, Himalayan and Japanese ivies.

In *Species Plantarum* (1753) the Swedish botanist Carl von Linne (1707–78) or Carolus Linnaeus as he termed himself, defined the ivy's generic name as *Hedera* taking the Latin name as used by Vergil, Ovid and others and derived from the verb *haerere*, to attach oneself. *Hedera* may well have been a general term for the plant but Theophrastus and Pliny writing more specifically on the plant used the word from the Greek, *helix*, which means twining. Although not particularly appropriate since ivy clings and does not twine, Linnaeus defined the common ivy using both words as *Hedera helix*.

As regards the common names of the plant there is some doubt as to the origin of the British word 'ivy'. According to Prior's *Popular names of British Plants'*, it was spelt 'Ivyne' in Anglo-Saxon manuscripts. In early times on the continent 'Ive' or 'Iven-Baum' belonged equally to Yew (*Taxus baccata*) and to ivy; in Britain they were gradually separated to the terms we know today. In old High German it was *Ebah* from which arose the present German name *Epheu*. The Icelandic name for ivy, a plant which does not occur in Iceland, is *bergfletta*. The French is *lierre*, the Russian *bljustach*. The Dutch *klimop*, appropriate to British ears, does indeed mean 'climbing up'. The Italian *edera* and the Spanish *hiedra* show links with the Latin. The Oxford English Dictionary extends *Hedera* to hederaceously – after the manner of ivy, hederated – crowned with ivy and hederigerent – bearing or wearing ivy.

VARIETIES AND CLONES

In the past the term 'variety' denoted a cultivated form of a plant, thus one spoke of sweet pea 'varieties' but since 1950 this has been replaced by the more descriptive 'cultivar', literally a cultivated variety. It is usually applied to seed-raised or hybridized plants rather than to plants arising from some form of mutation or natural variation. Thus one would speak of the rose 'Peace' as a cultivar whereas the Corkscrew

Hazel (*Corylus avellana* 'Contorta') is a clone, every plant being descended by vegetative propagation from the one found in 1863 in a hedgerow in Gloucestershire, UK. Most ivy variations are clones.

Ivy is a dimorphic plant (see page 25) and in this connection an interesting nomenclatural point arises. Cuttings taken from the adult stage give rise to shrubby and horticulturally useful plants; they were popular with the Victorians who often added the descriptive epithet 'Arborescens' to the varietal name. However, under the rules of the International Commission for the Nomenclature of Cultivated Plants, January 1st 1959 became a 'cut off' date for the use of Latinized cultivar names. Thus *H. helix* 'Arborescens' as published in a number of 19th-century catalogues is acceptable but, for example, to now publish *H. helix* 'Goldheart Arborescens' for the shrubby form of that plant would be invalid. It is however perfectly in order to publish *H. helix* 'Arborescent Goldheart' since the 'Arborescent' unlike 'Arborescens' is not Latin. Alternatively, a totally new name may be used, thus the arborescent form of *H. helix* 'Angularis Aurea' has been published as *H. helix* 'Mary Eggins'. Other forms of propagation are covered by this rule; the practice of grafting shoots from arborescent plants of *H. helix* 'Erecta' onto stocks of common ivy or onto *Fatshedera* so as to produce the dwarf clump-forming plants marketed as 'Humpty Dumpty' complies with the rules.

Botanists past and present have disagreed on the definition of the various *Hedera* species. For this book I have made my way through the maze of botanical floras and botanists' pronouncements but to an extent have followed, particularly as regards the somewhat controversial *H. canariensis*, what might be termed the status quo.

The summary of species, varieties and clones endeavours to unravel and evaluate their histories and to provide definitive descriptions. Most of these variations are clones that have been derived by vegetative propagation from a single individual. Such a clone will have been first seen as a 'sport' or mutation showing some distinct leaf or habit difference. Left to nature these mutations rarely persist; unless they are to the plant's advantage they die out, being overtaken by the usual and more useful growth. Noted however by keen gardeners, cuttings are taken and with care and subsequent propagation a uniform population is built up and the introduction given a name. Nowadays names must be factual or as the International Commission for the Nomenclature of Cultivated Plants puts it, 'fancy' names and not in Latin form although Latinized epithets such as 'Dentata' for example, if published before January 1st 1959, are valid and indeed must not be replaced.

IDENTIFYING IVIES

Most people when acquiring a new ivy or seeing one that is attractively different, seek its name. Indeed this is so with all plants; even non-gardeners admiring a plant or flower invariably ask 'What is its name?'.

Identification of ivies is a two-stage affair, first to ascertain the species, then the variety or clone. With some plants it is possible to identify species by means of a question-and-answer-type botanical key. Such a key is not very suitable for ivies because of the differences between juvenile and adult

The hairs of *Hedera helix* 'Angularis Aurea' (top) and *Hedera hibernica* (below) differ in the layout of their rays

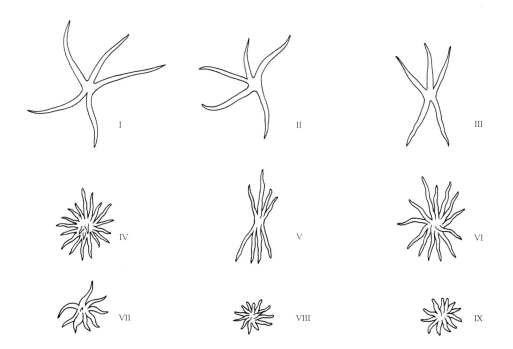

Leaf hairs of ivy species magnified 50 times:
I *Hedera azorica*; II *Hedera helix*; III *Hedera hibernica*;
IV *Hedera colchica*; V *Hedera maroccana*;
VI *Hedera canariensis*; VII *Hedera nepalensis*;
VIII *Hedera pastuchovii*; IX *Hedera rhombea*

leaves, also the flowering stage is not always available. Fortunately evolution has provided a built-in system of identification through the minute hairs or trichomes (see page 27). These hairs are usually discernible with a ten-times lens. Found on the young shoots and on the petioles and undersides of the leaves, their differing characteristics divide the genus into two groups.

In the first group the hairs are white and stellate, looking like ragged miniature stars with three to five rays like sprawling arms spread out in irregular fashion. The second and larger group has very small scale-like hairs. Rusty in colour and with 12–18 very short rays, they are about the same size as the dreaded red-spider mite and the two have been known to be confused!

In the first group, if the stellate hairs are very plentiful, almost like wool, and can indeed be scraped off, this indicates *H. azorica*. If the hairs are not so numerous, are scattered and the rays spread in irregular fashion, the species is *H. helix*. If the rays show a tendency to lie in a parallel fashion rather than haphazardly the species will be *H. hibernica*.

This is a tricky one since the only other factor separating *hibernica* from *helix* is their differing chromosome numbers, the counting of which is a highly specialized laboratory procedure, not a job for the potting shed!

Turning to the second group, if the leaves are large, say 6–8 x 7–9cm (3 x 3¼in), and the scale-hairs few in number the species is likely to be either *H. canariensis* or *H. maroccana*. A combination of similarly large leaves with rather more numerous scale-hairs and leaves that, when crushed, smell of resin or turpentine indicates *H. colchica*. Similar hairs and an aromatic leaf whose shape is long, unlobed and dark green suggests *H. pastuchovii*. The same long shape but lighter green and with often some indistinct lobing and scale-hairs so numerous as to give the shoots a 'rusty' appearance indicates *H. nepalensis*. Similar scales, not so numerous and combined with a small, delicate, unlobed or occasionally three-lobed leaf indicates *H. rhombea*.

The botanical varieties and clones of each species exhibit the same hair characteristics as their parent; in fact species other than *helix* have few varieties and clones. It is in *helix* that the great diversity of ivies becomes truly apparent, ranging from the non-climbing 'Erecta' to the minute-leaved 'Spetchley'.

Having identified the species the search can be narrowed by checking against the Index of Ivies (page 153). The descriptions given in the A–Z listing of species, varieties and clones (pages 39–135) contain a few botanical terms as illustrated right and on page 38. As regards colour, when two colours are recorded the first is assumed to be the dominant or more likely. Thus 'green-purple' might indicate a green stem with traces of purple. Similarly leaves described as 'cream-yellow' are those that veer towards white, while 'yellow-cream' suggests yellow as the dominant colour. Greens are given as light green, mid-green and dark green.

IVY COLLECTIONS

Interest in ivy developed rapidly during the 19th century. Nurserymen's stocks comprised what might be termed 'collections', thus in 1867 the nurseryman William Paul wrote of his collection of "more than 40 sorts".

Probably the first real collection was that of the Royal Horticultural Society at Chiswick, UK. Hibberd's 1890 report on the collection in the RHS Journal enumerated 46 kinds of ivy. Meanwhile at the Royal Botanic Garden, Kew, the Curator George Nicholson after the turn of the century established a collection on the Ivy Wall near the Natural Order Beds. It is thought that material from this collection was sent by Nicholson to G H M Lawrence and was the basis for his collection at the Bailey Hortorium, Cornell University, Ithaca, USA.

In 1979/80 the RHS conducted an invited Trial of Ivies but the 200 kinds submitted to their Wisley Trial Ground illustrated the confusion existing in ivy names. In the hope of easing this situation the RHS proposed that a *Hedera* collection be incorporated in the programme of the National Council for the Conservation of Garden Plants (NCCPG). With the cooperation of the National Trust this was established at Erddig, near Wrexham in Clwyd, Wales, a National Trust property with extensive garden walls. Material propagated from the Trial, duly verified for name, formed the basis of this collection.

A smaller collection was formed by the authorities at Newcastle Agricultural College and recently a very comprehensive collection has been formed by Fibrex Nurseries Ltd at Pebworth near Stratford-upon-Avon. All are under the NCCPG jurisdiction.

Ivy collections are not easy to maintain. The vining types need to be grown on walls at least 2m (6ft) high and varieties need to be well spaced to avoid their growing into one another.

It is desirable to have a soil area of at least 1.3m (4ft) wide in which the variety should be planted so as to demonstrate its ground-cover capabilities. Shoots are then led to the wall. Upon reaching the top of the wall most kinds will become 'adult' and that arborescent character will spread

PARTS OF LEAF AND STEM

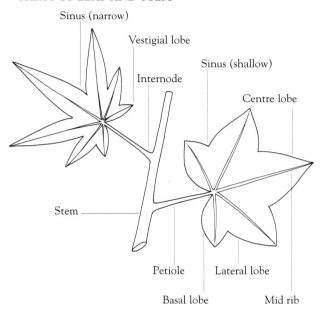

downward to encompass the whole plant. When plants become totally adult they cease to produce the juvenile growth that is usually the horticultural attraction; it also becomes difficult to find material for propagation. Growing the plants in a bed as suggested provides insurance against this, since at soil level some creeping shoots are sure to be found. If the purpose is to display the juvenile type of growth it may be necessary when the plant achieves arborescence to reduce growth to ground level and train the plant afresh.

While some house-plant-type ivies can be planted out in this manner, collections of such ivies are best maintained in pots in cold greenhouse conditions. Such a collection requires considerable attention in watering, cutting back and so on, and replacement every few years since the plants easily grow out of character.

In America the American Ivy Society has encouraged the establishment of ivy reference collections by distributing correctly named material (see page 157 for the location of collections). Details of these and of any others can be obtained form the American Ivy Society, PO Box 2123, Naples, Florida, 33939-2123, USA.

In Germany the Benedictine Monastery of Neuberg near Heidelberg retains and nurtures the very important collection which was established at the nursery there by the late Brother Ingobert Heieck.

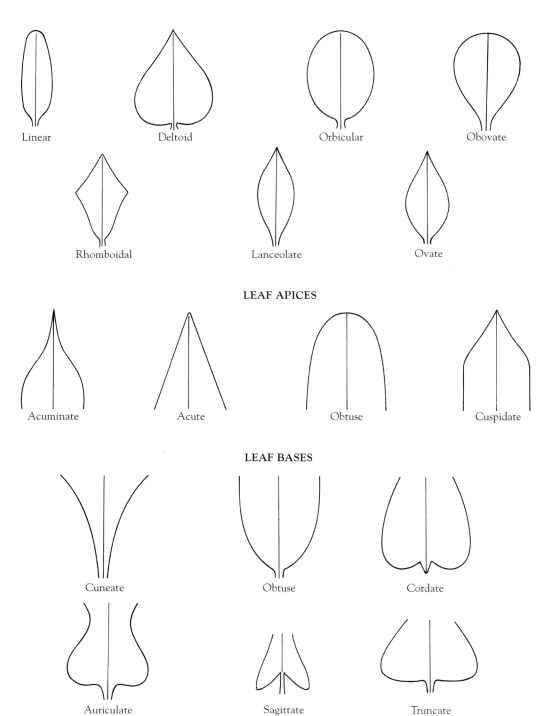

LEAF SHAPES

Linear   Deltoid   Orbicular   Obovate

Rhomboidal   Lanceolate   Ovate

LEAF APICES

Acuminate   Acute   Obtuse   Cuspidate

LEAF BASES

Cuneate   Obtuse   Cordate

Auriculate   Sagittate   Truncate

5
A–Z OF SPECIES, VARIETIES & CLONES

In the botanical descriptions given in this chapter, all leaf measurements are recorded as length x breadth.
The following abbreviations and symbol are also used:

AIS   American Ivy Society
BIS   British Ivy Society

♣   RHS Award of Garden Merit
FCC (T)   RHS First Class Certificate (at Ivy Trial)
PC   RHS Preliminary Commendation
HC   RHS Highly Commended

ICNCP   International Commission for Nomenclature of Cultivated Plants

Hedera azorica Carr

This species was introduced to Britain from the island of St Michael (São Miguel) in the Azores by Osborn & Sons of Fulham, London, some time prior to 1870 when they listed it in their catalogue as *Hedera helix azorica*. It circulated in the trade but became known generally, why is not clear, as *H. canariensis azorica*.

Hedera azorica was not mentioned by Hibberd in his report of the Ivy Trial at the RHS Chiswick gardens 1887/9 but, according to the Gardener's Chronicle of December 1889, it had by then received an FCC as *H. canariensis azorica* and had certainly been widely planted. The French botanist Elie Abel Carrière (1830–1922) described *H. azorica* in an article *Une Importante Collection de Lierres* published in Revue Horticole in 1890.

A few nurserymen followed his nomenclature in their catalogues but generally the plant retained its connection with *H. canariensis*. Indeed the entry in Bean's *Trees and Shrubs Hardy in the British Isles* (1914) reads

> *H. canariensis* var. *azorica.* A vigorous variety with leaves three to six inches across, vivid green, five or seven lobed, lobes ovate, blunt pointed, the

quite young wood and leaves covered with a thick tawny felt. Introduced from St. Michael in the Azores by the late firm of Osborn of Fulham.

This was repeated in subsequent editions and in other works. Doubts as to the accuracy of that name were resolved by Dr McAllister who in 1988 proposed specific status for *azorica* resurrecting Carrière's name accordingly. A large-leaved unlobed form found on the archipelagian island of Pico has been introduced (see 'Pico' below) and it may be that this is the more typical ivy of the Azorean islands. Ivy seen on São Miguel at present is mostly unlobed and it seems probable that the material upon which Carrière based his name was an isolated clone. Each island has slightly divergent forms: material collected on Faial is unlobed but is smaller in leaf than that of São Miguel or Pico. All have the extensive, almost felted, white stellate hairs.

The species was however based on the Osborn introduction and, despite the passing of the years, it is impossible to fault Bean's description. The pleasant bright matt-green colour and unusual lobing of its leaves give it an air of distinction and make it an excellent wall ivy.

Habit: Vining.
Stems: Green. Internodes 3–4cm (1¼–1½in).
Petioles: Green.
Leaves: 5–7-lobed, 9–11cm (3½–4⅓in) by 10–12cm (4–4¾in). Centre lobe only slightly larger than the 4 laterals, the 2 additional lobes when present are little more than protrusions. Sinuses fairly shallow, lobes bluntly acute. Stellate, long, 3–5-rayed hairs are extensive on young stems and leaves, sometimes giving a felted appearance. Colour bright mid-green and slightly matt, veins a lighter green. Chromosome No 2n=48.

Hedera azorica 'Pico'

The discovery in 1979 on the island of Pico of an ivy dissimilar to *H. azorica* suggests that the plant introduced by

Osborns in 1870 was not typical of the ivies of the archipelago; it is unlobed and markedly less hairy. In cultivation it appears reasonably hardy in Britain, not unlike *canariensis* in growth and fulfiling a similar horticultural role.

Habit: Vining.

Stems: Green-purple. Internodes 3–5cm (1¼–2in).

Petioles: Purple-green.

Leaves: Unlobed; 4–6cm (1½–2⅓in) by 6–8cm (2⅓–3in). Apices obtuse, leaf base slightly cordate. Young leaves appear flat in plane. Colour mid-green. Hairs similar to those of *H. azorica* but by no means so extensive.

Hedera azorica 'Variegata'

The origins of this variegated form are not certain. The first definite record appears to be that in the Kew Hand List of 1925 which shows *azorica* as a variety of *canariensis* and goes on to list var. *azorica variegata*. In the same list *algeriensis*, *maderensis* and *viridis* are given as synonyms of *canariensis*.

The 1932 catalogue of L R Russell Ltd of Surrey, listed "*H. canariensis* 'Azorica Variegata' – Medium-sized leaves, margined silver." In the Morris Arboretum Bulletin, Vol 7, No 2, 1956 the American botanist G H M Lawrence brought *algeriensis*, *maderensis* and *azorica* into synonymy as *H. canariensis* and went on to describe a clone with "Twigs and petioles green, leaves uniformly variegated with ivory- to cream-coloured margins, occasionally some leaves all white". He called this *H. canariensis* 'Canary Cream' but the description matches *H. azorica* 'Variegata' as we know it.

The plant is less vigorous than the type and benefits from a more sheltered situation. It is not widely planted and is probably of interest only to ivy enthusiasts. In 1980 I examined a large plant on the sheltered terrace at Tatton Park Garden, Knutsford, Cheshire, which I estimated then to have been about 30 years old.

There is a clone, rarely seen, that has a suffused and rather transient yellow variegation.

Habit: Vining.

Stems: Green. Internodes 3–4cm (1¼–1½in).

Petioles: Green.

Leaves: 5–7-lobed, 8–10cm (3–4in) by 8–10cm (3–4in). Centre lobe slightly larger than the four laterals, additional lobes little more than protrusions. Sinuses shallow, apices bluntly acute, hairs extensive as in the species. Colour light green, variegation cream-white and mostly at the leaf margin.

Hedera canariensis Willd

This, the Canary Islands and North African ivy, was the first ivy species (apart from *helix* named by Linnaeus in

1753) to be named and described in detail. The material was collected by Professor Broussonet (1761–1807) who collected in Morocco in 1794–9 and in the Canary Islands 1799–1803. Much of his material went to the botanist A P D Candolle but duplicates were sent to Willdenow who, in the Magazin Gesellschaft Naturforschender Freunde zu Berlin ii, 170 (1808) described *Hedera canariensis* as follows:

> The late Professor Broussonet showed me a branch of *Hedera helix* which he had collected from Tenerife which seemed astonishingly different; having made a very detailed study I find it an excellent species which I will exactly describe here under the name *Hedera canariensis*.

His Latin description translates as follows:

> Leaves of the flowering shoots roundish, pointed, with two equal lobes with branched veins, flowers in erect umbels. Stems smooth and round, leaves alternate, roundish, pointed and with a cordate base. Entire, glabrous and very shiny, veins branching. Petioles 1½in long, in transverse section semi-circular, glossy. Flowers in umbels terminal and unbranched. Peduncles thickened and one flowered.

By the middle of the century it was realized that the 'Canary Island' ivy was not confined to the Canary Islands. In 1865 writing in the Journal of Botany, Dr Berthold Seeman gave its range as the Canary Islands, North Africa, Madeira and the Iberian peninsula.

The existence of the North African ivy on the Canary Islands was confirmed by Dr Morris, Assistant Director of Kew, who wrote in the RHS Journal in 1896 that he saw it "truly wild in the Barranco de la Virgin on Grand Canary growing on rocks in large quantity". In 1912 Professor Friedrich Tobler described the North African ivy in considerable detail under the name *H. canariensis*.

Material collected by the Glasgow Naturalist Expedition of 1979 at La Mercedes, Tenerife and submitted to McAllister for identification appears to agree with that described by Willdenow in 1808 and indeed with the herbarium specimen.

H. canariensis can be grown as a climber in southern Britain but any garden value is far eclipsed by that of its botanical variant, var. *algeriensis*.

Habit: Vining.

Stems: Purple-green, smooth. Internodes 3–6cm (1¼–2⅓in). Hairs scale-like, 10–15 rays.

Petioles: Purple-green.

Leaves: Unlobed, occasionally 3-lobed but the lobes appearing little more than protuberances, 5–6cm

(2–2⅓in) by 5–7cm (2–2¾in). Leaf blade flat, leaf base slightly cordate, apices bluntly acute. Mid-green darkening with age, slightly glossy. Chromosome No 2n=96.

Hedera canariensis var. algeriensis

A slightly controversial issue in the nomenclature of ivies in recent years was the proposal by McAllister and Alison Rutherford to define the plant previously known as *H. canariensis* as *H. algeriensis*, largely on the basis that *canariensis* had not been found in Algeria. In the same publication (The Plantsman Vol 10, pt 1, 1988) they elevated the Madeiran ivy, known as *canariensis* var. *maderensis*, to species status as *H. maderensis*. I regard these proposals as not necessarily correct and in this book adhere to varietal status in both instances.

The origin of var. *algeriensis* was described in 1853 in the Belgian periodical La Belgique Horticole. It records the North African ivy, le lierre d'Alger, saying that it was introduced into France by M Joseph Auzende who in 1832 and 1835 found it very abundant around Algiers but that by 1840, due among other things to urbanization, it had become very rare (it is just as rare today). The article goes on to say that this "magnificent ivy" was extensively propagated by nurseryman M Rantonnet of Hyères and that it was totally different from the local French ivy and the Irish ivy. "M Rantonnet calls the ivy *Hedera algeriensis* but some wish to change it to *H. macrophylla*."

It would seem that following Rantonnet's efforts the plant became well established – indeed virtually naturalized – in southern France and Spain, with numerous clonal variations occurring. 'Gloire de Marengo' is probably one of the best known. Shortly after World War II the variety achieved popularity as a house plant, under the name 'Montgomery' or 'Monty'.

Habit: Vining.
Stems: Red-green, smooth. Internodes 3–5cm (1¼–2in). Hairs scale-like, 10–15 rays.
Petioles: Red-green.
Leaves: Unlobed or very slightly 3-lobed. 10–15cm (4–6in) by 8–12cm (3–4¾in). Leaf base cordate, apices bluntly acute. Light green, very glossy but a matt-leaved form is known.

Hedera canariensis var. algeriensis 'Gloire de Marengo'

This variegated form of the African or Canary Island ivy is probably the most extensively grown house-plant ivy in Europe, as well as being extremely popular in America and elsewhere, but the history of its name is as confused as any. In 1883 the celebrated French nursery firm of Vilmorin included a description of *H. canariensis variegata* in *Vilmorin's Illustrated Flower Garden*, but this name did not come into general circulation and for some 50 years catalogues and writers variously used the names *algeriensis*, *canariensis*, *grandifolia* and *hibernica* with *variegata* added for what was obviously the same plant.

Lawrence & Schulze (1942) in their analysis of *H. canariensis* cultivars combined *H. algeriensis variegata* and the *H. grandifolia variegata* of Hibberd as *H. canariensis variegata*, conceding in a footnote that the plant had been grown and distributed as 'Gloire de Marengo'. This was certainly true for in 1924 Hillier & Sons of Winchester, Hampshire, listed *Hedera canariensis* 'Gloire de Marengo' while in 1936 Jackmans of Woking, Surrey, in their influential *Planter's Handbook*, described *H. canariensis* 'Gloire de Marengo' as having "Large leaves, merging from green through silvery-grey to silver at the edge", a description that is hard to fault. The plant had therefore been in circulation as 'Gloire de Marengo' for 18 years prior to the Lawrence & Schulze analysis of 1942.

Brother Ingobert Heieck traced the origin of the name to Marengo Park in Algiers. He considered that although established as *variegata* in the 1880s it had been rediscovered in Algiers in the 1920s and acquired the name 'Gloire de Marengo'. The name would certainly have more appeal in France than *variegata*, for Marengo was the village in Italy where Napoleon won a crushing victory that resulted in northern Italy coming within his control. In 1927 W Fromow Ltd, wholesale nurserymen of Windlesham, Surrey, listed the plant as 'Souvenir de Marengo' a name still occasionally used.

In view of the plant's history and because of the well established use of the name, certainly since 1924, it seems appropriate to ignore the *variegata* of Vilmorin, despite the priority, and to retain the current name.

It is a fast-growing, decorative ivy, ideally suited to a high garden or house wall. In Britain it will survive very severe winters but with some loss of leaf and a resulting poor appearance until summer. Its prime use in Europe is indoors as a pot plant or a trained column or pyramid.

Habit: Vining.
Stems: Wine-red when young. Internodes 4–5cm (1½–2in).
Petioles: Wine-red, smooth.
Leaves: Unlobed, occasional vestigial signs of tri-lobing, leaf shape ovate, apices acute, 9–11cm (3½–4⅓in) by 9–11cm (3½–4⅓in). Light green with broken or large

areas of silvery grey-green. Some yellow-white variegation usually at the edges and far more pronounced in young shoots and plants. Leaves often slightly cupped, veins not very prominent.

Hedera canariensis var. algeriensis 'Margino-Maculata'

The name of this mottled mutant of 'Gloire de Marengo' was coined by Lawrence & Schulze in 1942; it was given varietal status and a Latin description. This was before the clarification of the use of the category *varietas* for botanical variations of wild origin rather than horticultural selections. However a further paper by Lawrence (1956) made amends by listing the plant correctly as a clone. Plants of 'Gloire de Marengo' will occasionally mutate to produce this clone, which in turn will often produce shoots identical to 'Gloire de Marengo'. In recent years the plant has become known in the trade as 'Marmorata' and unfortunately, since several ivies in the past have been given this name, it is confusing as well as invalid.

Grown mainly for the house-plant trade, its rapid growth and bright colouring make it a useful plant for large pyramids and general decorative work. It grows well and fast outdoors in good summers and survives mild winters in Britain but can be badly hit by cold winds or temperatures below -4°C (25°F). Pierot (1974) quotes it as grown outdoors on the West Coast of the USA but recorded that she would not grow it further north than South Connecticut.

Habit: Vining.

Stems: Wine-red when young. Internodes 4–5cm (1½–2in).

Petioles: Wine-red and smooth.

Leaves: Ovate, unlobed with vestigial signs of tri-lobing, apex acute, 9–11cm (3½–4⅓in) by 9–11cm (3½–4⅓in). Base colour light green, extensively mottled yellow-white. Occasional leaves particoloured.

Hedera canariensis var. algeriensis 'Ravensholst'

Plants of this large-leaved ivy began to circulate under this name from about 1972 but the origin of both clone and name remain a mystery. It is similar to several clones that are to be found in the south of France and Spain in the gardens of homes and hotels, indeed almost naturalized. These clones are probably descendants of a vigorous form of the North African ivy introduced into France according to La Belgique Horticole in the 1830s. Like 'Montgomery' it makes an effective large house plant when grown on moss-sticks or trellis. Its vigour and large leaves make it a good

Hedera canariensis var. *algeriensis* 'Margino-Maculata'

ground-cover plant in mild climates: *H. canariensis* itself is widely used as ground cover beside Californian freeways.

'Hispanica' is a three-lobed variation with a long acute centre lobe and almost equally long lateral lobes. The foliage reddens in cold weather.

Habit: Vining and vigorous.

Stems: Wine-red, smooth. Internodes 5–7cm (2–2¾in).

Petioles: Wine-red, green.

Leaves: 3-lobed, 10–13cm (4–5in) by 8–14cm (3–5½in). Centre lobe acute and broad. Laterals little more than protrusions, apices acute. Sinuses shallow, leaves occasionally unlobed and elliptical, leaf base truncate. Dark-green and glossy.

Hedera canariensis var. algeriensis 'Striata'

This is most probably the plant described by nurseryman William Paul in 1867 as "*Hedera canariensis aurea-maculata.* Leaves sometimes green but usually green finely clouded with gold, large, growth free and rapid."

Unfortunately *Hedera canariensis* and its varieties became confused with the Irish ivy (*H. hibernica*) and Paul's name was used to describe forms of *hibernica*. Hibberd substituted 'Grandifolia' for *canariensis* and in *The Ivy* (1872) this clone became 'Grandifolia Striata'. It was well therefore that Lawrence & Schulze in 1942, not recognizing Paul's name, described this ivy and selected for it a distinctive name. It is a vigorous grower, useful for walls or fences and suitable as ground cover for fairly sheltered areas. The faint streak of yellow in the leaf centre is somewhat fugitive and may not be present in every leaf. The plant has circulated in Britain under the synonyms 'Gold Leaf' and 'Golden Leaf'.

Habit: Vining.

Stems: Wine-red. Glabrous with few hairs. Internodes 5–7cm (2–2¾in).

Petioles: Wine-red. The petiole colour sometimes extends along veins on the leaf underside for 1–4cm (⅖–1½in).

Leaves: Unlobed and deltoid, 8–14cm (3–5½in) by 10–19cm (4–7½in). Occasional vestigial indications of tri-lobing. Margin slightly waved, apex often down-pointing. Lustrous dark-green with a slight yellow to light-green splash at the leaf centre. A spot of red at the petiole/leaf-blade junction, particularly in older leaves.

Hedera canariensis var. maderensis

An ivy with a slightly confused history, the name as *maderensis* is recorded by K Koch (1869); he cited no specimens and indicated that he did not believe it to be a species endemic to the island. Similarly when discussing *H. canariensis* (1870) he wrote "*H. canariensis* is also described under the name *H. maderensis* and it occurs in gardens."

The Rev R T Lowe in *Flora of Madeira* (1886) recorded the native ivy as "*H. helix*, 3–5-lobed, leaves smooth and shining" and commented that ropes for fishermen's boats were made of its stems but were neither strong nor durable. In an amending paragraph at the end of the work he quoted Seeman's work on ivy hairs and, commenting that it had 13–15 rays rather than the 6–8 of *helix*, he adjusted the entry to record the native ivy as *H. canariensis*.

The comments of Koch suggest that a plant from Madeira was circulating in the nursery trade, but looking at catalogues of 1880 to the 1930s it is certain that it was not the native ivy. All the catalogues describe *H. maderensis* or sometimes *madeirensis* as a plant with "silver variegation". From these descriptions it is evident that the plants were what we now know as *H. canariensis* var. *algeriensis* 'Gloire de Marengo'. This is not improbable: a wide range of tropical, semi-tropical and temperate plants had been introduced into Madeira. It is likely that the variegated form of *H. canariensis* would be among these.

It is apparent that the native Madeiran ivy was not in circulation and indeed, after Lowe's listing and description, received no attention until 1975 when it was collected by David McClintock from near Funchal, by Davis in 1984 from Poisa above Funchal and by Rose in 1985 from the Indigenous Botanic Garden at Ribeiro Frio. Following these introductions, McAllister in 1988 proposed it as a distinct species, *H. maderensis*, mainly by virtue of its chromosome count, 2n=144, as against those of *canariensis*, 2n=96 and *helix*, 2n=48. This however is the only factor to distinguish it from *canariensis* and in the *Flora of Madeira* (Press, Short & Turland, 1994) the proposal is refuted and the plant recorded as a variety of *H. canariensis*.

In Madeira the plant may be seen clothing the walls of terraced cultivated plots. From a distance the leaves are sufficiently glossy to reflect the light, noted by Lowe in 1886.

Habit: Vining.

Stems: Green-purple. Internodes 2–4cm (¾–1½in).

Petioles: Purple-green.

Leaves: 3-lobed, occasionally unlobed, 4–5cm (1½–2in) by 6–7cm (2⅓–2¾in). Sinuses very shallow or absent, lobes obtuse, leaf base truncate or slightly cordate. Mid- to dark green, initially very glossy. Adult leaves, flowers and fruit not seen. Hairs scale-like, white-brown, 10–16 rays.

Hedera colchica C Koch

The Persian or Colchic ivy is native to the region south of the Caspian and westward through the Caucasus to Asiatic Turkey. The definitive description is that of Caspar Koch, the German botanist who named it *colchica* from its habitat of ancient Colchis. The type specimen was reputedly in Berlin. The plant had reached Britain before 1859, certainly by 1851, and become known as *H. roegneriana* having been found, according to Seeman (1864) by Mr Roegner, "formerly Curator of the Botanic Gardens of Odessa". Although unpublished, this name was widely used and is still occasionally seen. Hibberd (1872) for no very good reason described the plant as *H. coriacea*, giving *colchica*, *roegneriana* and *cordifolia* as synonyms. *Caucasica* is another name invalidly used.

Typical of the species is the resinous odour of the leaves when crushed. The scale-type hairs can be described, as first noted by Seeman in 1864, as being very often two-lobed with some 6–10 rays in each lobe giving an average of 10–20 rays to each scale.

Hedera colchica is a useful ivy but its garden utility is often overshadowed by that of its larger leaved, more vigorous clone 'Dentata'. Slower growing and less easy to propagate than 'Dentata', *colchica* is the true bullock's heart ivy; elephant's ears is the name more appropriate to 'Dentata'. The true *colchica* is less often sold but is a suitable variety for situations in which a hardy, dark-green, relatively slow-growing ivy is required. 1993: ♔.

The plant called 'My Heart' by Pierot (1974) would appear to be identical to *colchica*.

Habit: Vining.

Stems: Green. Internodes 4–6cm (1½–2⅓in). Hairs rust-coloured, scale-like multiradiate in 2 lobes, 12–20 rays.

Petioles: Green.

Leaves: Ovate, generally unlobed, 6–12cm (2⅓–4¾in) by 6–8cm (2⅓–3in), margins entire, apices acute, leaf base cordate. Veins thick but recessed in the upper surface of the blade and correspondingly extruded on the under surface, Dark green. Adult leaves similar, more lanceolate. Inflorescence umbellate-corymbose, flower calyces triangularly toothed. Flowering mid- to late autumn, berry black. Chromosome No 2N=192.

Hedera colchica 'Batumi'

The clone described here was found in 1979 by Roy Lancaster (L.305) growing in woodland around the Botanic Garden of Russia's Black Sea port Batumi. It seems to be a half-way house between the heart-shaped leaved typical of *colchica* and the larger leaved and more lax 'Dentata'. Its colour and gloss make it a somewhat better garden plant than the slower growing, smaller leaved species.

Habit: Vining.

Stems: Purple. Internodes 4–8cm (1½–3in).

Petioles: Purple.

Leaves: 3-lobed, 9–13cm (3½–5in) by 9–12cm (3½–4¾in). Sinuses so shallow as often to suggest an unlobed leaf. In mature leaves the lobing is more apparent with the 3 lobes forward-pointing; lateral lobes ⅓ shorter than the centre lobe. Veins not particularly prominent; leaf plane flat, colour glossy dark green.

Hedera colchica 'Dendroides'

This ivy, usually seen only in botanic gardens or collections, has received little mention over the years. The only references I have found are those of Hibberd (1872) and Tobler (1912). Hibberd referred to it as "Dendroides – Tree-like thick-leaved ivy (Syn *roegneriana arborea*)" but proceeded to describe what appears to be an arborescent form of *H. colchica*, production and planting of which was popular at that time. However there does appear to be a form of *H. colchica* of considerable vigour, capable of producing stems 90–120cm (3–4ft) long in one season and with stem diameters of 1–1.5cm (½–¾in).

In the RHS Ivy Trial of 1978/9 some ivies submitted as *H. colchica* proved to be considerably more vigorous than others and these can be assumed to have been of this clone. Furthermore a clone collected in the Caucasus by Roy Lancaster in 1979 (L.310) would appear to be the dark-green form of 'Dendroides'.

The origin of Hibberd's name may be linked to references to 'Amurensis' and 'Acuta' that circulated towards the end of the last century. 'Amurensis' refers presumably to the Amur River region of Manchukuo, but I have been unable to find any authentic botanical references to it although one or two authors give the name as a synonym of *colchica*. A few catalogues have used the name, usually with a brief description such as a "large leaf", which could of course apply to *colchica*. *The Flora of the USSR* (1950) makes no mention of 'Amurensis' or indeed of any ivies from that region of the former USSR but due to past differences between the former USSR and China the area may not have been botanized extensively since the last century; certainly it could well be the eastern geographical limit of *H. colchica*.

I suspect that any connection between 'Dendroides' and 'Amurensis' is spurious and, as indicated by Lancaster's collected plant, 'Dendroides' is an appropriate name for the particularly vigorous clone of *colchica* occasionally seen.

Habit: Vining.

Stems: Purple-brown, thick, rapidly becoming woody. Internodes 6–8cm (2⅓–3in).

Petioles: Green.

Leaves: Ovate, 5–8cm (2–3in) by 6–8cm (2⅓–3in). Unlobed, apex acute, base cordate. Glossy dark green. Another form has light-green, slightly matt leaves.

Hedera colchica 'Dentata'

The most effective of all ivies, enormous glossy green drooping leaves... ascends to a great height and where an evergreen climber is required nothing can equal it as it will thrive on a north or east wall and quickly make a show.

This description is taken from a 1910 catalogue of V N Gauntlett & Co Ltd, then of Chiddingfold, Surrey, a celebrated firm of nurserymen whose plant list was prefaced by two pages of closely printed names of patrons, some 650 in all, commencing with Prince Henry of Battenberg and descending in order of nobility to Rev The Hon A R Parker. Gauntlett built up a vast trade, importing much of what he sold. It is probable that the plants making the impressive Ivy Wall at Polesden Lacey, Surrey, came from Gauntletts.

Hedera colchica is native to the Caucasus, the Balkans and Asia Minor and our knowledge of the discovery of 'Dentata', the much better plant, is scanty. An early record is that in the 1868 catalogue of the German nursery firm of Haage & Schmidt:

A new variety with very large leaves. Found in the Caucasus by the traveller Ruprecht. As hardy as the common ivy. The leaves are large, leathery and of a dark green, with their edges toothed; this distinguishes it from all other kinds.

The 'traveller' was presumably Franz Joseph Ruprecht (1814–70) the German botanist. This useful plant rapidly became known as *Hedera dentata* and appeared in British and continental catalogues from 1869 onwards. The Garden in 1893 recorded that it was unaffected by the great frost: as a variety of *colchica* this is what one would expect. Hibberd described it in 1890 as "*Hedera colchica* 'Dentata', a large ovate form of *colchica* characterized by a few sharp marginal spines".

One can add to Gauntlett's encomiums that the plant makes excellent ground cover for large areas; indeed, in parts of Britain it has naturalized itself. Completely hardy in Britain and most of Europe, one would expect it to be at home as far north as Zone 5 in USA. RHS Ivy Trial 1889: FCC, 1978/9: AM(T); 1993: ♚.

Habit: Vining, vigorous.

Stems: Purple-brown. Internodes 6–10cm (2⅓–4in).

Petioles: Green-purple.

Leaves: Large, mature leaves generally 15–22cm (6–8¾in) by 15–17cm (6–6¾in). Unlobed, ovate, the auriculate base gives an irregularly heart-shaped leaf. Leaf margin carries widely spaced fine teeth. On climbing plants the leaves hang down, older leaves curling inward at the edges. Colour rich pea-green, veins light green, not unduly prominent.

Hedera colchica 'Dentata Variegata'

This is not only the most spectacular of all the hardy ivies but is probably the most showy evergreen climber available. Many variegated ivies are less able to withstand frost and cold winds than their green counterparts, but the variegated form of *colchica* 'Dentata', whose geographical range is south-eastern Europe, Asia Minor, and the Caucasus to northern Iran, has shown no sign of being less hardy than the green plant. The large leaves hang in the same manner as the elephant's ears of 'Dentata' but are generously splashed with cream-yellow. As a wall plant it is superb, particularly on red-brick walls or as a backcloth for red-berried deciduous shrubs. It is admirable for ground cover since, unlike some ivies, it retains its variegation when on the ground. It is increasingly used for this purpose in architectural schemes where a large-scale plant is needed.

It was discovered by Mr Russell of L R Russell Ltd, who had seen the plant in a private garden near his Richmond nursery. Realizing its novelty and garden possibilities, he asked for a few cuttings and propagated it intensively to meet the demand he foresaw. Following its highly successful debut at the RHS Show in 1907, the firm listed it in their catalogue for 1908 in the following terms:

> In this variety is added to the grand glossy foliage of the type a broad marginal band of creamy yellow variegation in the young growth, changing to yellowish white as the leaves mature. The plant is of the same robust habit as the parent and is altogether the finest and most striking ivy in commerce, thoroughly hardy, constant in colouring and the foliage does not scorch in the hottest sun (3/6 to 10/6).

In 1908 10/6 (ten shillings and sixpence) would have equalled at least 20 pounds sterling today. The gardening public rushed to buy. For Russells it must have been for a brief period, as it were, a licence to mint sovereigns. The owner of the garden where the original plant grew approached Mr Russell, doubtless hoping for some share in the proceeds. Mr Russell's reply is not recorded and neither is any form of payment; it is likely and perfectly reasonable that he argued that it was he who saw the plant's potential and could justly claim the rewards.

Russell's description, although more eulogistic than scientific, at least did a service to botany in establishing the name and, as this was followed by descriptions in numerous catalogues, it came into general use. RHS Floral Committee 1907: AM; RHS Ivy Trial 1978/9: FCC (T); 1993: ♚.

Habit: Vining and vigorous.

Stems: Green-brown. Internodes 5–8cm (2–3in).

Petioles: Green to purple-brown.

Leaves: Ovate, unlobed, 15–20cm (6–8in) by 10–12cm (4–4¾in). Margins entire with a few scattered, very small, forward-pointing teeth. Leaf margins tend to fold under. Basic colour light green broken by patches of grey-green and with an irregular leaf-margin of deep cream-yellow. Texture leathery with a matt surface. When bruised the leaves have the spicy resinous smell associated with *colchica* varieties.

Hedera colchica 'Sulphur Heart'

The colchic ivies are dramatic, large-scale evergreen climbers. The plant was in cultivation in Britain before World War II as *H. colchica dentata aurea-striata*, but this name was never published. In Boskoop, Holland, the plant became known as 'Sulphur Heart' and under this name Nannenga-Bremekamp (1970) described it. In 1970 Roy Lancaster described it in Gardener's Chronicle as *H. colchica* 'Paddy's Pride', based on a plant growing in Ampfield, Hampshire. Upon further examination he decided this was the same clone as that already published as 'Sulphur Heart'.

PLATE III

All plants are shown at approximately ¾ size

H. helix f. *rhizomatifera*

H. helix 'Marilyn'

H. helix 'Donerailensis'

H. helix 'Pennsylvanica'

H. *helix* 'Big Deal'

H. *hibernica* var. *aracena*

H. *helix* 'Caenwoodiana Aurea'

H. *helix* 'Jasper'

H. *helix* 'Sark'

H. *helix* 'Obovata'

The spectacular *Hedera colchica* 'Sulphur Heart'

A fine plant for walls, fences, low balustrades or ground cover, it is sometimes listed as 'Gold Leaf' or 'Paddy's Pride'. As is the case with all *colchica* clones, a crushed leaf gives off a somewhat resinous fragrance. RHS Ivy Trial 1978/9: ♛ .

Habit: Vining, vigorous.

Stems: Light green to brown with age. Internodes 4–6cm (1½–2⅓in).

Petioles: Light green to purple-brown.

Leaves: Unlobed, large, 10–13cm (4–5in) by 9–12cm (3½–4¾in), cordate. Margin entire save for a few scattered fine teeth. Colour light green with central irregular splashes of yellow or lighter green. Veins slightly lighter green except where they traverse the variegated patch, where they are yellow.

Hedera helix L

The common or English ivy was named by Linnaeus who used the old Latin and Greek names. It is a native of western, central and southern Europe; northwards to southern Scandinavia to Latitude 60°; eastwards to Latvia and the Ukraine; south-east to Bulgaria and western Turkey, Greece, Cyprus and Crete. This wide distribution gives rise to several variations.

The British climate is particularly well suited to it and it is found almost everywhere below its altitude ceiling of 517m (1,700ft). In the west its place is taken by the larger leaved Irish ivy generally known as var. *hibernica* but now considered to be a distinct species, *H. hibernica*.

The species was described by Seeman in 1864 and by Tobler in 1912. It was Seeman who first used hair characteristics to separate ivy species and described the three- to five-rayed white stellate hairs of *helix*. The type described below is the typical common ivy and compares with the excellent plate and description in Sowerby's *English Botany* (1804). Despite the existence of many attractively leaved clones, large numbers of common ivy are grown and sold for landscape purposes. As hardy ground cover it is unharmed by temperatures down to -15°C (5°F); as cover for buildings it is an excellent choice. The purple-black berries are much favoured as winter food by blackbirds. It is said that the berries, boiled in water with a small quantity of alum, yield a red dye.

Hedera helix is extremely variable. Most garden and house-plant kinds are of this species, indeed one can find different leaf forms in a walk along almost any British country lane. Because of this variation it is not surprising that 'English' ivy sent to people living abroad often differs widely, each recipient assuming they have the typical form of the plant thus giving rise to names such as 'Old English' or 'Old Garden', names occasionally met in North America. It is the most unstable of the ivy species and has produced numerous mutations. Among these two are outstanding: one that in the 19th century gave the several erect non-climbing kinds and another which occurred in an American nursery in 1921 and produced the short-jointed 'ramulose' type, thereby establishing the multi-million pound industry of house-plant ivies.

Habit: Vining.
Stems: Purple-green. Internodes 4–6cm (1½–2⅓in).
Petioles: Purple-green.
Leaves: The juvenile leaves 3–5-lobed, 4–6cm (1½–2⅓in) by 6–8cm (2⅓–3in), the 2 basal lobes reduced in size to give the typical ivy-leaf shape. Lobes wedge-shaped, sinuses shallow, apices bluntly acute, leaf base cordate, colour dark green. Hairs stellate, white and 3–5-rayed. Adult leaves ovate or elliptic, 5–8cm (2–3in) by 4–7cm (1½–2¾in) broad, markedly narrower on shoots exposed to light, broader and more ovate on shaded shoots. Flowers borne on a panicle of globose umbels, pedicels and peduncle slightly hairy. Fruit a purple-black berry, mid-autumn to mid-winter, seeds 5. Chromosome No 2n=48.

Hedera helix 'Adam'

The source of the name is not known but it would be natural to link the plant with 'Eva', a clone to which it indeed bears some resemblance. The main difference is the fairly pronounced cordate leaf base as opposed to the cuneate leaf base of 'Eva'. In variegation, 'Adam' tends to be white-cream whereas 'Eva' is more cream-yellow.

The only published record appears to be that of Bean (1973). Available commercially in Britain since about 1968, 'Adam' is not recorded on the continent although the plant has certainly been exported to Britain, usually as 'Eva' or without a name. It is not mentioned in American ivy literature but two American clones, 'Silver Emblem' and 'Silver King' appear to be the same plant. The fairly white variegation makes it an excellent pot plant, it is generally hardy outside and is useful for low walls or even small areas of ground cover. RHS Ivy Trial 1978/9: HC(T).

A sport of 'Adam', similar in leaf but with at least 50 per cent more white-cream variegation, was introduced by the Danish nurseryman Frode Maegaard in 1980 under the name 'Glache'.

Habit: Self-branching.
Stems: Green-purple. Internodes 1–2cm (⅓–¾in).
Petioles: Green-purple.
Leaves: 3-lobed, 3–4cm (1¼–1½in) by 3–4cm (1¼–1½in). Lobes forward-pointing, more particularly in young leaves. A diagnostic clue is the slight sideways 'lean' of the acuminate centre lobe. Lateral lobes acute. Leaf base cordate; leaf centre light green, greying with maturity. White-cream variegation irregular and mostly at leaf edge.

Hedera helix 'Albany'

One of the first self-branching ivies, presumably a mutation from 'Pittsburgh', this was first described by Alfred Bates in the American National Horticultural Magazine, Vol XIX, p210, 1940. According to Bates it was first propagated in 1931 and introduced in 1935 by Fred A Danker, a florist in Albany, New York, who named it accordingly. A move to designate it 'Dankeri' was, quite rightly, repudiated by Bates and the name never achieved wide circulation.

A clone grown since 1978 by W Freeland of Columbia, South Carolina, under the name 'Alpha Carolinian' is very similar apart from the fact that it is generally three-lobed. It has been registered with the AIS, No 78182, as 'Alpha'.

An interesting link between 'Albany' and the clone 'Bunch' arose from an article by Bess L Shippy in the American Flower Grower, Vol 37, No 11 (1950), in which she referred to having a fasciated ivy that she called her "Bunch ivy". She pointed out that adventitious leaflets tended to appear on the central vein of the centre lobe; this is a distinctive feature in 'Albany' as seen today. The leaves tend to be variable in shape and the plant readily throws reverted shoots. It is grown as a pot plant but more for interest than decoration.

Habit: Semi-erect, self-branching.

Hedera helix 'Adam'

Stems: Green-purple, slightly flattened by fasciation. Internodes 2–2.5cm (¾–1in).

Petioles: Green-purple.

Leaves: 5-lobed, rarely 3, 6–7cm (2⅓–2¾in) by 6–8cm (2⅓–3in). Apices acute, leaf base cordate. Adventitious leaflets appear occasionally on the centre veins. Mid-green, veins lighter green and slightly raised.

Hedera helix 'Alt Heidelberg'

This cultivar was selected in 1972 by Brother Heieck. He described the leaves as being similar to those of *Quercus* x *schochiana*, which indicates the extent to which this plant differs from the usual conception of an ivy.

Short-jointed, compact and unusual in that the petioles are virtually non-existent, its leaves resemble small oak leaves.

It is most likely that 'Alt Heidelberg' was a mutation of a form of 'Pittsburgh', termed 'Chicago' or 'Chicago Minima'. Whatever its origin it is a first-rate and most interesting ivy. The proposed name was 'Heidelberg' but this was amended to 'Alt Heidelberg' (Old Heidelberg) to avoid confusion with *Hedera* 'Heidelbergensis' a plant grown at the beginning of the century at the Botanic Gardens, Kew, and at that time called the Heidelberg ivy. This large-leaved form of *H. colchica* is no longer grown.

Habit: Self-branching and very short-jointed, slow growing.

Stems: Red-brown, slender. Internodes 0.3–1cm (⅛–⅓in).

Petioles: Virtually non-existent, leaves accordingly are disposed regularly around the stem, rather than on one plane as is usual, by virtue of twisting petioles.

Leaves: Diamond-shaped with bluntly rounded apex and cuneate base. 2–3cm (¾–1¼in) by 1–1.5cm (⅓–⅝in). Entire, or with vestigial lateral lobes. The cuneate base runs out into a short, flat, fluted stalk so that the leaf is sessile. Colour deep green.

Hedera helix 'Alten Brucken'

The late Brother Heieck noticed one slightly different leaf on an ivy that was struggling to grow on the very lovely old bridge that crosses the river Neckar. Heieck nurtured the shoot and built up a stock of what is a pleasant, if not greatly striking, ivy. The variegation is white and suffused, it is a quick-growing clone with more green tissue in the leaf than the slower growing but more heavily variegated 'Minor Marmorata'.

Habit: Vining.

Stems: Green-purple. Internodes 1–2cm (⅓–¾in).

Petioles: Green-purple.

Leaves: 3-lobed, rarely 5-lobed, 3–6cm (1¼–2⅓in) by 4–6cm (1½–2⅓in). Sinuses shallow or almost non-existent, apices acute, centre lobe slightly prolonged, leaf base cordate. Dark green, some but not all leaves suffused and speckled with white variegation.

Hedera helix 'Ambrosia'

One of the most unusual variegated ivies and very much an enthusiast's plant. Closely set, slightly curled and twisted small leaves make this an interesting and excellent house-plant ivy but too slow-growing for nursery distribution.

'Ambrosia' was noted in 1980 at the Neuberg Monastery Nursery, Heidelberg as a mutation of 'Gertrud Stauss'.

Habit: Self-branching.

Stems: Green-purple. Internodes 0.5–1cm (¼–⅓in).

Petioles: Green-purple. Seldom more than 1cm (⅓in) long.

Leaves: Basically 5-lobed, 1.5–2cm (⅝–¾in) by 1–1.5cm (⅓–¾in); because of the twisted configuration often appearing unlobed. Centre light green; extensive yellow-cream variegation towards the leaf edge. Marked purple colouration at the base of the central vein.

Hedera helix 'Angularis'

First described by Hibberd (1872) and subsequently listed by several nurseries, the variety was growing in the RHS

The apple-green leaves of *Hedera helix* 'Ambrosia' make an admirable foil for the variegation of *Hedera helix* 'Schäfer Three'

gardens at Chiswick in 1890. Hibberd said "Angularis is a Jersey ivy with large leaves angular in form and of a light green colour". This differs from his earlier and, I think, more accurate description, "Leaves of medium size, bright green, and glossy, having no peculiarity of conformation sufficiently striking to arrest the attention of a casual observer ... boundaries of the side lobes approximate to straight lines."

The bright-green leafage of the variety, which is plentiful on the Channel Islands, makes it rather more interesting than the common ivy when an ordinary green climbing ivy is required. The arborescent form has recently been named as 'William Eggins'.

An ivy circulating as 'Emerald Gem' has been shown to be identical to 'Angularis'. The first description was in an article in The Garden (1888): "A splendid variety of great richness and beauty, it is very free and robust in growth. This is sometimes called 'Emerald Green' and it has other titles." The name subsequently appeared in catalogues but with descriptions confined to "bright green" or "bright glossy green". With a few exceptions those nurserymen listing it did not list 'Angularis' and vice versa, suggesting that the two may have been similar. The name was not mentioned by Hibberd. He did however refer to a Channel Island ivy, 'Smaragdina' as "Leaves large, three- to five-lobed and brilliant green". This he submitted to the RHS as 'Hibberd's Emerald' but this is the only mention of it. One may assume that this too was but a slight variation of 'Angularis'.

Habit: Vining.
Stems: Green-tinged purple. Internodes 3–4cm (1¼–1½in).
Petioles: Green-tinged purple.
Leaves: 3-lobed, 4–5cm (1½–2in) by 5–7 (2–2¾in). Centre lobe cuspid, occasionally wedge-shaped, lateral lobes wedge-shaped, sinuses shallow. Sides of lateral lobes often straight. Vestigial basal lobes occasionally produce a 'stepped' leaf outline. Leaf base slightly auriculate. Colour fresh bright green.

Hedera helix 'Angularis Aurea'
Hibberd (1872) described with some accuracy 'Angularis', the bright-green, glossy-leaved ivy that is generally conceded as being a Channel Islands form. Strangely, however, in the RHS Journal (1890), he described the golden variegated form of it which had been entered in the RHS Ivy Trial as 'Angularis Aurea', as 'Chrysophylla', causing thereafter confusion between the two names. Fortunately for us the description of 'Angularis Aurea' in the 1894 catalogue of William Clibran & Son of Altrincham, Cheshire, together with those of L R Russell Ltd in their catalogues from 1908–32, identify the plant grown today.

'Chrysophylla' was the earliest and therefore the correct name for a similar clone circulating in the 1890s and since as 'Spectabilis Aurea'. The variegated form of 'Angularis' would be easily confused with it.

'Angularis Aurea' is probably the best of the yellow-variegated ivies. The variegation is not always apparent in young plants. The arborescent form has recently been named as 'Mary Eggins' recording the Mother of the late Dr H Eggins who was greatly interested in ivies. 1993: ♔.

Habit: Vining.
Stems: Green, faintly tinged purple. Internodes 1.5–2.5cm (⅝–1in).
Petioles: Green.
Leaves: 3-lobed, 4–5cm (1½–2in) by 5–6cm (2–2⅓in). Centre lobe cuspid, occasionally wedge-shaped, sinuses shallow. Sides of lateral lobes often straight. Vestigial basal lobes produce a 'stepped' leaf outline; leaf base slightly auriculate. Bright green, some leaves suffused with interveinal yellow, surface glossy.

Hedera helix 'Anna Marie'
This clone originated in Denmark, probably during the 1960s. It gradually became widely grown, particularly in America; indeed the first records of the name are in the AIS Check-list of 1975 and in the catalogue of the Alestake Ivy Nursery then at Elkwood, Virginia, in the same year.

The plant – whose name is sometimes misspelt as 'Anne' or 'Ann', is presumed to be a mutation from 'Harald' which it resembles in colour but from which it differs in its larger, round-lobed leaves.

It is self-branching but makes sufficient trails to be suitable for hanging baskets, pots and troughs. It may be planted outside in sheltered spots as wall cover but in Britain can suffer in hard winters.

A particularly good form found by an ivy enthusiast Mrs Jill Butcher and named 'Brightstone' was described and illustrated in the 1989 BIS Journal. The clone 'Anne Borch' is said to be similar but with smaller leaves. A particularly striped variegation known as 'Harlequin' arose at the Whitehouse Nursery in 1987.

Habit: Self-branching with trails.
Stems: Green-purple. Internodes 2–3cm (¾–1¼in).
Petioles: Green.
Leaves: 5-lobed, 3–4cm (1¼–1½in) by 5–6cm (2–2⅓in). Sinuses are so shallow as to render the lobing indistinct. Apices obtuse to round. The basic colour is medium-green with grey-green areas. Clear cream variegation mostly at the leaf edge. Veins light green, not prominent.

Hedera helix 'Anna Marie'

Hedera helix 'Appaloosa'

This variegated form of 'Manda's Crested' was found in 1984 by Joyce Descloux of Dover, New Jersey. The plant was named because "like the Indian pony it is spotted with dark spots on a white background". Not quite correct, since the background is green and the spots – flecking really – are cream-yellow. Apart from this the plant is like 'Manda's Crested', but a little slower in growth and less hardy. AIS Reg No 840985.

Habit: Self-branching.
Stems: Green-purple. Internodes 2–2.5cm (¾–1in).
Petioles: Green-purple.
Leaves: 5-lobed, rarely reduced to 3, 3–4cm (1¼–1½in) by 4–5cm (1½–2in), typically star-shaped. Basal lobes back-pointing and almost the same length as the lateral lobes; this with the overlap of the basal lobes makes the petiole junction appear to be at the leaf centre. Sinuses shallow, all 5 lobes convolute with blunt, down-pointing apices. Light green with broken cream-yellow variegation.

Hedera helix 'Arborescens'

Cuttings taken from adult ivy shoots will produce plants of that stage which, lacking the ability to creep or climb, will grow into shrubs termed 'tree' ivies.

The name *arborea* (tree-like) was recorded as long ago as 1562 by Matthiolus in his *Neu Kreutterbuch*; and later by Richard Weston(1774). The more suitable epithet, *arborescens* (becoming tree-like) was first published in 1838 by J C Loudon in his *Arboretum et Fruticetum Britannicum*.

Catalogues from the 1860s to the 1920s listed many 'tree' forms indicating the extent and indeed popularity which these attained in an era when the time and expense of their production would be of little account.

Although occasionally used, these names are not in general circulation today and it is by no means certain to which clones they may refer. The list contains one or two curiosities; 'Arborea Fructu-luteo' and 'Baccifera Lutea' refer presumably to the orange-berried *H. helix* f. *poetarum*, named as 'Poetica' by Weston in 1774. The reference to 'Leucocarpa' is presumably the white-berried ivy which, as far as I am aware, has never been seen. It may stem from Hibberd's comment (1872) where he listed it saying "This variety is in my collection if labels may be trusted, but as it has not yet fruited, the mention of the name must suffice." The comment on labels is still pertinent today!

Arborescent forms were extremely popular in Victorian times. Kept in pots or tubs they were often used as a form of winter bedding. Nowadays few nurseries offer them since they are slow to root and take time to bring to a saleable size. The orange-berried poet's ivy is the exception, its colourful berries being its selling point. In the juvenile stage correct identification is difficult.

Habit: Shrubby.

Stems: Purple-green. Internodes 4–6cm (1½–2⅓in).

Petioles: Purple-green.

Leaves: Unlobed, 5–8cm (2–3in) by 4–7cm (1½–2¾in), markedly narrower on shoots exposed to light, broader and more ovate on shaded shoots. Apex acute, leaf base cuneate. Flowers borne on a panicle of globose umbels. Pedicels and peduncles slightly hairy with stellate *helix*-type hairs; leaves and petioles less so. Fruit a purple-black berry, mid-autumn to midwinter, seeds normally 5.

Hedera helix 'Ardingly'

This attractive short-jointed variegated ivy was found by Mrs Hazel Key of Fibrex Nurseries Ltd in the 1960s in a garden in Ardingly, Sussex. The leaf shape and colour suggest that it may be a mutation from 'Glacier'. Very close-growing, the pink-purple stems appear like a network among grey-green white-edged leaves. An excellent house-plant ivy.

Habit: Self-branching.

Stems: Pink-purple. Internodes 1–2cm (⅓–¾in).

Petioles: Pink-purple.

Leaves: Irregularly 3-lobed 1.5–2cm (⅝–¾in) by 2–3cm (¾–1¼in). One lobe often larger than the other, apex bluntly acute. Irregularly edged cream, basic colour mid-green with broken areas of grey-green.

Hedera helix 'Arran'

The credit for discovering this delightful little ivy belongs to the amateur botanist Alison Rutherford who, in the 1980s, noted and collected it on the Scottish isle of Arran.

Small, neat and exceptionally hardy, it is an excellent ivy for a low wall or a rock-garden. Sometimes listed as 'Aran' this spelling error has suggested that it originated on the Irish island of that name, which of course is not so.

Habit: Vining.

Stems: Purple-green. Internodes 2–3cm (¾–1¼in).

Petioles: Green-purple.

Leaves: 3-lobed, 2.5–3cm (1–1¼in) by 2–3cm (¾–1¼in). Sinuses very shallow, the 2 lateral lobes often barely discernible, leaf base truncate, apices bluntly acute. Colour mid- to dark green.

Hedera helix 'Asterisk'

Discovered by William Krekler of Somerville, Ohio, as a sport on an unknown ground-cover ivy, it belongs to what may be termed the 'Maple Leaf' group. When 'Maple Leaf', 'Lalla Rookh' and 'Asterisk' are grown side by side it can be difficult to differentiate between them but the feature that sets 'Asterisk' apart is the presence of two additional basal lobes, giving a seven-lobed leaf which, with imagination, can resemble the asterisk symbol.

Material was given by Mr Krekler in 1975 to Dr Sulgrove, the AIS Registrar who in 1979 named it 'Asterisk' and ensured its propagation and distribution. It is an ivy of interest to the specialist mainly as a pot plant but in the garden it can be used as a wall ivy in sheltered areas.

Habit: Short-jointed with trails.

Stems: Purple-green. Internodes 2–3cm (¾–1¼in).

Petioles: Purple-green.

Leaves: 5-lobed but frequently having 2 small lobes emerging from the basal lobes to give a 7-lobed leaf, 4–6cm (1½–2⅓in) by 4–6cm (1½–2⅓in). Sinuses wide, lobes particularly in young leaves rarely more than 1cm (⅓in) wide. Apices acuminate, lobe edges slightly waved, leaf base cordate. Colour mid-green, veins lighter and fairly pronounced. AIS Reg No 80282.

Hedera helix 'Atropurpurea'

The so-called purple ivy is sometimes listed under the erroneous names of 'Purpurea' or 'Nigra'. Its origin is reasonably certain as the following report by W Brockbank

(The Garden, January 1885), shows:

> The late Thomas Williams of Ormskirk found a wild variety with deep purple leaves which deepened in colour almost to black and he called it *Hedera purpurescens*. Mr Williams sold his stock of this ivy, I believe, to Messrs Backhouse of York and they brought it out as a novelty a few years back under the name of *Hedera atropurpurea*.

The plant had been mentioned in The Garden of 1884 as a suitable variety "to contrast with the large golden ivy" and from this time on various catalogues listed it either as *purpurea* or *atropurpurea*. The leaves are not "deep-purple" in summer, but certainly turn that shade in winter. RHS Ivy Trial 1978/9: ♔ .

Habit: Vining

Stems: Purple. Internodes 1.5–3 cm (⅝–1¼in).

Petioles: Purple.

Leaves: 5-lobed, 4–6cm (1½–2⅓in) by 5–7cm (2–2¾in). Basal lobes vestigial, sinuses shallow, centre lobe prolonged to acuminate, laterals bluntly acute. Leaf texture thin. Dull dark green in summer colouring to deep-purple in winter, depth of colour increases with exposure to cold and in an open situation.

Hedera helix 'Aureo Variegata'

Listed as long ago as 1770 by Richard Weston, this elegant, small-leaved vining ivy is surprisingly not mentioned by Hibberd in *The Ivy* (1872). It seems likely however that nurseries, overlooking or not knowing of Weston's description, were growing and listing the plant under a plethora of names including 'Aurea', 'Aureis', 'Aureola', 'Aurea Marginata', 'Aurea Maculata' and 'Aurea Densa', but all with little or no description. The clone often listed as 'Marginata Aurea' would appear identical.

Lawrence & Schulze in 1942 included it in what they readily admitted was a 'catch-all' name: 'Cavendishii'. In 1956 Lawrence recognized it as "One of those non-precocious clones whose leaves are variegated", meaning that it was not a ramosa or self-branching type. Jenny in 1964 provides perhaps the best modern description: "The leaf colours range from green to cream-yellow with patches of subtle nuances. Leaf-size varies from small to medium."

During the inter-war years, the name disappeared from catalogues; happily the plant persisted in various gardens and is presently catalogued by specialist nurseries. It is a quietly attractive ivy which could be more widely grown – particularly as cover for low walls.

Habit: Vining.

Stems: Purple-green. Internodes 1.5–3cm (⅝–1¼in).

Petioles: Green-purple.

Leaves: Unlobed, deltoid-triangular, 2–3cm (¾–1¼in) by 4–5cm(1½–2in). Apices bluntly acute, leaf base strongly cordate. Basic colour mid-green, generally comprising a central block edged with lime-green to cream-yellow; occasional leaves totally green.

Hedera helix 'Baccifer'

No one seems to know the origin of this rather unusual name. A clue exists in the fact that the nursery firm of H Cannell & Sons of Swanley, Kent, in their 1885 catalogue, or *Floral Guide* as they termed it, listed *Hedera baccifera* with the description "A peculiar shade of green" and continued to list it, certainly up to 1907.

In the early 1980s Fibrex Nurseries, then of Evesham, Worcestershire, received a plant from a private garden under the name 'Baccifer'. They listed it in their catalogue as "light green, five-lobed wavy leaves, close habit". By 1988 it was illustrated in the Whitehouse Ivies booklet, *Which Ivy* and Ron Whitehouse (BIS Journal 1994) said "It is distinctive, of a pea-green colour and has a leaf shape of its own", echoing in part Cannell's description of 109 years earlier.

Other names have been linked to the clone. Brother Heieck suggested that it may be the clone described by Nannenga-Bremekamp in 1970 as 'Smithii' – "Leaves with long lobes, pale green and with pale green nerves."

A closer comparison is that of Pierot (1974) where she describes a clone 'Ripples' as having five- to seven-lobed, slightly wavy leaves of "pea-pod green".

These writers would have been unaware of the Cannell plant but I suggest that it has persisted in cultivation and has surfaced under three names of which, by virtue of history and present attachment, 'Baccifer' is the one to be accepted.

Habit: Vining but reasonably compact.

Stems: Green-purple. Internodes 1.5–2.5cm (⅝–2in).

Petioles: Green-purple.

Leaves: 5-lobed, 4–5cm (1½–2in) by 6–7cm (2⅓–2¾in). The two basal lobes slightly back-pointing. Apices bluntly acute, leaf base cordate. Colour light green.

Hedera helix var. baltica

This variety, which differs from typical *helix* only in its hardiness, was discovered in the early 1900s by Alfred Rehder, Curator of the Arnold Arboretum Herbarium, growing in pine woods on the eastern edge of the Baltic sea near Riga, Latvia. Plants were sent to the Arboretum in 1907 where they proved to be hardy and quick growing. An excellent line drawing of the plant accompanied an article by Edgar Anderson in the 1932 Bulletin of Popular Information

Top: *Hedera helix* 'Baccifer'; above: *Hedera helix* 'Bill Archer'

Series (3,vi) published by the Arboretum. In addition to leaves and stem, the drawing depicts hairs having eight rays as opposed to the usual five of *helix*. This is possibly the only visible feature distinguishing the variety but Lawrence & Schulze (1942) warn that this difference is not always

consistent. At a latitude of approximately 56° the Riga collection is near to the northern limit of the genus. *The Flora of the USSR* (1950) states that in northern regions like Belorussia *H. helix* fruits only rarely. It describes *baltica* as a deviation distinguished by small rhombic-lanceolate leaves, having few and solitary flowers, resistant to cold and being the native ivy of the Baltic area.

In 1934 Anderson visited the Balkans to collect material of holly, ivy, yew and box that would survive the cold and dry of central USA. Two ivies were collected and named 'Rumania' and 'Bulgaria'. Anderson's descriptions were scanty but both clones resemble *baltica*, the centre lobe of 'Bulgaria' being rather larger and longer. These are almost indistinguishable from ordinary *helix*. Because hardiness is not a vital factor in the UK, little attention has been paid to these hardy clones.

Habit: Vining.
Stems: Green-purple. Internodes 3–5cm (1¼–2in).
Petioles: Green-purple.
Leaves: 3-lobed but the vestigial nature of the lobes often produces a triangular leaf 3–5cm (1¼–2in) by 4–6cm (1½–2⅓in). Apices bluntly acute, leaf base cordate. Dark green, light green veins show white in winter.

Hedera helix 'Big Deal'
This is one of those ivies with leaves totally unlike an ivy – wherein lies much of its fascination. Bess Shippy recorded in 1955 that it was introduced by Keith E Williams, a wholesale florist of Springfield, Ohio. She commented that the 5cm (2in) leaves are round, not unlike those of the greenhouse Geranium; in fact the first few plants were sold under the name 'Geranium'. Essentially a house-plant ivy, 'Big Deal' makes an interesting pot or trough plant. The stems are a little too stiff to recommend it for hanging baskets. The clone named 'Small Deal' differs only in having 5–7 leaves.

Habit: Self-branching with short trails.
Stems: Red-purple, noticeably smooth and slightly zig-zag from node to node. Internodes 3–6cm (1¼–2⅓in).
Petioles: Red-purple to green.
Leaves: Unlobed, 4–6cm (1½–2⅓in) by 3–6cm (1¼–2⅓in), sufficiently auriculate to hide the petiole junction. Colour medium-green. Veins radiating from the petiole, raised and thread-like. Leaf margins slightly puckered giving a slightly cupped effect to the leaf.

Hedera helix 'Bill Archer'
Found on a Surrey nursery in 1980 this clone was submitted to the AIS in 1982 by Stephen Taffler for registration under the name 'Excalibur' but it had meanwhile become casually

known as 'Archer's Lace', a name which would be invalid because of its apostrophe. Mr Archer, a nurseryman with a keen eye for plant variations, died in 1982 and several of those who had known him felt that 'Bill Archer' would be an appropriate name for this unusual ivy. By 1986 it was being sold as such by the specialist ivy nurseries.

Following AIS Registration (No 821987) the Registrar pointed out that in America they had similar plants under the names 'Pencil Point' and 'Spear Point', to which she said 'Bill Archer' tended to revert. One accordingly assumes that the origin of this clone was the very variable 'Spear Point'.

'Bill Archer' is an extreme variation that needs rigorous removal of reverted shoots to maintain its growth type.

Habit: Short-jointed, vining.

Stems: Purple-green. Internodes 0.5–1.5cm (¼–⅝in).

Petioles: Green-purple.

Leaves: Unlobed, but occasionally 2 vestigial lobes, varying 5–10cm (2–4in) by (consistently) 0.5–1.5cm (¼–⅝in). Apices acuminate, leaf base cuneate, colour dark green.

Hedera helix 'Boskoop'

This mutation from 'Green Ripple', found by J A Boer of Boskoop, was introduced by him in 1961 and awarded a Silver Medal at the Flora Nova in Boskoop in the same year. It was described and figured by Harry van de Laar in 1965 and by Dr Nannenga-Bremekamp in 1970. Tighter and less vining than 'Green Ripple' its curled leaves and rich green make 'Boskoop' a most useful pot plant. RHS Ivy Trial 1978/9: HC(T). A similar clone albeit with slightly less wavy leaves has circulated as 'Ustler' and a variegated form of this, at first called 'Ustler Variegated', has been recorded as 'Lemon Swirl'.

Habit: Self-branching.

Stems: Green-purple. Internodes 2–3.5cm (¾–1⅓in).

Petioles: Green-purple.

Leaves: 5-lobed, 5–8cm (2–3in) by 4–7cm (1½–2¾in). Lobes wedge-shaped, centre lobe longer than laterals and acuminate. Laterals forward-pointing and acute, leaf base cuneate, basal lobes reduced. All lobes down-pointing giving a 'claw' look. Sinuses narrow with leaf margin raised at the cleft giving a frilled appearance. Bright green, veins raised but similar in colour.

Hedera helix 'Brokamp'

Any grower of 'Brokamp', 'Garland', 'Gavotte' and 'Sylvanian' will find all to be unstable, each readily producing sports resembling the others and all needing great care in propagation if their individual differences are to be maintained. All can trace their origins to the old variety 'Star', itself a derivative of 'Pittsburgh', the first short-jointed, thin-leaved mutation. 'Brokamp' was selected from what has been known in America and Europe as 'Sagittifolia'. The selection was made at the Brokamp Nursery, Ramsdorf, Westfalen, Germany, and described by O Koch in Gartenwelt in 1959.

In Britain the plant became known for a time as 'Salicifolia' and in America as 'Imp', but inevitably Koch's description and name have priority.

Provided that the stock can be maintained by propagating only from the characteristic willow-leaved shoots, this can be a useful ivy, very suitable for hanging baskets.

Habit: Self-branching with long trails.

Stems: Green-purple. Internodes 1.5–3cm (⅝–1¼in).

Petioles: Green. 0.5–2cm (¼–¾in).

Leaves: Mostly entire and lanceolate, 5cm (2in) by 1–1.5cm (⅓–⅝in), acuminate. Occasional leaves with an asymmetrical lateral lobe also some sagittate leaves. Centre vein prominent, lateral veins running almost parallel. Medium- to dark green.

Hedera helix 'Boskoop'

Hedera helix 'Bruder Ingobert'

This mutation from 'Glacier' was selected by Brother Ingobert Heieck in 1962 at the Neuburg Abbey Nursery, Heidelberg. Primarily useful as a house plant or for hanging baskets, it is suitable also for low walls.

Habit: Vining and moderately branching.

Stems: Purple-red. Internodes 1.5–3cm (⅝–1¼in).

Petioles: Purple-red. Shorter than those of 'Glacier'.

Leaves: Indistinctly 3–5-lobed. Many irregularly shaped and indented. 2–3.5cm (¾–1⅓in) by 3–5cm (1¼–2in). Lobes rounded, sinuses shallow or non-existent. Leaf blade undulating, leaf base deeply cordate. Colour grey-green with irregular dark-green patches. Often a dark-green rim area and an inner rim of cream-white, centre grey-green. Veins light green, not prominent.

Hedera helix 'Buttercup'

One of the most useful and decorative of garden ivies, this can be effective in combination with other plants while remaining a superb ivy in its own right. 'Buttercup' is a climbing ivy but not to be recommended for ground cover where, in shade, it will lose its unique golden colouring.

The first record of the name is in the 1925 list of the nursery firm of T Smith of Newry, Ireland. There is nothing more until 1948 when it was exhibited before the RHS Floral Committee by Hilling & Co, then of Chobham, Surrey. It did not receive an award but gradually circulated through the nursery trade. In his book *Three Gardens* (Collingridge, 1983) Graham Thomas records of his 'Buttercup' plant that "The shady side of the plant was a uniform dull green and it was a surprise to find how brilliant it could be in sun, having been propagated from an old plant, some 5ft high and wide, at Sunningdale Nurseries, which being under trees was always green." It is likely that Sunningdale Nurseries, where it remained until Thomas spotted its potential, received it from Smith of Newry before the war.

The firm of L R Russell Ltd, who specialized in ivies between 1900 and 1939, listed various golden-leaved kinds. Russell, like all British nurseries, was badly hit by the restrictions of World War II which limited the growing of ornamentals and they lost many interesting ivies. Some may have survived the war years in America, a theory suggested by the comments of Lawrence & Schulze (1942) who, describing an ivy 'Russell Gold', stated that it was donated by C McK Lewis of Sloatsburg, New York, who had obtained the material from Russell in 1934. It is possible that the clone imported from America in the 1970s under the name 'Gold Cloud' was in fact 'Russell's Gold', a clone which has some resemblance to 'Buttercup'.

When propagating 'Buttercup' it is best to use green material. It roots easily but plants tend to 'hang' for a while when potted on and take a year or so to attain any yellow colour. The yellow leaf portions can suffer from sun-scorch; a north-facing aspect suits it best. 1993: ♔.

Habit: Vining.

Stems: Green to yellow-green in sun. Internodes 1–2.5cm (⅓–1in).

Petioles: Green.

Leaves: 5-lobed, 5–7cm (2–2¾in) by 6–8cm (2⅔–3in). Apices acute, sinuses shallow, centre lobe slightly prolonged. Leaf base cordate. Colour lime-green in shade, in sun some leaves green-yellow, others completely yellow.

Hedera helix 'Caecilia'

Resembling a variegated 'Parsley Crested', this striking clone was a mutation from 'Harald' that arose on the nursery of Franz Rogmans of Geldern, Germany, in 1976. Sometimes sold under the erroneous and invalid name of 'Clotted Cream' it has also been catalogued as 'Sicelia' and 'Silicia'.

Individual stocks can vary but the best, those having a high degree of variegation and leaf-edge cresting, make superb house-plant ivies.

Habit: Self-branching.

Stems: Green to light purple. Internodes 2–3.5cm (¾–1⅓in).

Petioles: Green to light purple.

Leaves: 5-lobed, basal lobes often vestigial; 3–4cm (1¼–1½in) by 3–5cm (1¼–2in). Leaf base strongly cordate, centre lobe twice the length of laterals. Sinuses shallow, leaf edge frilled and crisp to the touch, convolution at the cleft tends to disguise the lobing.

Hedera helix 'Caecilia'

Cream-yellow variegation mostly at the leaf edge, remaining areas light green with grey-green portions.

Hedera helix 'Caenwoodiana Aurea'

In 1863 the 'bird's foot' ivy was listed, without a description, in the catalogue of James and John Fraser of Leebridge Nurseries, Essex, as 'Caenwoodiana'. It circulated under this name until 1872 when Shirley Hibberd in *The Ivy* described it in detail as *H. helix* 'Pedata'.

In 1905 a reference to a yellow-leaved form was listed, without description, in Robert Veitch's catalogue. A descriptive note appeared in the 1908 catalogue of L R Russell Ltd: "'Caenwoodiana Aurea' – foliage heavily blotched yellow." This became the first published name of the yellow-variegated clone and by the rule of priority has precedence over 'Pedata Variegata' sometimes quoted. The clone was listed thereafter in various catalogues, the last being Hillier's of Winchester, Hampshire, in 1924. Their catalogue of 1928, while listing the usual green 'Caenwoodiana', said "The golden form is not sufficiently constant" and the last reference is in the RHS Journal (1930) where it is noted among plants suitable for a north wall.

The suffusion of light-yellow is seen in spring in the young leaves. In young plants this is rapidly replaced by the normal green colour but in older plants, and particularly in an open sunny position, the colour is retained in some leaves at least. It is essentially a wall ivy.

Habit: Vining.
Stems: Green-purple. Internodes 2–5cm (¾–2in).
Petioles: Green-purple.
Leaves: 5-lobed, the central lobe approximately ⅓ longer than the laterals and tending to be narrower at the base, broader at the middle, tapering to the tip, 4–5cm (1½–2in) by 5–6cm (2–2⅓in). Lobes back-pointing giving the 'bird's foot' appearance. Younger leaves take on a yellow colouration as they develop, subsequent leaves may attain the usual grey-green associated with 'Pedata'; similarly the veins are light green.

Hedera helix 'California'

This clone was discovered in 1939 as a sport of 'Merion Beauty' at the Weber Nurseries, Los Angeles. It was first named as 'Weber's California' and as such was described by Shippy in the American Flower Grower (Vol 37, No 11, 1950). In that publication in 1955 she referred to it as 'California', under which name it appeared in the AIS Checklist of 1975 and is generally catalogued. Somewhat unstable, it often produces sports similar to existing clones. Named clones considered to be synonymous with 'California' are:

'Abundance', 'Berlin', 'Brigette', 'Ideal', and 'Patricia'. A fasciated form is listed as 'Astin'; 'Baden-Baden', rather like a large 'Irish Lace', was selected from 'California' by Gebr Stauss of Möglingen in 1980. 'Crinolette', a clone with crimped, crumpled and curled leaves was selected by Ron Whitehouse in 1993.

So much for the name; what of the plant? The leaves are slightly convoluted at the sinuses and closely set on short trails. It is a good house-plant ivy but not recommended for outside where it tends to romp and lose character.

Habit: Short-jointed and self-branching.
Stems: Green-purple. Internodes 1–2cm (⅓–¾in).
Petioles: Green-purple.
Leaves: 3- but sometimes 5-lobed, 3–4cm (1¼–1½in) by 4–4.5cm (1½–1¾in). Centre lobe triangular, lateral lobes markedly convolute, apices bluntly rounded, colour mid-green.

Hedera helix 'Cathedral Wall'

Described by Freeland in the American National Horticultural Magazine, Vol 50, No 1, 1971 as having been received by him in 1961 from Mr A Rosenboom, gardener at the Washington Cathedral in Washington DC. For garden purposes it has little advantage over common *helix* or *hibernica*.

Habit: Vining.
Stems: Purple-green. Internodes 4–6cm (1½–2⅓in).
Petioles: Purple-green.
Leaves: Unlobed, 3–6cm (1¼–2⅓in) by 3–5cm (1¼–2in). Deltoid, apex bluntly acute, leaf base cordate, veins fairly prominent. Colour mid- to dark green.

Hedera helix 'Cavendishii'

The first record of this name is in the list of ivies grown by William Paul and published in the Gardener's Chronicle (1867). I have been unable to trace the origin of the name but it may be assumed to honour the family name of the Dukes of Devonshire. At this period the Duke's gardener, Joseph Paxton (later Sir Joseph) had distinguished himself as the gardener at Chatsworth and as the architect of the Crystal Palace. Various plants bear the specific *cavendishii* in honour of the celebrated gardens and the equally noted gardener and one can assume that Paul, a leading nurseryman of his day, named the plant which was already in circulation.

It was Hibberd in 1872 who queered the nomenclatural pitch. He described the plant as 'Marginata Minor', listing *cavendishii* as one of its synonyms, his aversion to personal names asserting itself once more. Nicholson (1855) followed Hibberd's lead, but Bean (1914) described the plant as *cavendishii*. Nurserymen, understandably, were confused;

PLATE IV

All plants are shown at approximately ³/₄ size

H. rhombea 'Variegata'

H. helix 'Succinata'

H. helix 'Alt Heidelberg'

H. pastuchovii

H. azorica
shoot (left) and older leaves

H. helix
'Anna Marie'

H. hibernica 'Rona'

some managed to list both 'Cavendishii' and 'Marginata Minor'! Regardless of this, by virtue of its good constitution and good variegation, the plant persisted in gardens.

I suspect that 'Cavendishii', although listed as 'new' in catalogues of around the 1870s may be the original 'Silver Striped' ivy of Richard Weston (1770) and the 'Striped Leaved' ivy listed in the 1783 catalogue of Archibald Dickson of Roxburgh, Scotland. Doubtless it was also the 'Striped' ivy of the 1790 catalogue of William Thompson of York and the 1801 catalogue of Whitely and Brames, nurserymen of Old Brompton, London. Indeed, going back some 1900 years, it may have been the variegated ivy of Pliny's *Natural History* (23–79 AD). My reasoning for this is the fact that the plant never seems to revert. If the 'Silver Striped' of Weston and the variegated of Pliny are still with us, I suggest it must be in the form of a non-reverting kind such as 'Cavendishii'.

It remains an excellent, easy, hardy variegated climber. In arborescence, which it achieves fairly readily, it produces black fruits profusely and in this form can be used as a focal point. It is not suited to ground cover. 1993: ♔.
Habit: Vining.
Stems: Light green. Internodes 1–3cm (⅓–1¼in).
Petioles: Green.
Leaves: 3-lobed, 5–6cm (2–2⅓in) by 6–7cm (2⅓–2¾in). Lobes acutely pointed and angular in young leaves, less so with maturity. Sinuses shallow, leaf base truncate, lobes sometimes vestigial in older leaves. Variegation sharply defined, leaf centre medium-green with grey-green streaks. Occasionally the green breaks through to the irregular margin of cream-yellow.

Hedera helix 'Ceridwen'

Some ivies are described as 'interesting' or 'effective', others as 'pretty'; this clone falls very definitely into the last category. The bright yellow variegation is similar to that of 'Goldchild' but it differs and is made distinctly elegant by the sharp points to the three-lobed leaves.

The name is Welsh and means pretty, the plant however originated on the Danish nursery of the pot-plant specialist Frode Maegaard as a sport from 'Ester' and appeared in Britain during the late 1980s as 'Golden Ester'. The clone 'Ester' is cream variegated and thought by Heieck to be a synonym of 'Ingrid' and possibly only a slight variation of 'Eva', which may be taken to be the base type. The probable 'family tree' is 'Eva'–'Ester'–'Goldchild'–'Ceridwen'.

The plant was being marketed in Britain by Whitehouse Ivies who realized that the name 'Golden Ester', or indeed 'Golden Ann' which had occasionally been used, would not

be totally acceptable under the ICNCP which does not look kindly on names that qualify existing names. The firm gave it this most appropriate name.
Habit: Self-branching.
Stems: Purple-green. Internodes 2–3cm (¾–1¼in).
Petioles: Green-light purple.
Leaves: 3-lobed, 3–4cm (1¼–1½in) by 3–4cm (1¼–1½in). Apices acute. Leaf base truncate, occasionally cuneate or slightly cordate. Light green irregularly variegated cream-yellow, a fair proportion of totally yellow leaves.

Hedera helix 'Chester'

This clone appears to have originated and been named in Denmark but the name has been attributed in error to Chester in England as well as Chester in Pennsylvania. In 1977 I received the plant from a British house-plant nursery, one of whose directors spent much of his time in Europe and periodically sent back container-loads of house-plants of all kinds. 'Chester' was one of these plants. The then President of the AIS, Henri Schaepman, visited me in 1979 bringing plants from the USA and taking back plants, one of which was 'Chester' as recorded in the AIS Journal, Vol 5 pt 2, 1979. The name became connected, wittingly or unwittingly, with the Pennsylvanian town of that name.

In 1977 the nurserymen Gebr Stauss of Möglingen in Germany sent material to Heieck in Heidelberg. As 'Chester' the plant was described in *Ivies* (1980) and in *Hedera Sorten* (1980). The same clone was submitted to the AIS Research Center in 1982 as 'Citronella' but inevitably the first published name has priority.

This is a useful and widely grown clone.
Habit: Self-branching with short trails.
Stems: Green-purple. Internodes 2–2.5cm (¾–1in).
Petioles: Green-purple.
Leaves: Remotely 3-lobed, 3–3.5cm (1¼–1⅓in) by 4.5–5cm (1¾–2in). The shallow sinuses give a leaf almost triangular in outline. Apices acute, leaf base deeply cordate. Ground colour lime-green in young leaves with dark-green central splash. As the leaf ages the ground colour turns cream-white and the central portion darkens.

Hedera helix 'Chicago'

Several clones under this name have circulated in Europe from about 1962 and been catalogued by various nurseries. The published references of Jenny (1964), van de Laar (1965) and Nannenga-Bremekamp (1970) all describe it as a small-leaved clone of 'Pittsburgh'. It is probable that the original 'Pittsburgh' is now seldom seen, most nurseries having consciously or unconsciously selected the smaller-

Hedera helix 'Chicago'

leaved material when propagating so that 'Chicago' has supplanted its parent largely through selection. A most useful and widely grown pot plant, it will also make good ground cover. Stocks vary but that described below is judged to be typical. RHS Ivy Trial of 1978/9: C.

Habit: Self-branching.
Stems: Red-green. Internodes 2–4cm (¾–1½in).
Petioles: Pink-green.
Leaves: 3-lobed, 3–4cm (1¼–1½in) by 3–4cm (1¼–1½in). Centre lobe only slightly longer than laterals, lobes acute, sinuses shallow. Most leaves show two very slight basal lobes. Leaf base cordate, colour light green.

Hedera helix 'Chrysophylla'

This yellow variegated ivy is sometimes referred to as 'Spectabilis Aurea' or 'Aurea Spectabilis'. No record appears to exist of any early published description under these names. A yellow-variegated ivy was listed in the 1755 catalogue of Christopher Gray, nurseryman at Fulham, Middlesex, as "Yellow Bloatched Ivy". This name, usually written as 'Gold Blotched', together with 'Gold Striped' and 'Gold Leaved', appeared in various early catalogues but with only scant descriptions. An ivy named 'Gold Blotched' is among a number from the Lincoln nursery of Messrs Pennell & Sons that were illustrated in the Gardener's Chronicle (1909). It appears identical to the plant we know as 'Chrysophylla' and it seems probable that the names given above were among those applied to this clone.

'Chrysophylla' is described in the 1867 catalogue of Robert Veitch & Sons of Exeter: "Some of the leaves of *H. helix* chrysophylla are yellow, others green and others blotched with yellow, it is very rich and distinct."

Reporting on the RHS Ivy Trial of 1890 Hibberd wrote:
'Chrysophylla' is variable and uncertain and needs to be kept to the best possible character by propagating from the best coloured growths obtainable. It is well known as a fast-growing ivy of robust habit; the leaves occasionally richly coloured deep yellow in patches or in mottled form, justify one of its names of 'Clouded Gold'. Contributed by Mr Turner as 'Spectabilis Aurea' and by Mr Fraser as 'Gold Clouded'. The plant sent by Mr Turner as

'Angularis Aurea' is 'Chrysophylla' in one of its
many forms differing but little from the type".
In fairness to "Mr Turner" (Charles Turner, 1818–85, the
Slough nurseryman who 'promoted' the then unknown
Cox's Orange Pippin apple) it should be said that the ivy
generally known in the trade as 'Spectabilis Aurea' had been
offered as such in various catalogues since about 1870. Hibberd's last comment of shows that confusion between this
clone and 'Angularis Aurea' is by no means new. Colouring
and habit are indeed similar but the leaves of 'Angularis
Aurea' tend to be thinner, the green parts a lighter green and
the primary veins less noticeable. As the leaves age they
take on an angled appearance with typically an elliptic centre lobe terminating in a slightly drawn-out apex.

Differentiating between the two clones is a slightly acad-
emic exercise; both are excellent for wall cover; 'Chryso-
phylla' probably shows more colour as the plant matures.
'Angularis Aurea' shows better yellow colour when young.
Habit: Vining.
Stems: Green-purple. Internodes 2.5–4cm (1–1½in).
Petioles: Green.
Leaves: 3-lobed, 4–6cm (1½–2⅓in) by 5–8cm (2–3in).
Lobes wedge-shaped and almost equal, leaf base trun-
cate. Mid- to dark green, some leaves suffused light-
yellow. In the adult state whole trusses of leaves can
show up as clear yellow. Main veins fairly pronounced.

Hedera helix 'Cockle Shell'

One of the most interesting ivies in that it is utterly unlike
an ivy. In place of the usual three- or five-lobed leaf is an
almost round leaf, attractively veined and concave.
Recorded in 1976, 'Cockle Shell' is a mutant of 'California'
and was found by Paul Taylor of Rosemeade, California.

The plant was registered (No 762) by Marion Vincent of
La Habra, California as 'Cockle Shell'. Reputedly hardy in
Zone 7 in America, it has proved hardy in Britain. Essen-
tially a house-plant ivy, it is an attractive clone for hanging
baskets and indoor cultivation.
Habit: Self-branching.
Stems: Light purple. Internodes 2–2.5cm (¾–1in).
Petioles: Light purple.
Leaves: 3–5cm (1¼–2in) by the same in breadth, often
unlobed and appearing almost circular but occasionally showing 3–5 vestigial lobes, often as little more than
marginal protrusions. Leaf margins upturned giving the
leaf blade the concavity aptly described by its name.
Light green maturing to dark green. Veins light green,
prominent, raised, radiating in digital fashion from the
petiole junction.

Hedera helix 'Congesta'

The earliest description of this clone is in the 1956 catalogue of Burkwood & Skipwith, nurserymen then of Wal-
ton, Surrey, which listed "*Hedera congesta* (formerly known
as 'Minima'), short stiff branches, erect growing and reaching up to two feet. Deep olive-green leaves." This reference
to a former unpublished name of 'Minima' is supported by
the existence in the Kew Herbarium of a specimen collected
by M Young in 1887 and labelled *Hedera helix* 'Minima', Milford Nursery, Godalming. This specimen is plainly of the
clone 'Congesta' and shows the existence of an erect ivy
some ten years prior to Dr Master's exhibit of an erect ivy
before the Scientific Committee of the RHS in 1898.

Bean (1973 ed) quotes neither 'Erecta' nor 'Congesta' but
refers to 'Conglomerata' and 'Conglomerata Erecta', owning that the latter had been known by the invalid name
'Minima'. Bean (1988) uses the correct nomenclature of the
erect ivies, quoting *Ivies* (Rose, 1980) and The Plantsman
Vol 8, pt 1, 1986 where they were surveyed in detail.

Whatever its nomenclatural history, this ivy is of considerable value as a rock-garden plant and better for the small
garden than its larger cousin 'Erecta'. The leaves are smaller,
the stems tend to have more colour and the two-ranked leaf
arrangement is tighter. It is widely grown on the continent
where the larger 'Erecta' is seldom seen. 1993: ♛.
Habit: Non-climbing, erect.
Stems: Green-purple. Internodes 0.5–1cm (¼–⅓in).
Petioles: Purple-green.
Leaves: 3-lobed, 3–4cm (1¼–1½in) by 2–3cm (¾–1¼in).
Sinuses shallow, young leaves often unlobed. Apices
acute, the leaf margins lift to give a folded effect, this
combined with the distichous arrangement gives a
formal, closely erect plant. Colour dark green, veins
only slightly lighter.

Hedera helix 'Conglomerata'

The origins of many ivy clones are elusive, few more so than
this. The first record is that in the Gardener's Chronicle
(1871) which reported it as "...being an interesting addition
to this class of plants on account of its distinct habit." *La Belgique Horticole* of 1873 commented, "It is one of the most
curious and distinct varieties of ivy" and in 1875 it was listed
by the celebrated German nursery firm of Haage & Schmidt.

William Clibran & Son of Altrincham listed it in 1880 as
"very distinct with curiously distorted foliage". Thereafter it
was in wide circulation and references appeared in the horticultural press. The Garden (1881) wrote of it as

The clustered ivy... a peculiar ivy and quite distinct
from its congeners both in foliage and habit. The

leaves are very thick and have a curious crimped appearance, while the plant instead of climbing forms a low shrub suitable for the shady parts of rockwork and similar places.

In 1889 Hibberd wrote in the RHS Journal,

'Conglomerata' has the merits of distinctness and though scarcely beautiful is immensely interesting. The growth is in a somewhat geometric plan the branches radiating regularly. The leaves are ovate, curled and frilled and overlap so as to form a dense imbricated mass, the result as may be seen of a peculiar fasciation. The colour is a deep rich green. When trained to a wall its character is destroyed, it should be left perfectly free to spread in its own way on an open border or on a broad shelf in the rockery. It requires a moist warm climate to ensure full development.

Hibberd did not mention the plant in his monograph of 1872 so it is fair to assume that the record of June 10th 1871 was the clone's first public appearance. In Nicholson's *Dictionary of Gardening* (1885) it is described as "A marked slow growing erect variety with small wavy leaves and very short internodes. An excellent subject for rockwork." The word 'erect' seems a misnomer and may refer to the plant's characteristic of producing short erect shoots from the recumbent stems. This may have bred the confusion, seen to this day in some catalogues where 'Conglomerata' is marketed as 'Erecta'. Unlike the erect ivies it can be trained to wall, rock or tree; after a century and a quarter it has retained its identity, it does not revert and has not thrown any variegated form. It remains the "clustered ivy suitable for rockwork" and as such can be strongly recommended. RHS Floral Committee, 1872: FCC; RHS Ivy Trial 1978/9: AM.

Habit: Creeping and climbing, very short-jointed.
Stems: Green, often slightly flattened. Internodes 0.5–1cm (¼–⅓in).
Petioles: Green.
Leaves: Unlobed to obscurely 3-lobed, 1–3cm (⅕–1¼in) by 2–4cm (¾–1½in). Margins undulate and waved, arranged in two ranks, texture leathery, colour dark green. Veins raised giving a puckered appearance.

Hedera helix 'Corrugata'

Described by Hibberd in 1872 together with an illustration that corresponds exactly with plants seen today and particularly with material at the Royal Botanic Gardens, Kew. Hibberd's figure appears to be of adult shoots and it is true to say that the forward-pointing, almost toothed lobing and the attenuated leaf base are more evident on older material.

An interesting wall ivy of which 'Mrs Pollock' would seem to be the variegated form and more commonly grown today.
Habit: Vining.
Stems: Green. Internodes 3–5cm (1¼–2in).
Petioles: Green.
Leaves: 5–7-lobed, 5–7cm (2–2¾in) by 6–8cm (2⅖–3in). Lobes often appear as little more than forward-pointing projections or large teeth at the apex of a leaf whose cuneate base makes it like an inverted triangle with its apex at the petiole/leaf-blade junction. The lobes are short and acuminate with deep sinuses. Mid- to dark green.

Hedera helix 'Crenata'

This clone was one of the "40 sorts" grown by the nurseryman William Paul of Cheshunt, London. In the Gardener's Chronicle of 1867 he described it as "Leaves green, broad, regularly cleft; the veins very conspicuous, similar to but larger than those of *H. helix* 'Palmata'. Growth free and rapid." In fact there appears little difference between this and his description of *H. helix* 'Pennsylvanica'.

Hibberd (1872) called it the "wrinkled ivy" and suggested it was intermediate between 'Palmata' and 'Digitata'. "The leaves are broad, usually five-angled and digitate, but less distinctly so than those of 'Digitata'; the edges are much crenated and the colour a light grass green."

'Crenata' appeared in a few catalogues from 1865–90 but rarely thereafter. Lawrence & Schulze however thought it sufficiently distinct to warrant listing together with an illustration in *Cultivated Ivies* (1942) commenting that the lobes bore one or two teeth at the wavy margins.

From this history of some 126 years I think it may be deduced that there are several digitate-type ivies with slight differences that have been noted over the years, 'Crenata' with its very slightly notched leaves being one of these.
Habit: Vining.
Stems: Purple-green. Internodes 2–4cm (¾–1½in).
Petioles: Purple-green.
Leaves: 5-lobed, 2–6cm (¾–2⅓in) by 5–7cm (2–2¾in), palmately digitate, apices acute, strongly undulate, leaf base truncate, glossy light green.

Hedera helix 'Curvaceous'

Discovered in 1980 by Elise Everhardt of Baltimore, Maryland as a sport of 'Manda's Crested'. The parent plant was over-wintered indoors but a rooted shoot developed into this excellent cream-variegated, curly-leaved clone.

Whilst primarily of value as a house plant it has proved to be an excellent outdoor clone. It retains the habit and

Hedera helix 'Crenata'

comparative hardiness of 'Manda's Crested'; in cold weather the leaf margins take on a reddish tint, a possible inheritance from its parent which colours so well in cold weather.
Habit: Self-branching with short trails.
Stems: Green-purple. Internodes 2–3cm (¾–1¼in).
Petioles: Green-purple.
Leaves: 3-lobed, sinuses virtually absent giving a roughly triangular leaf averaging 4–5cm (1½–2in) by 5–6cm (2–2⅜in). Leaf base cordate, apices bluntly acute, leaf margins waved, apices equally waved and down-pointing. Mid-green with broken areas of grey-green, cream variegation at leaf edge. AIS Reg No 810384.

Hedera helix 'Cuspidata Major'
This ivy is easily identified from the illustration in Hibberd's *The Ivy* (1872) and from his description,

> The lobes uniformly three-lobed, all the lobes project forward, the centre being the largest; they are cuspid in outline and peculiarly 'cockled' at the bifurcation. The leaf is thick and hard like parchment, colour deep, full cheerful green.

The plant has been found as a climber on walls at a few stately homes in Britain, doubtless planted around the turn of the century. Its fresh green colour and its almost trident-like leaves are its attributes. 'Cuspidata Minor', also described by Hibberd, was similar but with smaller leaves. The clone 'Tomboy' described by Nannenga-Bremekamp (1970) and marketed in the USA appears to be the same ivy.
Habit: Vining.
Stems: Green. Internodes 3–5cm (1¼–2in).
Petioles: Green-purple.
Leaves: 3-lobed, 6–7cm (2⅜–2¾in) by 5–9cm (2–3½in). Lobes cuspid or acuminate. Forward-pointing so that often the tips of the 3 lobes are parallel. Sinuses narrow, margin convolute at the cleft. Leaf base cuneate to attenuate. Colour fresh bright green. Veins light green, pointing forward in slowly diverging lines from the petiole/leaf-blade junction.

Hedera helix 'Dealbata'

This ivy was described by Hibberd (1872) as

> A very distinct and peculiar plant occurring frequently in a wild state in the woods on the Eastern slopes of Snowdonia, where it frequently carpets the ground with a profuse growth of dark green leafage, dotted with leaves of a pure white. The leaves are usually equally three-lobed small and varying but little in size or form; many of them dark green, with a faint powdering of white; others wholly blanched and semi-transparent; when grown in a good soil, the growth becomes wholly green, but when grown in a soil consisting chiefly of potsherd, broken stones, and coarse grit, it continues faithful to its sylvan character.

There is no subsequent reference in literature or catalogues of the day to the plant. Reviewing the genus Lawrence & Schulze (1942) assumed it to be the same plant as 'Discolor' and the 'Minor Marmorata' of Paul, although Hibberd had named both 'Discolor' and 'Dealbata' and with different descriptions of each. All rather unsatisfactory.

The picture clears when we examine another of the early varieties. In 1928, L R Russell Ltd catalogued *H. helix* 'Howardiana' which they described as "Edge mottled silver, very pretty in the young growth". In later catalogues the name is given as 'Howardii'. There the matter might rest but for the existence at the Royal Botanic Gardens, Kew, of an ivy labelled 'Howardii'. Examination of this very old plant and of cuttings rooted from it show it to have all the characters of Hibberd's 'Dealbata', which in fact is not an outstanding clone being typical of the variegated forms of *helix* frequently found in the wild in Britain. 'Dealbata' differs from 'Minor Marmorata' in that the leaf is consistently three-lobed while that of 'Minor Marmorata' is five-lobed, broad and with more consistent variegation.

Habit: Vining.
Stems: Purple-green, thin. Internodes 3–4cm (1¼–1½in).
Petioles: Purple.
Leaves: 3-lobed, triangular to arrow-shaped, 3–5cm (1¼–2in) by 4–6cm (1½–2⅓in). Apices acute, sinuses shallow or non-existent. Dark green irregularly spotted and splashed cream-white, more so on young leaves.

Hedera helix 'Diana'

This mutation from 'Sylvanian' appeared in 1977 at the nursery of Franz Rogmans of Geldern, Germany, and was named in 1981 to honour his daughter Diana. It is a most unusual ivy in that the lobes terminate in a finely drawn-out wispy point not unlike a small tendril. A good house-plant ivy with fairly broad leaves, it is easy and quick to root.
Habit: Self-branching with long vigorous trails.
Stems: Purple-green. Internodes 1–3cm (⅓–1¼in).
Petioles: Green-purple.
Leaves: 3-lobed, 5–8cm (2–3in) by 3–6cm (1¼–2⅓in), shape very variable. Lobes often show as mere protrusions, they and the vein endings often terminate in a fine piliferous point. Colour dark green, veins raised and prominent, lateral veins sometimes joined at their termination. AIS Reg No 811782.

Hedera helix 'Dick von Stauss'

Introduced by the firm of Gebr Stauss in 1975/6, this sport from the clone 'Stuttgart' was awarded a silver medal at the Bundesgartenschau (BUGA) Horticultural Show in 1977.

It is similar to 'Astin' but has larger leaves. It makes a good pot plant and can be treated like bonzai, it is also attractive as ground cover for small areas.
Habit: Self-branching.
Stems: Purple-green. Internodes 1–1.5cm (⅓–⅗in).
Petioles: Purple-green.
Leaves: 5-lobed, 5–6cm (2–2⅓in) by 7–8cm (2¾–3in). Convoluted at the sinuses to give a wavy and curled leaf, apices acute, leaf base cordate. Colour mid-green.

Hedera helix 'Digitata'

This name is one of the earliest applied to an ivy variety. It was one of seven catalogued by Conrad Loddiges of Hackney, London in 1826, and was mentioned by the Edinburgh nurserymen, Peter Lawson & Sons, in their *Arboretum et Fruticetum* of 1846. It was among ivies offered for sale in 1838 by James Booth who had established his Flottbeck Nursery in Hamburg, Germany and whose English language catalogue listed the ivy at 9d (ninepence) a plant.

In the Gardener's Chronicle of 1867 William Paul described 'Digitata' as "Leaves dark green, long and pointed, broad at base, deeply cleft, growth rapid. Shoots less numerous than in most others." Lawrence & Schulze (1942) give a detailed description and illustration saying that it was first recognized in Ireland, "Made known by Mr Hodgens and noticed by Dr Mackay (*Flora Hibernica*, 1836)". It was said to have been found growing wild near the former nursery gardens at Dungas Town, Wicklow and listed as *H. helix* 'Hodgensii' or *H. helix* 'Incisa'. If this were so Loddiges would seem to have had the variety before Mr Hodgens.

Along with his description of 'Digitata' Paul described two other 'fingered' ivies, 'Digitata Nova' and 'Pennsylvanica'. He recorded 'Digitata Nova' as having smaller leaves and in my opinion this is the clone depicted by Lawrence

& Schulze. Furthermore I suspect that the 'Digitata' of Loddiges and Hodgens was in fact a clone of what we now term *H. hibernica* and which now circulates as 'Rottingdean'.

From 1899 to 1932 a few nurseries listed 'Digitata Aurea', Russell described it as having "Deeply cut golden foliage". Hibberd in 1872 had quoted this name as a synonym of 'Chrysophylla' of which he wrote that it has "Broad lobes, obtuse and few in number". Plainly the Russell plant was different from this but would seem to have been lost, certainly no golden-leaved digitate vining ivy is extant today.

Habit: Vining.

Stems: Purple-green. Internodes 3–5cm (1¼–2in). Profuse 4–6-rayed stellar hairs.

Petioles: Green-purple.

Leaves: 5–7-lobed, 4–5cm (1½–2in) by 5–7cm (2–2¾in). Centre lobe roughly equal to lateral lobes, basal lobes a little smaller. Apices acute, leaf base shallow to deeply cordate. Dull dark green with grey-white veins.

Hedera helix 'Direktor Badke'

Charming and unusual, the leaves of this ivy sometimes seem to be made up of three circles, so rounded are the leaves. The clone was selected by Hans Schmidt, nurseryman of Bockum-Hövel, Germany, and exhibited in 1960 at BUGA, the large flower show at Dortmund. The name commemorates Richard Badke, Director of the Horticultural College and Gardens at Wolbeck, Germany, from 1930 until his death in 1956.

The clone is similar to 'Ralf' but has smaller, more rounded leaves. The compact growth and neat foliage make it a useful pot plant. A similar clone was later selected at the Stauss nurseries and named 'Christian'. This name was withdrawn when it was realized that the clone already existed and had been named. 'Frizzle', a sport in which the leaves are wrinkled and rumpled and slightly cristate, was selected in 1993 by Ron Whitehouse.

Habit: Self-branching.

Stems: Red-purple. Internodes 1.5–2cm (⅝–¾in).

Petioles: Green, pink at base.

Leaves: 3-lobed, 1.5–2.5cm (⅝–1in) by 3–3.5cm (1¼–1⅜in). Lobes rounded and not pronounced, often merging to produce a rounded, deltoid leaf. Leaf base strongly cordate, basal lobes sometimes overlapping slightly. Soft light green with lighter veins. Centre vein occasionally red-purple in strong sun or in cold.

Hedera helix 'Donerailensis'

According to Bean (1973) this ivy was in cultivation in 1854 "and may have originated at Doneraile, County Cork".

I suggest that it is possible to elaborate on this statement. Volume 84 of *Curtis's Botanical Magazine* of 1858 was dedicated by Sir William Hooker, Director of Kew, to the Countess of Doneraile "A great admirer and successful cultivator of plants". Lady Doneraile was in constant communication with Kew and, with her husband, visited Sir William frequently. She gave many items to the museum, in particular unique examples of Irish Lace made from various plant fibres, a fashion at that time. In return there was a constant flow of plants from Kew to Doneraile and it is interesting that in a letter of 1858 she sought cuttings "of the palmated ivy". This interest suggests that 'Donerailensis' may well have originated at Doneraile Court under the watchful eye of 'May Doneraile' as she signed herself.

On the death of her husband Lady Doneraile moved to Gresy-sur-Aix in France where she created a fine garden. She died in 1907. That we have this plant today with the same characteristics described by writers of over 100 years ago illustrates the stability of clones of the *helix* 'vining'-type ivies.

Our plant as 'Donerailensis Minor' was included in the list of ivies grown by Paul and published in the Gardener's Chronicle (1867) and as 'Donerailensis' was listed in the 1867 catalogue of Haag & Schmidt.

There is an attractive illustration in *The Ivy* (Hibberd, 1872); Hibberd obviously admired the plant for he used it as a motif bordering the pages of his book but despite this, showing his customary aversion to names recording people or places, renamed it 'Minima' thereby causing confusion.

The plant's characteristics are summarized by Bean (1973) whose description can hardly be bettered.

> Leaves small, usually three-lobed, the central lobe narrowly triangular, the lateral lobes similar in shape to the central one, margins wavy. This clone only retains its character if grown as a pot plant. Allowed to grow freely on a wall the leaves eventually become much larger and very like those of 'Pedata'.

In youth it is rather like a miniature 'Pedata', in age the leaves become large, flat and rather like 'Pedata' trying to be 'Crenata'! Whilst it has the virtue of turning purple readily with the onset of cold weather, its unpredictable leaf shape does not recommend it for garden use.

Habit: Vining.

Stems: Purple-green. Internodes 1–2.5cm (⅓–1in).

Petioles: Purple-green.

Leaves: 3-lobed, 4–5cm (1½–2in) by 3–4cm (1¼–1½in), central lobe 1½ times the length of the laterals and tending to curl. Lateral lobes wedge-shaped, margins wavy. The occasional presence of 2 vestigial basal lobes give a 'bird's foot' appearance. Leaf base cordate, colour dark green colouring purple in cold weather.

Hedera helix 'Dragon Claw'

Found in the early 1970s in a park in Norfolk, Virginia by the daughter-in-law of Leo Swicegood (1906–81), the clone has some affinity with 'Manda's Crested' but is larger in all its parts. Swicegood, then at Rescue, Virginia, named the ivy. At some time it was known in Britain under the unpublished name 'Curly-Q'. AIS Reg No 751 (1977).
Habit: Self-branching with long trails.
Stems: Green-purple. Internodes 1.5–2cm (⅝–¾in).
Petioles: Green-purple.
Leaves: 5-lobed, 3–4cm (1¼–1½in) by 5–7cm (2–2¾in). Sinuses so shallow as to give the impression of an unlobed leaf, lobes down-turning with fluted margins. Apices bluntly acute, leaf base cordate. Mid-green.

Hedera helix 'Duckfoot'

An engaging little ivy whose leaves do indeed rather resemble the webbed foot of a duck. It is a good house-plant ivy but not very effective for outside cultivation. The clone occurred on the nursery of Ballas and Tillender at Bound Brook, New Jersey, as a sport from 'Merion Beauty' in 1976/7. Initially it was sold as 'Baby Merion Beauty' but locally gained the name of 'Duckfoot', a name confirmed by the AIS in 1978. The plant came to Britain in 1980 and has sometimes been known by the invalid name of 'Fiddle Leaf'.
Habit: Self-branching, short-jointed.
Stems: Green-purple. Internodes 0.5–1cm (¼–⅓in).
Petioles: Green-purple. 1–1.5cm (⅓–⅝in).
Leaves: 3-lobed, sinuses extremely shallow, leaf base cuneate. 1–2cm (⅓–¾in) by 2–2.5cm (¾–1in), colour light green, veins not unduly pronounced.

Hedera helix 'Dunloe Gap'

First listed as a *hibernica* clone, examination of the hair structure shows it to be a form of *H. helix*. It was collected by Roy Lancaster in July 1986 near the beauty spot of Dunloe Gap just north of Killarney in County Kerry, Ireland. Examining the local flora, Roy had climbed the cliffs above the Gap when he slipped, sliding down some way but coming to rest between a rocky outcrop where a curtain of this small-leaved ivy hung. Recognizing it as something different he listed it (L.351) and circulated it as 'Dunloe Gap' since when it has proved to be a useful little ivy, well suited as ground cover for rock-garden situations. It has an affinity in leaf size, shape and habit with *H. helix* 'Arran'.

Hedera helix 'Duckfoot'

Habit: Vining and readily branching.
Stems: Purple-green. Internodes 1.5–3cm (⅝–1¼in).
Petioles: Purple.
Leaves: 3-lobed, 2–4cm (¾–1½in) by 3–4cm (1¼–1½in). Sinuses very shallow, apices bluntly acute, leaf base truncate to cuneate. Colour dark green.

Hedera helix 'Elegance'

Discovered as a sport of 'Pittsburgh' in 1968 in the nursery of Hage & Co of Boskoop, Holland, it differs in having a more pointed centre lobe and shallow sinuses, giving a more 'open' leaf. It has been confused with 'Carolina Crinkle', which has a more undulate leaf and which was introduced in 1971 by W O Freeland of Columbia, South Carolina.
Habit: Self-branching.
Stems: Green-purple. Internodes 2–4cm (¾–1½in).
Petioles: Green-purple.
Leaves: 5-lobed, basal lobes occasionally vestigial, 3–7cm (1¼–2¾in) by 5–7cm (2–2¾in). Centre lobe twice as

long as wide. Sinuses shallow, apice of centre lobe acuminate, of lateral lobes acute. Colour mid-green.

Hedera helix 'Elfenbein'

This clone can well be described as a variegated 'Parsley Crested'. It was selected at the nurseries of Stauss Bros in 1977. The name 'Elfenbein' has a connection with elves and refers to the plant's spindly mode of growth. This character makes it unsuitable as a pot plant; it is likely to be as hardy as 'Parsley Crested' and worth trying outside.

Habit: Self-branching but with long trails.
Stems: Green-purple. Internodes 2–4cm (¾–1½in).
Petioles: Green-purple and long: 4–8cm (1½–3in).
Leaves: 5-lobed but the sinuses so shallow as often to produce an unlobed leaf, 3–6cm (1¼–2⅓in) by 4–5cm (1½–2in). Colour light-grey-green with defined patches of light-grey. Yellow-cream variegation confined to the leaf edge which is heavily cristate.

Hedera helix 'Erecta'

The *Transactions of the RHS* (1898) contain the report of a meeting of its Scientific Committee held in that year:

Ivy Sports. Dr Masters exhibited sprays of a peculiar small leaved dwarf ivy remarkable for sending up vertical shoots with distichous leaves, though unattached to a wall. The habit appears to have become fixed, even in free growing branches.

Unfortunately we do not know the source or nature of Dr Master's plant for we have inherited three distinct erect ivies, 'Erecta', 'Congesta' and 'Russelliana'. Hibberd did not mention an erect ivy in *The Ivy* (1872) but in his report on the RHS Trial 1888 he wrote, "'Fasciata' is a form of *conglomerata* distinct enough but not so far away as to be particularly desirable". He did not indicate that the plant was erect in habit. He called it 'Fasciata' but it had been submitted by the nurseryman Maurice Young of Milford, Surrey, as 'Minima'. Evidence that this may have been an erect clone is provided by the 1894 catalogue of William Clibran & Son of Altrincham, Cheshire, which listed "'Minima' – each shoot forms a perfect column of small leaves". 'Minima' was an invalid name because Hibberd had published it in *The Ivy* to describe what had previously been called 'Donerailensis'.

The plant thereafter was much confused with 'Conglomerata'. Various catalogues of the period describe an erect-growing variety as 'Minima', 'Conglomerata Erecta' or 'Congesta'. The first authoritative description of *H. helix* 'Erecta' is that of Lawrence & Schulze (1942) but their description and illustration is more typical of the closer growing, sharp-leaved form which has acquired the name

'Congesta' on the Continent. 'Erecta' is stronger growing, has larger leaves and thicker, lighter coloured stems, it is suited to the bigger rock garden and as a front plant for a shady shrub border; 'Congesta' is more suitable for the smaller situation. Both are plants of great architectural value, they can never be confused with 'Conglomerata' since they resolutely refuse to climb, however closely planted to walls. RHS Ivy Trial 1978/9: HC(T); 1993: ♛.

Whilst not a climber, established plants of 'Erecta' will develop arborescent shoots although I have never seen these shoots produce flowers. Such shoots taken as cuttings will develop into curious little dumpy plants. Such rooted cuttings or possibly grafted plants have been produced commercially in Holland and marketed as 'Humpty Dumpty'.

Habit: Non-climbing, erect.
Stems: Short-jointed, green, freely producing adventitious roots. Internodes 1cm (⅓in).
Petioles: Light green.
Leaves: 3-lobed, occasionally unlobed, 4–6cm (1½–2⅓in) by 4–6cm (1½–2⅓in). Distichous, though this is less noticeable in older shoots. Leaf sinuses usually shallow, centre lobe slightly longer than laterals. Apices bluntly acute. Dark green, veins light green to grey.

Hedera helix 'Eugen Hahn'

According to Krussman (1977) this was a mutation from 'Pennsylvanian'. There is no plant of that name in the AIS Check-list nor in other available lists and I suspect the parent variety to be 'Sylvanian' (US Patent variety 430, 1940). The similarity of the leaves to 'Sylvanian' is mentioned by Brother Heieck in his Check-list of the clones grown by Gebr Stauss and in fact the clone was introduced by them at the BUGA Horticultural Show of 1977 and described in *Gartenwelt* (1977). Brother Heieck's description of "Leaves dappled and speckled with light green, dark green, grey-green and white to yellowish white distributed in large or small patches over the whole leaf", can hardly be bettered.

The powdered 'pepper and salt' effect may not be to everyone's taste but it is certainly distinct. A vining clone producing fairly compact trails, it is useful for decoration, particularly troughs and baskets. The newer introduction 'Domino' however, a mutation from 'Eugen Hahn' selected by Gebr Stauss in 1879, may well supplant it.

Habit: Short-jointed but throwing strong vining trails.
Stems: Purple. Internodes 1.5–3cm (⅝–1¼in).
Petioles: Green-purple, rarely more than 2cm (¾in).
Leaves: Remotely 3-lobed, more often unlobed with frequently a lobe-like protrusion to 1 side of the leaf base. Heart-shaped to triangular, 3–4cm (1¼–1½in) by

3–5cm (1¼–2in), noticeably thin. Base colour cream, densely stippled and marbled with medium green.

Hedera helix 'Eva'

The first record of this popular clone is in Gartenwelt und Zierpflanzenbau (1966), where it appears that Tage Melin of Hjallese, Denmark, selected it from the clone 'Harald' in the early 1960s. Large quantities are now grown for the house-plant trade because growth is rapid and the small leaves make it suitable for pot work and particularly for bottle gardens.

In common with 'Harald' it has proved reasonably hardy in Britain, albeit with some damage to the variegated portions in frost and cold winds. On the continent it is considered an indoor plant and its USA limit is probably Zone 8. It is described by Nannenga-Bremekamp (1970) as 'Pittsburgh Variegated' but in view of the earlier record this name should be disregarded. Reversion to totally green leaves occurs occasionally: these can be identified as 'Pittsburgh' and one may assume that this clone and 'Harald' are variations of 'Pittsburgh Variegated' described by Bates (National Horticultural Magazine) in America in 1940. In Europe its extensive cultivation has given rise to numerous mutations. The name 'Liz' has been quoted as a synonym.

Habit: Self-branching.

Stems: Green-purple. Internodes 2–3cm (¾–1¼in).

Petioles: Green-purple.

Leaves: 3-lobed, 2.5cm (1in) by 2.5–3.5cm (1–1⅓in). Centre lobe usually acuminate and up to twice the length of laterals. Sinuses shallow, lateral lobes often wedge-shaped, centre lobe occasionally so. Leaf base cuneate. Colour, grey-green centre blotched darker green, bordered with cream-white, this extending sometimes to ½ the leaf.

Hedera helix 'Fallen Angel'

Discovered as a sport of 'Emerald Globe' in 1980 by Frank Batson of Woodburn, Oregon. The name is derived from Batson's nursery, Angelwood; 'Fallen' suggests its mutant status! The small spade-shaped leaves are very closely set, almost overlapping, on flattened, somewhat fasciated stems. These trail but the tips turn up giving a candelabra effect. An attractive house-plant ivy but prone to reversion. AIS Reg No 822683.

Habit: Self-branching.

Stems: Green-purple. Internodes 0.5–1cm (¼–⅓in).

Petioles: Green.

Leaves: Rhomboid or ovate, occasionally 3-lobed with very shallow sinuses; 2–4cm (¾–1½in) by 2–4cm (¾–1½in).

Top: *Hedera helix* 'Eva'; above: *Hedera helix* 'Fan'

Apices bluntly acute, leaf base truncate, occasionally cuneate. Mid-green, the lighter coloured veins slightly prominent.

Hedera helix 'Fan'

An interesting ivy whose name indicates the shape of its leaves and their radiating veins.

According to Dr Sulgrove, Registrar for the AIS, the stock of 'Fan' in their collection matches 'Weber's Fan'. This, according to Shippy (1950), was a sport from 'Weber's Californian' which was introduced by the Weber Nurseries of Los Angeles, California in 1939 and was supposed to have come from 'Merion Beauty'.

A good pot or trough plant 'Fan' throws out short vining trails with a cluster of small leaves at virtually every node. Its close habit makes it a good house plant. 'California Fan' is a slightly more compact form. 'California Gold' is a yellow-cream sport with slightly waved lobes.

Habit: Self-branching with short trails.

Stems: Purple-green. Internodes 3.5–4cm (1⅓–1½in). Miniature shoots with leaf clusters at every node.

Petioles: Pink-green.

Leaves: 5-lobed, 3–4.5cm (1¼–1¾) by 5–7cm (2–2¾in). Short, fat lobes often reduced to forward-pointing protrusions. Apices blunt, leaf base truncate to cuneate. Soft apple-green, veins prominently raised, radiating fan-like from the petioles.

Hedera helix 'Fantasia'

A cream-mottled clone that has circulated under the names 'Aalsmeer' and 'Pittsburgh Variegated'. Whilst it may have arisen in Holland, the first written references appeared in the 1975 catalogue of the Alestake Nursery of Elkwood, USA which described a freely branching 'Pittsburgh'-type ivy with fine white specks on the leaves and pinkish vines. Its name only was included in the AIS Check-list (1975).

In Britain it is at its best as an indoor plant, outside it will survive hard winters but with severe damage to the variegated areas and a greater tendency to green reversion.

Habit: Self-branching.

Stems: Pink-purple. Internodes 1.5–2cm (⅝–¾in).

Petioles: Green-pink.

Leaves: 5-lobed, 3–4cm (1¼–1½in) by 4–6cm (1½–2⅓in). Apices acute, sinuses wide, leaf base deeply cordate. Basic colour bright-green heavily mottled cream. Veins light green.

Hedera helix 'Filigran'

A most distinctive ivy. The back-pointing tendency of the heavily curled and crimped leaves gives an impression of a series of curly leafy balls. Fairly quick growing and easily propagated but not as self-branching as some house-plant ivies. The plant arose on the nursery of Stauss Bros in 1975 as a mutation from 'Boskoop'. It was named by them in 1977 and exhibited with success in Germany. The very appropriate name is of course German for filigree.

Habit: Short-jointed with trails.

Stems: Purple-green. Internodes 1–3cm (⅓–1¼in).

Petioles: Purple-green, slightly flattened, 3–5cm (1¼–2in).

Leaves: 5-lobed, 3–5cm (1¼–2in) by 4–5cm (1½–2in). Sinuses extremely deep, sometimes cut almost to the centre vein. Leaf edges of each lobe deeply waved, base generally cuneate, sometimes extremely so. Apices acute and back-pointing to the petiole. Mid-green.

Hedera helix 'Flamenco'

Introduced by Henri Schaepman of the then Alestake Ivy Nursery, Elkwood, USA during the mid-1970s it is presumed to have been a mutation from 'Ivalace'. The name refers to the ruffled petticoats of Flamenco dancers, an allusion to the superimposed style of the almost stemless leaves and ruffled leaf margins. A faster growing, more vigorous and larger leaved mutation was discovered by Frank Batson of Woodburn, Oregon, in 1982 and registered as 'Pirouette'. It is less stiff stemmed than 'Flamenco'. AIS Reg No 80581.

Habit: Short-jointed, self branching.

Stems: Purple-green. Internodes 1–2cm (⅓–¾in).

Petioles: Purple-green. 1cm (⅓in). Some leaves almost sessile, often thickened.

Leaves: Often unlobed, otherwise basically 5-lobed, 1–1.5cm (⅓–⅝in), 1–3cm (⅓–1¼in). Often divided into 3 with a distinctly thickened, fasciated petiole. Margins convolute, dark glossy green, red colouration at the petiole junction.

Hedera helix 'Flavescens'

Identification of this clone has been heavily dependent on nursery catalogues, particularly those of L R Russell Ltd. Descriptions dating from 1901–32 refer variously to "lasting golden foliage" and "slow growing, foliage entirely bright gold". These descriptions fit the ivy still occasionally found in gardens and include the plant growing on the Ivy Wall at Kew, recorded there as 'Flavescens'. The only firm apart from Russell to have listed the plant in Britain appeared to be Gauntletts of Chiddingfold in Surrey.

The leaves of 'Flavescens' differ from other 'golden' ivies in being of a more uniform pale yellow-green; as the leaves age they become light to mid-green. Slow growing, the old catalogues suggest that the arborescent form was a favourite for 'bedding out' and 'yellow gardens' in pre-1914 days.

Habit: Vining.

Stems: Green-purple. Internodes 2.5–4cm (1–1½in).

Petioles: Green-purple.

Leaves: 3-lobed, 3–4cm (1¼–1½in) by 3–4cm (1¼–1½in). Lobes not prominent but showing more as protrusions on the small leaves. Leaf base slightly cordate. Colour very light green to pale yellow ageing to mid-green.

Hedera helix 'Fleur de Lis'

Recorded by Shippy in the American Flower Grower of 1950 (Vol 37, No 11) as having the "appearance of a greatly

Hedera helix 'Fluffy Ruffles'

enlarged 'Meagheri'" ('Green Feather'). Probably a muta-tion from that clone, it is extremely variable. At its best it resembles the figure in Pierot's *The Ivy Book*. This shows a spray with five-lobed leaves that make a good representa-tion of the fleur-de-lis of tradition. It is not always seen like this for without rigorous selection in propagation it can deteriorate into 'Shamrock' or 'Green Feather'. It is best suited for indoors.

Habit: Vining.

Stems: Purple-green. Internodes 3–5cm (1¼–2in).

Petioles: Green-purple.

Leaves: 5-lobed, 3–4cm (1¼–1½in) by 3.5–4cm (1⅓–1½in). Lateral lobes often split to the mid-rib, basal lobes small and back-pointing. Centre lobe apex acute and prolonged, laterals bluntly wedge-shaped. Leaf base cordate. Colour dark green.

Hedera helix 'Fluffy Ruffles'

A most distinctive ivy of whose origin little seems to be known save that it is American. It was listed by Graf (1963) and described by Pierot (1974).

Looking at this plant it is difficult to believe it to be an ivy. The leaves are deeply waved and convoluted and, because the lobes almost encircle the petiole, appear almost like pom-poms. Although hardy it is definitely an indoor ivy and highly suitable as an attractive specimen pot plant. 'Fiesta', found by Yolanda de Silva of Valinda, California in 1977 (AIS reg No 81282), is similar but less self-branching and will climb to about 2m (20ft).

Habit: Branching, open growth.

Stems: Green-purple. Internodes 2–3cm (¾–1¼in).

Petioles: Green-pink, sometimes thickened as if fasciated.

Leaves: Basically 5-lobed, but so convoluted as to appear like frilled circular rosettes, 4–6cm (1½–2⅓in) by 4–6cm (1½–2⅓in). Leaf base so auriculate as to appear almost circular. The prominent veins radiate from the petiole/leaf-blade junction, light to yellow-green. Leaf blade mid-green.

Hedera helix 'Garland'

The first description of this clone appeared in an article by Shippy, *English Ivy Keeps Changing Faces* in the American Flower Grower in 1955. From this it appeared that Carl Frey of Lima, Ohio, discovered the clone as a mutation of 'Pitts-burgh' in 1945. The plant is described by Graf (1963), Pierot (1974) and in the AIS Bulletin No 4 (1978). All descrip-tions emphasize its compact bushy habit, variable leaves and their close setting like "wide plaited garlands" to quote Bess

PLATE V

All plants are shown at approximately ³/₄ size

H. helix 'Natashja'

H. helix 'Tess'

H. helix 'Asterisk'

H. helix 'Golden Curl'

H. helix 'Dunloe Gap'

H. *helix* 'Midas Touch'

H. *helix* 'Crenata'

H. *helix* 'Bill Archer'

H. *helix* 'Little Witch'

H. *helix* 'Russelliana'

Hedera helix 'Gertrud Stauss'

Shippy. The AIS report it as tolerating -12°C (10°F) and suggest it as ground cover for Zone 7 areas or warmer. It has proved hardy in Britain. A good easy pot plant but also ground cover for small areas.

Habit: Compact and bushy.

Stems: Green-pink. Internodes 1–3cm (⅓–1¼in).

Petioles: Green-pink.

Leaves: Sometimes 3-lobed but often unlobed and ovate, 5–6cm (2–2⅓in) by 4–5cm (1½–2in). Leaf blade slightly folded at leaf-blade/petiole junction and waved. There is a distinct downward dip in the main lobe. Leaves closely set on the stem, bright green with lighter green, well defined veins.

Hedera helix 'Gavotte'

This ivy is often confused with 'Brokamp' although it arose as a mutation from a different clone. 'Gavotte' was introduced from America into Holland in 1953 as a sport from 'Star'. The clone was propagated in Holland and Britain from 1956 onwards and described by van de Laar (1965) as having small, single-lobed leaves, sometimes with one or two side lobes and being two to four times as long as wide. Nannenga-Bremekamp (1970) recorded it as having "distinct entire leathery leaves, 5cm long, 2½cm at base,

base weakly cordate, occasional asymmetrical lateral lobes."

These descriptions illustrate the clone's similarity to 'Brokamp' and, as in the case of that clone, the need to propagate from typical material.

The leaf of 'Gavotte' is slightly more linear than that of 'Brokamp' and possibly less auriculate at the leaf base. For all practical purposes they are the same and the comments made in respect of 'Brokamp' apply, namely that it is an interesting and useful clone for hanging baskets or similar situations.

Habit: Self-branching with long trails.

Stems: Green-purple. Internodes 1.5–3cm (⅝–1¼in).

Petioles: Green, 0.5–2cm (¼–¾in).

Leaves: Mostly entire and linear-lanceolate, acuminate. Occasional lobed to heart-shaped leaves. Generally averaging 5cm (2in) by 1–1.5cm (⅓–⅝in). Dark green, leaf base cordate.

Hedera helix 'Gertrud Stauss'

Introduced in 1977 by the ivy nursery of Gebr Stauss, Möglingen, Germany, this clone was reputed to be a sport from 'Pittsburgh' but Brother Ingobert Heieck suggests that it is closer to 'Harald'. Certainly the fairly broad, flat leaves with their cordate leaf base suggest a 'Harald' connection. A good and unusual ivy for hanging baskets, window boxes and the like, it is also sturdy enough for outdoors.

Habit: Self-branching with long trails.
Stems: Green to light purple. Internodes 2–3cm (¾–1¼in).
Petioles: Green.
Leaves: 5-lobed, 2.5–4cm (1–1½in) by 3–5cm (1¼–2in). The centre lobe often divided to give virtually a 7-lobed leaf. Sinuses shallow, apices bluntly acute to rounded, leaf base cordate. Centre vein often divides at or about the leaf centre. Colour mid-green with grey-green areas, white-cream variegation irregular but mostly at the leaf edge.

Hedera helix 'Ghost'

Introduced to Britain in 1970 by Stephen Taffler from America where it was in the Lawrence collection at the Bailey Hortorium, having been planted as 'Cavendishii'. Lawrence & Schulze in 1942 made something of a 'catch-all' of 'Cavendishii', it is probable therefore that the plant in the Lawrence collection was by no means typical. 'Cavendishii' as accepted has a firm pronounced variegation with a sharply defined dark-green centre, nothing like the rather misty colouring of the present plant. Not particularly striking or garden worthy.
Habit: Vining.
Stems: Green. Internodes 2–3cm (¾–1¼in).
Petioles: Green-purple.
Leaves: 3-lobed, 2.5–3cm (1–1¼in) by 3–6cm (1¼–2⅓in). Apices blunt, sinuses shallow often presenting an unlobed triangular leaf. Basic colour mid-green but having a certain amount of chlorophyll reduction. Combined with variable cream-yellow variegation this give the pale effect indicated by the clonal name.

Hedera helix 'Glacier'

This widely grown house-plant ivy is stated to have originated in the Weber Nurseries, Los Angeles, around 1943. Before World War II Webers were active in growing and introducing ivies; 'California', first named as 'Weber's California', was a sport of 'Merion Beauty' and introduced in 1939; its sport 'Weber's Fan' was introduced in 1944. They also raised the yellow variegated 'Gold Dust', the first description of which was that by the American ivy enthusiast Bess Shippy (Flower Grower Vol 37, No 11, 1950).

A ramulose type, 'Glacier' will climb quite readily and in favourable areas of Britain is planted out of doors. When such plants achieve height, which can be some 3.5–5m (10–15ft), the leaves become larger and more irregular. The plant usually fails to achieve true arborescence and persists in what one might term an 'adolescent' state in which mutations sometimes appear. The name 'Paper Doll' (AIS Reg No 77280) was given by Leo Swicegood to the irregularly margined, often unlobed mutation which frequently appears. 'Hahn's Variegated', synonymous with 'Silver Garland', was almost identical to 'Glacier' but had less grey in the leaf. A mutation that arose at the Neuburg Monastery was known for some years as 'Glacier Mutant 3'. It had dark-green, slightly asymmetrical leaves and was registered in 1982 as 'Laubfrosch'.

The first official description of 'Glacier' is that by Nannenga-Bremekamp (1970). In the RHS Ivy Trial of 1978/9, four stocks were entered, all were somewhat variable. The stock typified below received an AM. Fairly hardy, 'Glacier' makes an excellent silvery-grey foil for colourful shrubs or plants. It is probably hardy in USA Zone 7. ♡.
Habit: Short-jointed with trails.
Stems: Green-purple. Internodes 2–3cm (¾–1¼in).
Petioles: Green-purple.
Leaves: 3-lobed, 3.5–5cm (1⅓–2in), 4–6cm (1½–2⅓in). Apices acute, sinuses shallow. Leaf base slightly cordate, occasionally cuneate. Basic colour mid-green, overlaid grey-green with slight cream variegation.

Hedera helix 'Glymii'

The glossy purple winter leaves, veined light green, make this an ideal flower arranger's ivy. That early connoisseur of ivies, William Paul, described it in the Gardener's Chronicle of 1867 as "Leaves pale green, of medium size, almost entire; very glossy looking as if varnished. Growth very rapid, forming masses of foliage." Who was Glym? We do not know; Nicholson (1885) and one or two 19th-century catalogues refer to it as 'Glym's Ivy' but to date I can trace no nursery or horticultural person of that name.

Following Paul's description it was occasionally catalogued, increasingly so after about 1880. Hibberd (1872) described it, but on the slender pretext of a slight twisting of the leaves in winter, named it 'Tortuosa' (RHS Ivy Trial 1889: FCC). In the Society's Journal (1890) Hibberd described it as 'Tortuosa' adding a footnote that it was "Submitted by Mr Fraser as Glymii". Because of its gloss it is the best of the purple ivies; Nicholson suggested it as suitable for pot culture; it is a vigorous grower and one would need very large pots, possible probably in 1885; nowadays I think it is better as a wall ivy or in its adult form as a bush.
Habit: Vining.
Stems: Green in summer to purple in winter. Internodes 2–4cm (¾–1½in).
Petioles: As stems.
Leaves: Remotely 3-lobed, short: 4–5cm (1½–2in) by 5–6cm (2–2⅓in). Sinus virtually absent. Centre lobe

acute and short. Leaf base truncate, sides of the leaf tend to be straight, ie parallel with the centre vein. Deep green with a very glossy upper surface. Veins lighter but not prominent until winter when they stand out against the deep purple of the leaf blade.

Hedera helix 'Gold Knight'

Originating in Denmark and distributed and named by Whitehouse Nurseries in 1991, the leaf shape and pattern suggest it to be of 'Shamrock' parentage. It is probably a mutation or selection from what was exported as 'Golden Shamrock'. Smaller in all its parts than 'Ursula' it is outstanding by reason of the pale-yellow colouration that develops as the plant ages. As in other yellow-coloured ivies this appears more readily when the plant is in a good light situation. Very much a house-plant ivy.

Habit: Self-branching.

Stems: Green-purple. Internodes 0.5–1cm (¼–⅓in).

Petioles: Green-purple.

Leaves: 5-lobed, 2–3cm (¾–1¼in) by 2–3cm (¾–1¼in). Centre lobe wedge-shaped, lateral and basal lobes occasionally split to the centre vein so as to appear almost detached. Apices bluntly acute, leaf base usually cordate. Colour mid-green to yellow-green as the plant and leaves age.

Hedera helix 'Goldchild'

The origin of this clone is not known for certain; it was acquired by Thomas Rochford Ltd of Hertfordshire among a selection of house-plant ivies purchased from a continental supplier (RHS Show, 1971: AM). The clone as yet was unnamed; Rochford, discussing the plant with Stephen Taffler, revealed that he had just become a proud grandfather and Taffler suggested the very suitable name 'Goldchild'. The clone proved however a disappointment to the trade: it was a weak grower and most intolerant of any over- or under-watering. At about the same time the Danish nurseryman Frode Maegaard developed a yellow sport from 'Harald'. The Danish marketing organization accepted that it was identical to the ill-fated original 'Goldchild' whose name it acquired. With its vigour and good colour it was rapidly taken up by the trade in the UK and elsewhere.

A good house-plant ivy and useful outside on low walls. The name 'Gold Harald' occasionally seen is incorrect. 1993: ♛.

Habit: Self-branching.

Stems: Purple-green. Internodes 1.5–2cm (⅝–¾in).

Petioles: Purple-green.

Leaves: 3-lobed but 2 vestigial basal lobes often give a 5-lobed appearance, 3–4cm (1¼–1½in) by 4–5cm (1½–2in). Lobes wedge-shaped, centre lobe only slightly longer than laterals, sinuses shallow, leaf base cordate. Variegation yellow mostly at the leaf margin, central area broken mid- to grey-green.

Hedera helix 'Goldcraft'

The history of this useful clone is unusually well documented. Thought to be a mutation of the common ivy it was found in 1969 by Mr Curren Craft Jnr of Cayce, South Carolina, and named 'Craft's Golden'. Later, with the raiser's approval, it was introduced and named 'Goldcraft' by Mr W O Freeland of Columbia. The clone was registered in 1976 with the AIS as 'Goldcraft' (No 761) – one word, not two as sometimes quoted. It is one of the few yellow-leaved ivies that have a green splash in the leaf centre. It is deemed hardy in USA Zone 8 and possibly 7, but while it would probably succeed in sheltered parts of Britain it is more suitable and very attractive for pot culture or hanging baskets.

A mutation of the clone was found in 1982 by Ruby L Williams of Trinidad, California, and named 'Regency' (AIS Reg No 82484). In accepting it for registration the Registrar admitted that it was little more than a slightly compact version; my own observations agree with this.

Habit: Self-branching with short trails.

Stems: Green. Internodes 1.5–3cm (⅝–1¼in).

Petioles: Green.

Leaves: 3-lobed, 3–4cm (1¼–1½in) by 3–4cm (1¼–1½in). Centre lobe broad wedge-shaped, laterals ¼ length of centre lobe. Sinuses shallow, apices acute. Lime-yellow with green 'splash' irregularly placed. Leaves darken with age, veins light green, not pronounced.

Hedera helix 'Golden Ingot'

In 1987 Maegaard of Denmark introduced onto the European pot-plant market three excellent yellow variegated ivies. They were distributed as 'Golden Ester', 'Golden Kolibri' and 'Golden Inge'. The ICNCP precludes adjectival prefixes to existing names so the only acceptable name of the three would have been 'Inge' which, unlike 'Ester' and 'Kolibri' has not been previously published. 'Golden Inge' would have been in order.

'Inge' is a popular name for a girl in Denmark but unlikely to be well known in English-speaking pot-plant markets. When the first consignment appeared on an English market a smudge of peat or something had obliterated the 'e' of 'Inge' on the hand-written label. A market salesman, perhaps not unreasonably, wrote in 'ot' to produce 'Ingot'. The plant's bright variegation assured its brisk sales;

'Golden Ingot' became known as such and has been registered under that name, which is actually a better 'selling' name.

Of the other two ivies, 'Golden Kolibri' was unnamed when first seen in Britain but was given the very appropriate and acceptable name 'Midas Touch'. 'Golden Ester' in most situations appears indistinguishable from 'Goldchild' and the name is best disregarded. 'Golden Ingot' has the same fine colour as 'Goldchild' and attractive, often crumpled and wavy leaves. Essentially a pot-plant ivy. 'Golden Gate' is a good yellow-edged variation but not a strong grower.

Habit: Self-branching.

Stems: Purple-green. Internodes 1.5–3.5cm (⅝–1⅓in)

Petioles: Green-pink.

Leaves: 3-lobed but the sinus so shallow that it presents an unlobed leaf, 3–5cm (1¼–2in) by 4–6cm (1½–2⅓in). Apices bluntly acute and often down-pointing giving a slightly curled leaf. Leaf base cordate; medium-green with grey-green areas and heavily variegated yellow often towards the leaf edge, which retains an irregular band of green. The pink of the petiole occasionally seeps into the base of the centre vein.

Hedera helix 'Golden Snow'

A distinctive ivy, the first to be recorded in which yellow and white variegation occur side by side in the same leaf. This combination with the medium-green basic leaf colour has given a most interesting and unusual house-plant ivy.

The clone first appeared in Britain in 1987 among ivies imported from Denmark but it was not until 1990 that Frode Maegaard of Ringe, Denmark, at whose nursery the mutation had occurred, named it 'Golden Snow'. Its origins are not known but the leaf shape suggests a link with 'Harald'. Despite the substantial area of variegation the clone roots and grows reasonably well.

Habit: Self-branching.

Stems: Purple-green. Internodes 2–3cm (¾–1¼in).

Petioles: Green-purple.

Leaves: 3-lobed with rarely 2 additional somewhat vestigial lobes, 3–4cm (1¼–1½in) by 4–5cm (1½–2in). Sinuses shallow, apices bluntly acute, leaf base cordate. Ground colour mid-green with broken areas of grey-green. Cream-white variegation is overlaid in places, generally towards the leaf edge, with light-yellow.

Hedera helix 'Goldheart'

One of the best vining ivies ever introduced, the pink of the young stems and dark green leaves splashed in the centre with clear yellow combine to make a superb picture. Essen-

tially a wall ivy, it is occasionally grown as a pot plant on moss-sticks but does not fill in sufficiently for it be recommended for that purpose. It is not suitable for ground cover, tending to produce green leaves when on the ground. Colour is usually well maintained on wall plants, particularly in the early stages of growth, but it is worthwhile to cut out any all-green shoots when they appear. It is hardy in Britain and probably in most of Europe and reportedly grows well in the USA as far north as Zone 7.

The origin of the plant is not certain. It first appeared in Italian catalogues in the 1950s as 'Oro di Bogliasco' (Bogliasco Gold), apparently having originated in a nursery near Bogliasco, a town east of Genoa on the Italian Riviera.

It was certainly grown in Switzerland in 1954 where it acquired the name 'Jubilaum Goldherz' and in Holland in 1955. Later in Britain it was exhibited as 'Jubilee' (RHS Show, 1970: AM). Shortly after it was realized that the name 'Jubilee' had been given as long ago as 1900 to a plant honouring the 1899 Diamond Jubilee of Queen Victoria and furthermore that the plant had been listed in Holland by van de Laar in 1965 as 'Goldherz'. The exhibiting firm accordingly gave their plant the English equivalent name 'Goldheart' and a note to that effect was published in the Proceedings of the RHS (Vol 95, 1970). The plant is listed in Italian, French, Spanish and Portuguese catalogues as 'Oro di Bogliasco' but despite that name's priority, the vagueness of the Italian catalogue descriptions followed by the detailed descriptions of Nannenga-Bremekamp (1970) in Holland, Bean (1973) in Britain and in the AIS Bulletin (1975) suggest that the name 'Goldheart' should stand.

It is possible that by virtue of its earlier publication the name 'Goldherz' has priority and that the ICNCP will adjudicate on the situation; meanwhile it is listed here as 'Goldheart' with 'Oro di Bogliasco', 'Goldherz' and 'Jubilee' accepted as synonyms.

The variegation of 'Goldheart' is periclinal (see page 31) consequently the leaves develop with an outer area of green and a centre portion of yellow. It is interesting to note that this chimaeral state persists in the ivy 'berries': some are all green, some yellow and yet some particoloured. All eventually ripen to the usual black of *H. helix*. Green shoots appear from time to time and this reversion has been selected by Freeland and named by him 'Teena'. I regard this as an unnecessary name; all indications are that 'Goldheart' was a mutation of *H. helix* and that the reverted leaves are *helix*.

Habit: Vining.

Stems: Pink-red, browning with age. Internodes 2–3cm (¾–1¼in).

Petioles: Mostly pink, occasionally light green or yellow.

Hedera helix 'Golden Ingot'

Leaves: 3-lobed, 4–6cm (1½–2⅓in) by 4–6cm (1½–2⅓in). Centre lobe longest and acuminate, lateral lobes bluntly acute, vestigial basal lobes sometimes apparent, leaf base truncate. Colour dark green, irregularly splashed centrally clear yellow. Veins not prominent.

Hedera helix 'Goldstern'

This is a striking arrowhead-leaved counterpart of 'Goldcraft'. It has the same lime-green colour but in this case a consistent darker green central splash. Like 'Goldcraft', the leaf darkens with age. A mutation from 'Star', it was noted by a gardener at Luisen Park, Mannheim, Germany and named and distributed by Heieck in 1979.

The thin, well defined arrowhead leaves with their lime-green colour make this a most useful pot plant but the light colour and contrasting green splash are not sufficiently marked to be appreciated in outdoor situations.

The yellow-variegated, self-branching, arrowhead-leaved clones 'Goldfinger', 'Golden Fleece', 'Goldtobler' and 'Sterntaler' are so close to 'Goldstern' as to be classed as synonymous. The sport 'Rauschgold', introduced in 1982 from the Neuburg Monastery nursery (Reg No 821183) is identical to 'Goldstern' except that the leaf margins are slightly rolled under. The name translates as 'Tinsel'.

Habit: Self-branching and compact.
Stems: Green-purple. Internodes 1–2cm (⅓–¾in).
Petioles: Green-pink.
Leaves: 5-lobed, 3.5–5cm (1⅓–2in) by 4.5–6cm (2–2⅓in). Centre lobe prolonged to twice the length of the 2 laterals which stand at right angles to it; apices acuminate. The 2 basal lobes are small and back-pointing. Lime-green with a darker green splash in or around the leaf centre.

Hedera helix 'Goldwolke'

This is an interesting ivy by virtue of the fact that the yellow variegation is centrally placed, that is to say it is periclinal as is the case with 'Goldheart'. 'Goldwolke' however is a sport of the ramulose-type ivy 'Harald' whereas 'Goldheart' was a mutation of the common *H. helix*.

Discovered in 1979 by Heieck in Heidelberg, Germany, it is described and illustrated in the AIS Journal Vol 9, No 3, 1983 and also in *Hedera Sorten* (1980).

The variegation is not sharp and defined as with 'Goldheart' and is not always constant. Some leaves can be entirely green, in others the variegation might be termed

'chartreuse'. An ivy primarily of interest to ivy enthusiasts.
Habit: Self-branching with trails.
Stems: Green-purple. Internodes 2–3cm (¾–1¼in).
Petioles: Green-purple.
Leaves: 5-lobed but with such shallow sinuses as to seem unlobed, 3–5cm (1¼–2in) by 4–5cm (1½–2in). Apices bluntly acute, leaf base cordate. Colour mid-green, soft yellow variegation at leaf centre in a smudge radiating from the centre vein.

Hedera helix 'Gracilis'

First described by Hibberd (1864) no synonyms were given and one may assume this was a name Hibberd gave to any ivy grown in his day but unnamed. The plant began to appear in catalogues: Hendersons of London listed it in 1865 as "slender branched"; William Clibran(1894) described it as a "small cut leaved variety veined rich bronze in autumn". Hibberd (1890) described it as having "a singularly elegant appearance. It is a minor *helix* of wiry habit with purple stems and leaf stalks; the leaves conspicuously veined. An excellent rockery plant." Nicholson (1885) wrote "*H. h gracilis* [slender] leaves usually three-lobed, colour rather light dull green, richly bronzed in autumn. Stems wiry, purplish. A very pretty variety for covering a wall or a tree stump." Not widely grown, it can be termed a 'pretty' ivy, too loose and spreading for ground cover but good for covering tree stumps and for large walls. It is as hardy as *helix,* of which it is a leaf variant. RHS Ivy Trial 1889: AM.
Habit: Vining with long spreading trails.
Stems: Purple. Internodes 3–6cm (1¼–2⅓in).
Petioles: Purple.
Leaves: 3, occasionally 5-lobed, 2–4cm (¾–1½in) by 3–4cm (1¼–1½in). Leaf base truncate to cordate. Lobes wedge-shaped, apices acute, centre lobe only slightly longer than laterals. Sinuses generally shallow, margin slightly convolute at cleft. Colour deep green, veins light green.

Hedera helix 'Green Feather'

A classic mutation and the forerunner of many interesting clones, this was spotted by Mr Meagher, an employee on the nursery of Mr Fred Danker of Albany, New York, who in 1939 introduced it to the trade, honouring his employee by giving it the unpublished name of 'Meagheri'.

Bates in the American National Horticultural Magazine in October 1940 described the plant under the name 'Green Feather'. This was an authentic publication and although Lawrence & Schulze (1942) rejected Bates' name and described the plant as 'Meagheri', the first published name

has priority. Plants now in circulation do not show the extremely short internodes of 3mm (⅛in) quoted by Bates, or the smallness of leaf he suggested. Nevertheless this remains a most useful pot plant, excellent for hanging baskets and low wall cover. It is still often listed as 'Meagheri' and sometimes 'Megheri'.
Habit: Vining, moderately self-branching.
Stems: Purple-green. Internodes 1–3cm (⅓–1¼in).
Petioles: Purple-green.
Leaves: 3-lobed, 3–5cm (1¼–2in) by 3–4cm (1¼–1½in). Sinuses narrow, occasionally split almost as far as the vein. Centre lobe long, acuminate to cuspidate. Lateral lobes bluntly acute and sometimes slightly folded upward. Dark green, veins lighter green, the purple of the petiole occasionally seen at the lower end of veins on upper surface but never on the under surface.

Hedera helix 'Green Ripple'

The inspired name of 'Green Ripple' well describes the rippling green of the strongly veined leaves.

'Green Ripple' was a mutation from 'Maple Queen' discovered in 1939 by Louis Hahn of Pittsburgh, Pennsylvania, and introduced by him. The plant was very well described by Shippy as 'Green Ripple' in 1950 and again in 1955. In Holland, Harry van de Laar described it in 1965 as "'Hahn's Green Ripple' imported from America in 1952," while Nannenga-Bremekamp (1970) using the same name, grouped it with 'Green Feather' and 'Shamrock'. The first name given, 'Green Ripple', is however the correct name. A well established clone it has proved its worth in various situations; as a pot plant it vines and branches sufficiently to cover moss-sticks or canes or to furnish hanging baskets. It is a reasonable wall plant though tending to show reversion over a period. It makes good ground cover and is hardier than might be expected. The AIS suggest it is a possibility for USA Zone 5. RHS Ivy Trial1978/9: AM(T).
Habit: Vining but branching well.
Stems: Green-purple. Internodes 2–3cm (¾–1¼in).
Petioles: Green-purple.
Leaves: 5-lobed, 5–10cm (2–4in) by 5–7cm (2–2¾in). Lobes forward-pointing, acuminate, sinuses shallow, margin at the cleft raised in an upward pleat. Leaf base cordate. Veins prominent on the leaf surface, pale green. Leaf colour bright deep green.

Hedera helix 'Gruno'

Introduced in 1986 and described by Ing G Fortgens and H J van de Laar in *Dendroflora* No 26, 1989, this vigorous ivy is in some respects similar to 'Green Survival' described in the

Hedera helix 'Harald'

same publication and introduced in 1977. The leaf of 'Green Survival' is three-lobed with very shallow sinuses giving an almost heart-shaped leaf.

Both are excellent for rapid coverage and with leaf shapes that give rather more interest than the ordinary *H. helix*.

Habit: Vining.

Stems: Green. Internodes 2cm (¾in).

Petioles: Green.

Leaves: 5-lobed, 5–8cm (2–3in) by the same broad. Centre lobe prolonged twice the length of laterals. Apices acute, leaf base cordate. Colour dark glossy green.

Hedera helix 'Harald'

As 'Harold', 'Herold' or 'Harald' this ivy is widely grown for the European pot-plant trade, indeed with 'Eva' and 'Anna Marie' it accounts for the bulk of the trade in variegated *helix* ivies at the present time. 'Harald' was grown in 1958/9 in Denmark but its origin seems vague. Heieck (1977) points out that on the Stauss Ivy Nurseries in Germany this clone has been selected out of 'Eva' suggesting, since 'Harald' is the older, that 'Eva' was a mutation from 'Harald'. I have seen 'Eva' revert to 'Pittsburgh' and assume it to have come from 'Pittsburgh Variegated'. The clone 'Chicago Variegated' appears to be the same plant. Synonyms include 'Anne Borch', 'Ester', 'Ingrid' and 'Hahni'. In leaf size 'Harald' is mid-way between 'Eva' and 'Anna Marie'.

Habit: Self-branching.

Stems: Green-purple. Internodes 2–4cm (¾–1½in).

Petioles: Green-purple.

Leaves: 3-lobed with occasionally vestigial basal lobes 4–6cm (1½–2⅓in) by 4–5cm (1½–2in). Lobes wedge-shaped, rounded or bluntly acute, sinuses shallow. Leaf base truncate or slightly cordate. Central portion grey-green, bordered irregularly with cream-white sometimes extending into a larger area. Veins light green, not prominent.

Hedera helix 'Harrison'

One of the older ivy clones it was listed in the 1939 American *Plant Buyer's Guide* as being sold by Jackson and Perkins Roses of Newark, New York, a long-established nursery firm who incidentally were responsible for introducing in 1901 that favourite rose of the Edwardian era, 'Dorothy Perkins'.

We have no knowledge of the origin of the name 'Harrison' nor how the plant came into being. The description by Dr Sulgrove (AIS Journal Vol 12, No 3, 1986) is the first we have of this useful, hardy ivy. The fairly slight variation in leaf shape is the only distinguishing feature of this clone.

Habit: Vining.

Stems: Purple-green. Internodes 3–5cm (1¼–2in).

Petioles: Purple.

Leaves: 3-lobed, 3–5cm (1¼–2in) by 4–6cm (1½–2⅓in). Centre lobe usually prominent and triangular, lateral lobes half the length of the centre lobe and slightly back-pointing. Apices acute, leaf base cordate; a slight upward curl at the base of the sinus. In older leaves the centre lobe may be less prolonged. Dark green, veins white; the leaves readily colour purple in cold weather.

Hedera helix 'Hazel'

A mutation from 'Adam' selected by Thomas Rochford & Sons Ltd of Broxbourne, England, around 1975 and named by them to mark the contributions to ivy cultivation of Mrs Hazel Key of Fibrex Nurseries Ltd. The cream-white leaves speckled and marbled green resemble 'Kolibri' in colour but are broader and shorter. Very much a house-plant ivy.

Habit: Self-branching.

Stems: Green-pink. Internodes 1.5–2cm (⅝–¾in).

Petioles: Green-pink.

Leaves: 3-lobed, 2.5–3cm (1–1¼in) by 2.5–4cm (1–1½in) with two vestigial basal lobes. Centre lobe twice as long as laterals, apices acute, leaf base cordate. Basic colour cream-white, substantially covered grey-green with darker green patches. Some leaves have only scattered areas of green.

Hedera helix 'Helena'

The origin of this American clone is not known but it was introduced by David Clark of Jarretsville, USA, in 1980 and named for his wife. In Britain it makes a useful house-plant ivy but seems more short-jointed than the American comments indicate. The AIS Registrar drew attention to similarities with 'Williamsiana' and 'Lancelot', a clone described by Shippy (1955) but certainly no longer in circulation. The Registrar found sufficient differences between both these clones to Register 'Helena' as a distinct clone, No 80181.

Habit: Self-branching with trails.

Stems: Green-purple. Internodes 1–2.5cm (⅓–1in).

Petioles: Green.

Leaves: 5-lobed, the 2 basal lobes sometimes vestigial; 2–4cm (¾–1½in) by 2.5–3cm (1–1¼in). The centre lobe twice as long as the lateral lobes, tapering, down-pointing and slightly curved. Colour mid-green with patches of grey-green. Variegation white-cream and mostly around the leaf edge.

Hedera helix 'Heron'

In the late 1950s Roland Jackman of the celebrated firm of that name in Woking, Surrey, found and named this selection of 'Pedata'. Similar in habit and colour, it differs in its attenuated leaves, long internodes and wiry habit; indeed the small narrow-lobed leaves on the younger shoots look almost like the barbs on barbed wire. More interesting than beautiful it shows to best effect against a white wall or in a situation where its long stems can hang over a wall or bank; it can be grown into a wiry tangle on a wood or wire lattice.

Habit: Vining, extending rapidly.

Stems: Grey-green. Internodes 3–6cm (1¼–2⅓in).

Petioles: Generally short, 1–3cm (⅓–1¼in). Dull purple.

Leaves: 5-lobed, basal lobes back-pointing, 3–5cm (1¼–2in) by 4–5cm (1½–2in). Centre lobe 1½ times the length of the lateral lobes. Sinuses very shallow, in extreme cases the lateral lobes are at right angles to the centre lobe. Leaf blades attenuated sometimes almost to the veins. Dark grey-green, veins green-white.

Hedera helix 'Hester'

Introduced by the nursery firm Kwek Woudengroep, Drachten, Holland, in 1995 this linear-leaved clone is outstanding by virtue of its long internodes as well as the uniformity of its narrow leaves. These combined with trails 45–90cm (1½–3ft) long make it ideal for hanging baskets.

Habit: Self-branching with trails.

Stems: Green-purple. Internodes 4–7cm (1½–2¾in).

Petioles: Green-purple and very short.

Hedera helix 'Irish Lace'

Leaves: Unlobed, 4–6cm (1½–2⅓in) by 1cm (⅓in). Apex acuminate, leaf base cuneate. Colour light to mid-green.

Hedera helix 'Irish Lace'

The origin of this clone is not known. Pierot (1974) described it as having delicate, long, thin, five-lobed leaves. It was figured in the AIS Journal (Vol 7, pt3, 1981) as very short-jointed, leaves having a long, narrow centre lobe, vestigial basal lobes and a cuneate leaf base.

'Irish Lace' has produced numerous variations, the following have acquired names but in my opinion do not merit separate descriptions.

'Needlepoint', described in *Exotica* in 1959, is similar to 'Irish Lace' but with slightly broader lobes. 'La Plata', registered by Henri Schaepman in 1977 is similar but the lobes are bluntly acute. 'Midget', registered by Leo Swicegood in 1978 is a very compact form of 'Needlepoint' but prone to reversion. A slightly larger leaved clone showing less self-branching has circulated as 'Perfection'. All these are sometimes marketed as 'Irish Lace', all are good house-plant ivies and may be said to form a group of self-branching, 'bird's foot'-type ivies whose leaves are characterized by an extended and often acuminate centre lobe. A sport called 'Misty' originating at the nursery of Herman Engelmann

Hedera helix 'Ivalace'

Greenhouses, Apopka, Florida has centre lobes tending to droop downwards, grey-green with cream-yellow variegation at the leaf edge.

A variation registered by Patricia Hammer of Longwood Gardens, PA in 1987 as 'Innuendo' (No 870188) has lobes slightly rolled under, the leaves variable, some attenuated, leaf base cuneate. Dark green with a slight variegation of lighter green. Pierot and some others describe 'Plume d'Or' as a larger form of 'Irish Lace' but the clone submitted to the RHS Ivy Trial 1979/80 had a closer resemblance to 'Très Coupé'. 'Plume d'Or' translates as 'Golden Feather' but is a misnomer, for it has not been recorded as having any yellow colouration, and is best disregarded. As far as 'Irish Lace' is concerned the following may be taken as a typical description.

Habit: Self-branching.
Stems: Green-purple. Internodes 1–1.5cm (⅓–⅝in).
Petioles: Green-purple.
Leaves: 5-lobed, 2–2.5cm (¾–1in) by 1.5–2cm (⅝–¾in), basal lobes often vestigial. Centre lobe prolonged, 1½ times the length of laterals and averaging 1.5–2cm (⅝–¾in) by only 0.5cm (¼in). Apices acuminate, leaf base cuneate, colour mid-green.

Hedera helix 'Ivalace'

This is an outstanding ivy unlikely to be confused with any other; this being so it is surprising that it has circulated under many erroneous names; names that are not synonyms in the true sense of the word but rather just mis-applied. These include 'Green Gem', 'Laceveil', 'Lace Leaf', 'Wilson' and 'Little Gem'.

For a brief description it is hard to better the first one of all written by Shippy in the American Flower Grower of September 1955:

> Mr William's 'Ivalace' is a most enchanting ivy. The medium-sized bright-green leaves are five-lobed and the margins are finely crimped, making the edging look like fine lace. The young branches, which are produced freely, stand upright until seven or eight inches long.

"Mr Williams" is a wholesale florist in Springfield, Ohio, who introduced 'Ivalace' to the trade. I do not know the source, but it has something of the characteristics of 'Green Feather' and may be a mutation of that ivy. It was introduced into Europe around 1958 and has become universally popular as a pot plant.

A mutation discovered in 1988 by Mr Coon of Fremont, California and named 'Chalice' (AIS Reg No 900193), has a stiff, fasciated, upright habit and slightly cupped leaves. 'Jasper' introduced by Fibrex Nurseries in 1989 has similarly convoluted leaves but a more spreading habit. 'Stuttgart', discovered by Stauss Bros in Germany in 1972 is but a closer growing and more vigorous form of 'Ivalace'.

'Ivalace' is a good all-purpose ivy; the upright branching habit makes it an excellent house-plant ivy. Its readiness to throw trails makes it a useful clone to use when creating standard ivies by grafting, the long trails 'weeping' attractively. It is reasonably hardy and can be used as ground cover for small areas. It is useful for low north-facing walls where it will make a curtain of glossy green, lacy leaves. RHS Ivy Trial 1978/9: FCC(T); 1993: ♛.

Habit: Vining but readily self-branching.
Stems: Purple-green. Internodes 1.5–2.5cm (⅝–1in).
Petioles: Purple-green.
Leaves: 5-lobed, 4–6cm (1½–2⅓in) by 4–5cm (1½–2in). Centre lobe acuminate, lateral lobes sharply acute. Leaf margins strongly undulate, sinuses shallow, leaf margin convolute at the sinus-cleft giving a crinkled 'lace' effect. Colour dark green, a lighter bright green on indoor plants. Leaf texture stiff, upper surface glossy, veins light green.

Hedera helix 'Jack Frost'

An ivy whose variegational flecking and leaf distortion may well be due to a systemic virus. Interesting but with little horticultural appeal, it was submitted to the AIS in 1976 under the name 'Silver Queen' by W O Freeland. That name however had been used in the past; it was therefore registered as 'Jack Frost' (No 78283).

Habit: Vining.
Stems: Purple-green. Internodes 1.5–2.5cm (⅝–1in).
Petioles: Purple-green.
Leaves: 3-lobed, 3–5cm (1¼–2in) by 5–7cm (2–2¾in). Centre lobe twice as long as laterals. Apices acute, leaf base cordate, margins and leaf surface puckered. Colour mid-green, flecked grey-cream.

Hedera helix 'Jersey Doris'

Discovered in 1966 on the island of Jersey by Stephen Taffler, President of the BIS. The eponymous name includes that of the lady upon whose house the ivy grew.

The plant's origin is not known but it seems possible that it is a sport of a house-plant ivy growing outside, indeed Mr Taffler commented that it was very close to the clone 'Sally' which was a sport from 'Sagittifolia Variegata' and it may be that the latter holds the origin of 'Jersey Doris'.

The variegation is very attractive but the plant is not over robust and is slow to branch.

Habit: Vining.
Stems: Green-purple. Internodes 2–3cm (¾–1¼in).
Petioles: Green-purple.
Leaves: 3–5-lobed but the basal lobes often vestigial, 3–5cm (1¼–2in) by 4–6cm (1½–2⅓in). Apices acute, sinuses shallow, leaf base cordate. Colour dark green mottled and speckled cream-yellow.

Hedera helix 'Jubilee'

Since the turn of the century there have been two 'Jubilee' clones, inevitably a source of some confusion. In 1900 the nurseryman William Barron of Elvaston, Derbyshire, listed 'Jubilee' as a clone having "a small variegated leaf". In the following year David Russell of Brentwood, Essex also listed it, describing it as a "beautiful silver-edged variety, very neat". Other nurseries continued to offer the clone, L R Russell Ltd listing it under variegated ivies as "Silver edged".

In 1927 Tobler gave the origin as from the Hesse Nursery of Weener, Hanover, and its introduction as 1912. His description was brief, agreeing with those above. In Britain the clone continued to be listed and sold until the outbreak of World War II.

After the war however, and crossing the Atlantic, we find Beth Shippy (1951) recording that a variety 'Jubilee' had recently been introduced by Weber Nurseries of California, that it was "more self-branching than 'Glacier' with medium sized leaves, variegated, some totally white". Other than the self-branching characteristic her description and photograph would fit the clone described above. So in the 1950s there were two very similar clones both circulating as 'Jubilee' but with, I suggest, a very basic difference: the

Hedera helix 'Jubilee'

earlier one was a vining-type ivy, typical of several circulating toward the end of the 19th century; the post-war clone was self-branching. Turning to the German reference by Tobler it seems likely that the plant was introduced by Hesse from Britain, particularly since it was listed under its British name. From the date of the British catalogue listings one may safely assume that the name celebrated Queen Victoria's Diamond Jubilee of 1899.

The Weber Nursery made a number of first-rate introductions and doubtless the naming was purely coincidental. It is reasonably certain that the plant seen today is from the Weber clone, although from time to time the earlier vining type may be found growing in old gardens.

One more event remained to muddy the nomenclatural pool. When the yellow-centred ivy 'Goldheart' first circulated in northern Europe it was named in Holland 'Jubilaum Goldherz'. Introduced to Britain it was exhibited by L R Russell Ltd as 'Jubilee' (AM). Russell, however, realized the error and re-submitted it under the new name 'Goldheart'. The following description is of what one might term the modern 'Jubilee', illustrated in Pierot's *The Ivy Book* (1974).

Habit: Self-branching.

Stems: Green-purple. Internodes 1.5–2cm (⅝–¾in).

Petioles: Green-purple.

Leaves: Unlobed, elliptic to ovate, 2cm (¾in) by 3–4cm (1¼–1½in). Apices bluntly acute, leaf base cuneate. Grey-green with patches of dark-green, edged cream-white.

Hedera helix 'Kolibri'

The name is German for hummingbird but was presumably a purely fanciful name for this valuable clone which arose as a mutation from 'Ingrid' (syn 'Ester') during the 1970s on the nursery of Firma Brokamp of Ramsdorf, Westfalen, Germany. The clone 'Ester', said to have come into commerce in 1959–62, was a variation of the better-known 'Eva' and certainly the similarity to 'Eva' is seen in 'Kolibri'. The most striking feature however is the extent and whiteness of its variegation; against this white ground the flecks and spots of mid-green stand out sharply.

The plant is an excellent pot plant for room, greenhouse or conservatory decoration; variable in lobing and the extent of variegation so that individual stocks can differ considerably. (1993: ♔.) A sport found in 1984 by Frank Batson of Woodburn, Oregon, has plain mid- to dark-green slightly thickened leaves with a prolonged 'nose'-like centre lobe, hence its clonal name 'Cyrano de Bergerac'.

Habit: Self-branching and short-jointed.

Stems: Pink-purple. Internodes 1–1.5cm (⅓–⅝in).

Petioles: Cream-pink.

Leaves: 5-lobed, 2–4cm (¾–1½in) by 2–4cm (¾–1½in). Basal lobes not prominent. Centre lobe acuminate and ⅓ longer than the bluntly acute lateral lobes. Basic colour light green with flecks of grey-green; areas of white variegation so extensive as to appear almost the basic colour.

Hedera helix 'Königer'

Originally known as 'Königer's Auslese' this ivy, according to Hahn, was selected or found in 1935 by Hermann Königer of Aalen, hence 'Auslese', the German for 'selection'. Such a noun is excluded under the ICNCP, accordingly it should be designated 'Königer', a name which in any event records the plant's finder.

Heieck (1980) points out that because of its variability it is difficult to find the distinct type. According to Heieck, Eugen Hahn depicted a dense ivy with small leaves similar to 'Itsy Bitsy' (now reckoned as synonymous with 'Pin Oak'). Heieck noted that 'Königer' frequently bore mutations identical to 'Itsy Bitsy'. Other mutations that were

Hedera helix 'Kolibri'

frequent resembled 'Irish Lace', 'Needlepoint' and one with strong shoots and larger leaves resembled 'Star'.

In 1965 van de Laar drew attention to the plant's propensity to vary and suggested that the original selection had long been superseded by variations. Some of these, 'Anchor' for example, found in the 1960s near Dumbarton Oaks in Washington DC, have shown differences worthy of clonal naming, in others they are too slight to record.

The clone was being grown in Belgium in 1952 under the name 'Heraut'; other synonyms include in addition to 'Königer's Auslese', 'Königer's Rhum', 'Sagittifolia' and 'Feastii'.

'Königer' remains a popular house-plant ivy that is also suitable for ground cover or low-wall coverage and its capacity for variability, although a nomenclatural hazard, gives it an added interest.

What is assumed to be a sport of Königer was discovered by Ken Frieling in the Glasshouse Works nursery at Stewart, Ohio. It has an effective but sometimes transient splash of greenish-yellow at the base of the leaf centre vein. It was registered in 1983 as 'Tiger Eyes'.

Habit: Self-branching and vining.

Stems: Green-purple. Internodes 1–2cm (⅓–¾in).

Petioles: Green-purple.

Leaves: 5-lobed, 3–7cm (1¼–2¾in) by 5–8cm (2–3in). Centre lobe twice as long as laterals. Lobes tapering acuminate. Basal lobes back-pointing. Colour mid-green, veins light green but not pronounced. Veins of the lateral lobes often make a right angle with the centre lobe vein.

PLATE VI

All plants are shown at approximately ³/₄ size

H. helix 'Sub-marginata'

H. helix 'Goldchild'

H. helix 'Dragon Claw'

H. helix 'Caecilia'

H. helix 'Königer'

H. maroccana

H. helix 'Trinity'

H. helix 'Persian Carpet'

H. helix 'Minty'

H. helix 'Ovata'

H. helix 'Ivalace'

Hedera helix 'Kurios'

This interesting clone, the result of a mutation from 'Shamrock', was isolated by Brother Heieck and named by him in 1979. 'Kurios' is similar in leaf type to 'Big Deal' but differs markedly by its thick fasciated petioles and its stiff branching habit which is similar to that of 'Big Deal' but less zig-zag. It makes a fascinating pot plant and a point of interest in any ivy collection. Another mutation, 'Shamrock III', was selected at the Neuburg Monastery in 1977 and subsequently named 'Knülch', a German name for a scallywag. It differs mainly in the irregular leaf margins and petioles flattened near the base of the leaf blade. These differences are slight and have not persisted over the years so that it has become indistinguishable from 'Kurios'.

Habit: Stiffly branching.

Stems: Thick and comparatively rigid; purple. Internodes 3–7cm (1¼–2¾in).

Petioles: Fasciated and greatly thickened in comparison to other ivies, 4mm (³⁄₁₆in) wide compared to the average of 2mm (⅛in). Colour green-purple.

Leaves: Unlobed, rounded to a blunt slight apex, 4cm (1½in) by 4–5cm (1½–2in). Surface wrinkled and concave or convex on different leaves. Colour mid-green, veins radiating from the very visible petiole/leaf-blade junction, becoming purple on older leaves.

Hedera helix 'Lady Kay'

Listed by Graf (1963) and mentioned in the AIS Journal of 1979 as one of the clones that survived a winter hardiness test in 1978/9. Rarely seen, the clone has survived in specialist ivy nursery catalogues. On occasion the name has been transliterated as 'Lucy Kay'. A useful small-leaved ivy.

Habit: Vining.

Stems: Purple-green. Internodes 2–3cm (¾–1¼in).

Petioles: Purple-green.

Leaves: 3-lobed but sinuses so shallow as to appear usually as an unlobed leaf, 2–3cm (¾–1¼in) by 1.5–2cm (⅝–¾in). Apex rounded, leaf base cuneate. Dark green.

Hedera helix 'Lalla Rookh'

Discovered as a sport of 'Cascade' in 1974/5 by the ivy enthusiast Leo Swicegood in Rescue, Virginia, this clone honours his wife's maiden name.

The extremely decorative and interesting leaves appear to have more than five lobes due to the deeply cut teeth on the lobe edges. The clone makes a good pot plant and since it is hardy (in Britain) is a pleasant ivy for low walls or small areas of ground cover. AIS Reg No 80281.

Habit: Short-jointed with trails.

Stems: Green-purple. Internodes 2–3cm (¾–1¼in).

Petioles: Green-purple.

Leaves: 5-lobed, 4–6cm (1½–2⅓in) by 6–7cm (2⅓–2¾in). Sinuses deep, almost to the centre vein. Lobes often irregularly toothed, waved at the sinus cleft, apices acuminate. Light to mid-green, veins slightly lighter.

Hedera helix 'Lee's Silver'

The existence of this clone recalls a time when the site of the Olympia Exhibition Hall in West London was the Vineyard Nursery. Founded in 1745 by Lewis Kennedy and James Lee it became, under the management of Lee and then his sons and grandsons, one of Britain's foremost nurseries.

There is no record of the date of introduction of 'Lee's Silver' but it is mentioned in an article on ivies in the Gardener's Chronicle of November 1888. There is a reasonably good leaf picture in the Gardener's Chronicle of January 1909 which agrees with the description given by Lawrence and Schulze (1942). The clone seemed to be reasonably popular in America and was listed in the UK.

Another 19th-century clone, 'Lee's New Silver' would seem to be a different and possibly misnamed plant for Hibberd (1890) described a clone 'Lacteola' as having leaves smaller than *H. canariensis* with much creamy white variegation and "sent by Fraser as 'Maderensis Variegata' and 'Lee's New Silver'". From this one might reasonably infer that the clone in question was *H. canariensis* var. *algeriensis* 'Gloire de Marengo'.

In 1901 the Lee nursery empire was broken up and James Russell (1822–1902) purchased the Isleworth nursery which, according to the account of the day, "specialised in propagation and the growing of ivies in great quantities". The clone then appeared more frequently in nursery lists, often as described by Russell: "Medium sized leaves with a broad white edge".

The period 1900–1914 was the heyday of the Russell nursery business and in 1912 they expanded by taking over Thomas Cripps & Son of Tunbridge Wells, Kent. At some time, probably around 1882, Cripps had introduced *H. helix* 'Crippsii' a green-leaved, silver-edged clone. It appeared in many catalogues up to 1939 and is sometimes listed today. Opinions on its leaf size varied thus in 1883 William Fell of Hexham, Northumberland, described it as "large leaved, silver edge" but Kelways of Langport, Somerset, listed it in 1896 as "small leaved variegated". In 1898, Fisher Son and Sibray of Handsworth, Sheffield, described it as "silver edged and robust"; they also sold it in tree form. The Southampton firm of Rogers and Son opted for a medium sized leaf and, nearer to the present day, Fibrex Nurseries drew attention in 1986 to its "small leathery leaves" and the fact that it was a slow grower, but by 1990 had ceased to list it. A clone entered in the RHS Ivy Trial of 1979/80 as 'Crippsii' proved to be 'Tricolor'.

Adding further confusion to these white-edged clones of yesteryear there was 'Cullisi', first recorded in an article by Hibberd in the *Floral World* of 1858. He extolled the clone as having "markings that are delicate white, cream, and blush crimson, very regularly disposed and the leaves of a neat outline." Among nurseries listing it Dillistone & Woodthorpe from Essex catalogued it in 1866 as "Cullissi, Cullis's Silver Margined." This indicates, as one might assume, that it originated from a nurseryman and this may well have been John Cullis who had a nursery at Ranelagh Gardens, Leamington Spa, Warwickshire, in the late 19th century. Russell in 1914 was still listing it but without any description and thereafter it appears in fewer catalogues and is lost from sight apart from a brief description by Mathias Jenny(1964). Within *Hedera helix* he described 'Cullisi', "broadish long centre lobes and often reddish margins and stalks, cream-coloured margins and grey-green to dark green centre."

In summary of these three silver-edged clones, 'Lee's Silver' appears fairly distinct and is described below from material that I received from America in 1976. The other two were probably variations of what we know as 'Tricolor', a clone which to this day can vary according to nursery and stock as was shown in the RHS Ivy Trial of 1979/80.

Habit: Vining but slow growing and with short trails.

Stems: Purple-green. Internodes 1.5–2.5cm (⅝–1in).

Petioles: Purple-green.

Leaves: 3-lobed, 2–3.5cm (¾–1⅓in) by 4–5cm (1½–2in). Centre lobe cuspid in outline, sinuses shallow, apices acute, leaf base cordate. Colour mid-green with white-edged variation varying in depth.

Hedera helix 'Leo Swicegood'

This linear-leaved ivy resembles somewhat the clone 'Bill Archer' but has a softer, more grassy type of leaf and appears to be more stable. A good house-plant ivy it arose as a mutation from 'Spear Point' selected by Brother Ingobert Heieck in 1979. It was named by him to honour the late Leo Swicegood, a very capable, friendly and generous American ivy enthusiast. AIS Reg No 821289.

Habit: Self-branching and short-jointed.

Stems: Purple-green. Internodes 0.5–1cm (¼–⅓in).

Petioles: Purple-green.

Leaves: Elliptically linear and unlobed, 4–6cm (1½–2⅓in) by 0.5–1.5cm (¼–⅝in) at the broadest part. Apices acute, colour mid-green.

Hedera helix 'Leo Swicegood'

Hedera helix 'Little Diamond'

The origin of this popular clone is not known but it occasionally throws shoots resembling 'Glacier' from which it may have been a mutation. Whatever its origin 'Kleiner Diamant', as it is sometimes known in Europe, has been grown since the early 1960s. It is a useful house-plant ivy and suitable for the rock garden if variegated ivies are accepted! The leaves closely set on the stem are diamond-shaped, grey-green with good cream-white variation. As plants mature the little shoots assume an almost arborescent form, the leaves tending to 'spiral' in the way they come off the stem. Heieck noted that occasionally small stunted flowers appear, evidence that this clone may be close to the adult phase. RHS Ivy Trial 1978/9: AM(T); 1993: ♛.

A triangular, pointed-leaved clone named 'Needle Diamond' was introduced in 1995 by the Dutch nurserymen W Streng BV of Boskoop.

Habit: Self-branching.

Stems: Green. Internodes 0.25–1.5cm (¹⁄₁₀–⅝in).

Petioles: Green, short, rarely more than 3cm (1¼in).

Leaves: Unlobed, 3–4cm (1¼–1½in) by 1.5–2cm (⅝–¾in). The acute apex and attenuated leaf base produce a diamond-shaped leaf, very few show vestigial lobes. Grey-green variegated cream-white mainly at the leaf edge.

Hedera helix 'Little Diamond'

Hedera helix 'Little Gem'

An attractive ivy whose small leaves and fairly close habit make it suitable for ground cover over bulbs in small areas. If the vining stems are pinched back it makes a useful house-plant ivy. The restriction of the leaf base at the petiole junction gives the leaf its slightly crimped, subtle attraction. A mutation from 'Pittsburgh', it was noted and described in 1965 by the Dutch horticultural botanist van de Laar.

Habit: Self-branching with short trails.

Stems: Purple. Internodes 1.5–2cm (⅝–¾in).

Petioles: Red-purple, the colour extending a short way up the leaf mid-rib.

Leaves: 3-lobed, 3–4cm (1¼–1½in) by 4–4.5cm (1½–1¾in). Centre lobe acute, lateral lobes bluntly acute. Leaf base depressed so that the leaf folds slightly upwards at the base, the centre lobe tends to point downward. Mid-green, veins light green with red colouration extending up to 1cm (⅓in) from the petiole junction.

Hedera helix 'Little Witch'

This is a novel but very charming house-plant ivy selected by Ron Whitehouse in 1992 from a sport of 'Telecurl'. An unusual feature is the tendency of the comparatively long petioles to grow almost parallel to the stems, the leaf blade then standing out almost at right angles. This and the wrinkled, almost malformed nature of the leaves combine to create an amusing albeit very useful house-plant ivy.

Habit: Short-jointed but upright-growing.

Stems: Green-purple. Internodes 0.5–1.5cm (¼–⅝in).

Petioles: Green-purple.

Leaves: 3-lobed, 2–3cm (¾–1¼in) by 2cm (¾in), lobes often divided to the mid-rib. Occasional single-lobed leaves of some 3cm (1¼in) by 0.5cm (¼in), lobes often twisted and curled. Apices acuminate, leaf base strongly cuneate, colour mid- to dark green.

Hedera helix 'Luzii'

This plant, originating at the Ernst Luz nursery in Stuttgart-Fellbach, Germany, was put on the market by the firm of Hausmann and exhibited at the Hanover Show in 1951. It has given rise to a number of similarly mottled clones but remains a valuable variety in its own right, widely grown for the house-plant trade. Its lightly mottled leaves are interesting and the plant is more forgiving of ill-treatment than many more highly variegated clones. If planted outside it loses some of its mottle. Described by Dr Nannenga-Bremekamp in 1970 as 'Luzii' it has been variously misnamed as 'Lutzii', 'Lutzei' 'Minima Luzii' and sometimes

Hedera helix 'Luzii'

'Marmorata'. Names such as 'Gold Dust', 'Golden Pittsburgh', and 'Masquerade' have been applied to derivatives of 'Luzii', they vary only in the amount of leaf mottle, a factor that can vary in individual plants. 1978/9: HC(T).

'Little Luzii', reputedly a more compact clone, tends to revert rather readily to the original clone.

Habit: Self-branching.

Stems: Purple-green. Internodes 2–3cm (¾–1¼in).

Petioles: Purple-green.

Leaves: 5-lobed, 3–4cm (1¼–1½in) by 3–4cm (1¼–1½in). Lobes not pronounced, leaf base cordate to auriculate and tending to overlap. Centre lobe rather longer than lateral lobes. Colour light grey-green, mottled and speckled yellow-green.

Hedera helix 'Malvern'

An ivy whose attraction rests in its extreme hairiness. A mutation from 'Olive Rose', it was found and introduced by Fibrex Nurseries in 1989. The profusionhairs is so great that the newly opened leaves appear silvery-white. As the leaves grow the hairs become slightly outspaced. Although a vining ivy it is more suited as a slightly novel house-plant ivy.

Habit: Vining.

Stems: Purple-brown. Internodes 2–3.5cm (¾–1⅓in).

Petioles: Green, heavily hirsute and long: 6–8cm (2⅓–3in).

Leaves: 5-lobed, 5–6cm (2–2⅓in) by 6–8cm (2⅓–3in). Apices acuminate, leaf base truncate to cuneate, margin twisted and convoluted to give a heavily curled leaf. Dark green but the closely spaced white stellate hairs give the leaves a grey appearance.

Hedera helix 'Manda Fringette'

An attractive house-plant ivy suitable for troughs and hanging baskets. It was listed by Graf in *Exotica* (1963) and is one of a number of clones introduced by the firm of W A Manda Inc, South Orange, New Jersey during the 1950s.

Listed in the AIS Check-list (1975) it is better known as 'Fringette' under which name it appeared in the RHS Ivy Trial (1977/9). In the mid 1970s a very similar clone was found in Morocco by Henri Schaepman the then President of the AIS. It was named and distributed by him as 'Miss Maroc'. In fact material and various descriptions, including an illustration in the September 1983 AIS Journal, show it to be identical to 'Manda Fringette'.

Habit: Self-branching with long trails.

Stems: Purple-green. Internodes 1.5–2.5cm (⅝–1in).

Petioles: Purple-green.

Leaves: 5-lobed, basal lobes reduced and often back-pointing, 3.5–5.5cm (1⅓–2¼in) by 4–6cm (1½–2⅓in). Centre lobe and the 2 lateral lobes attenuated for the uppermost third of their length. Sinuses shallow so that lateral lobes are almost at right angles. Leaf edges slightly crisped; lobes slightly twisted and sometimes 'fluted'. Some reversions to a broader leaf pattern. Colour light green; main veins slightly raised.

Hedera helix 'Manda's Crested'

In many families of cultivated plants there arise varieties or clones that become virtually 'classics', plants of character, pioneers that often break new ground. In the genus *Hedera*, 'Manda's Crested' is just such a clone. The American horticulturist botanist Alfred Bates coined the group name 'ramosa' to cover the kinds that were appearing as sports from the first self-branching clone 'Pittsburgh'. Prominent among these was 'Merion Beauty' and on the nursery of W A Manda Inc at South Orange, New Jersey, this sported to give 'Manda's Crested'. Bates described and illustrated it in the National Horticultural Magazine of October 1940. He remarked that it was not on the market then but Mr Manda had lent him a potted plant for "observation and photographs". The latter show that the clone has retained its stability remarkably over the past 55 years.

It was the first of the 'curlies': clones in which the leaf sinuses have an upward curvature while the lobes point downward. The plant was introduced to Europe and in Britain given the erroneous albeit descriptive name of 'Curlilocks'. 'Permanent Wave' and 'Pin Up' are very similar and are here treated as synonyms. It is a superb ivy for troughs, pots or baskets indoors or for ground cover outside where in winter it attains a delightful coppery colour. Its thin leaves indicate a certain tenderness; in Britain it has survived -12°C (10°F) with no problems but suffers far more from cold winds. RHS Ivy Trial 1978/9: FCC; 1993: ♔.

Habit: Self-branching but vining sufficiently to make slowly spreading cover.

Stems: Green-purple. Internodes 2–2.5cm (¾–1in).

Petioles: Green-purple, long: 7–8cm (2¾–3in).

Leaves: 5-lobed, rarely reduced to 3, 5–6cm (2–2⅓in) by 7–8cm (2¾–3in). Typically star-shaped, basal lobes back-pointing and almost the same length as the laterals, this with the overlap of the basal lobes makes the petiole junction appear to be at the leaf centre. Sinuses very shallow, all 5 lobes convolute with blunt down-pointing apices giving the curly appearance. Colour light green turning coppery-brown in cold weather.

Hedera helix 'Maple Leaf'

Until this plant's re-discovery in 1983 by Brother Heieck, the name was often bestowed in error on the totally different 'Maple Queen'. The clone was introduced to Germany from the USA around 1956/7 by the nurseryman Königer of Aalen. Both the name and a note in Gartenwelt in 1959 suggest that it was a North American clone (the maple leaf is the Canadian symbol). It appeared to be out of circulation until 1965 when the German nurseryman Klaus Friedrich noted it in Essen Botanic Garden. In 1983 he gave cuttings to Brother Heieck, who distributed material and registered it with the AIS (No 84-11b). A similar clone named 'Ahorn' was selected by Gebr Stauss of Möglingen, Germany, in 1974; *ahorn* of course is German for maple.

'Maple leaf' is sufficiently short-jointed to serve as a house plant, the leaf shape is unusual and attractive; it is hardy enough to make useful but not too vigorous ground-cover.

Habit: Short-jointed with trails.

Stems: Purple-green. Internodes 2–3cm (¾–1¼in).

Petioles: Purple-green.

Leaves: 5-lobed, 4–5cm (1½–2in) by 4–5cm (1½–2in). Sinuses shallow, centre lobe 1½ times the length of laterals which have vestigial lobes below the basal lobes. Apices acuminate, leaf edges irregularly indented. Colour mid-green, veins prominent by being lighter.

Hedera helix 'Maple Queen'

A mutation from 'Pittsburgh', this long-established clone was introduced by Mr Sylvan Hahn of Pittsburgh, Pennsylvania, and issued with the US Plant Patent No 429 in 1940. An easy grower, the leaves are typical of most people's idea of ivy while the red-purple stems make a pleasing contrast. A reliable, trouble-free indoor ivy for pots, troughs or baskets, it is reasonably hardy surviving -7°C (19°F) and cold winds in Britain. According to Pierot (1974) it can be grown outdoors as far north as New York City. The ivy sold as 'Kobby' is the same plant. A linear-leaved sport discovered by Allen C Haskell of New Bedford, Massachusetts was registered in 1989 as 'Iantha'. An effective plant provided that reversions are rigorously removed.

Habit: Self-branching with short trails.

Stems: Purple-red. Internodes 2–2.5cm (¾–1in).

Petioles: Purple-red.

Leaves: 3-lobed, 3–5cm (1¼–2in) by 3.5–5.5cm (1⅓–2¼in). Centre lobe prolonged, basal lobes vestigial, apices bluntly acute. Sinuses variable, slightly waved at the cleft. Leaf base truncate. Dark green with light green veins.

Hedera helix 'Marginata Lactea'

One of the 'Marginata' clones recorded in the late-19th century that can still be identified with some certainty. It was first recorded by Hibberd who in 1872 drew attention to the reddish petioles and the cream-white leaf-edge variegation which readily acquires a pink tinge in autumn. It may also have been the 'New Silver' and 'Osborn's New Silver' sometimes listed in early catalogues. A plant answering Hibberd's description was submitted to the RHS Ivy Trial of 1978/9 as 'Lisney's Silver'.

A reliable climbing ivy, the variegation is noticeable in young growth, less so on older leaves.

Habit: Vining.

Stems: Green-purple. Internodes 2–4cm (¾–1½in).

Petioles: Purple.

Leaves: 3–5-lobed, 5–8cm (2–3in) by 8–10 cm (3–4in), basal lobes occasionally asymmetrical, apices acute, leaf base cordate. Colour mid-green with slight areas of grey green; a thin margin of cream-yellow variegation with a discrete pink edge that becomes darker in cold weather.

Hedera helix 'Marginata Major'

Twenty-two different ivy names having 'Marginata' in their make-up can be selected from catalogues and horticultural literature. This emphasizes the confusion that has over the years prevailed with regard to marginally variegated ivies. In 1867 William Paul listed seven; in 1872 Hibberd listed eight; later in 1890 he recorded seven, rejecting 14 names then current under which some had been submitted to the RHS. In 1942 Lawrence & Schulze, faced with this plethora, made one 'catch all' of 14 names as 'Cavendishii'.

The marginate ivies that can be identified with some certainly are 'Marginata Major', 'Marginata Minor' and 'Marginata Lactea'. The picture can be confused because some of the variegated house-plant ivies will, in a sheltered situation outside, behave similarly to 'Marginata'-types and climb with some vigour. They can usually be distinguished by the fact that they seldom reach a truly flowering stage.

Habit: Vining.
Stems: Green-purple. Internodes 2–5cm (¾–2in).
Petioles: Green-purple.
Leaves: 5-lobed, 4–5cm (1½–2in) by 5–6cm (2–2⅓in), basal lobes often vestigial. Apices acute, becoming more blunt on older leaves. Leaf base cordate; colour mid-green with areas of grey-green, irregularly variegated cream-white towards the leaf edge.

Hedera helix 'Marginata Minor'

Widely grown in Victorian times, 'Marginata' attracted as many as 22 descriptive names as nurserymen distinguished or introduced their own variants. Few have survived, indeed any distinctive features may well have been slight. However with 'Marginata Minor', still offered today, we are more fortunate: it is distinct and moreover was described with a reasonably accurate illustration in Hibberd's *The Ivy* (1872).

A pleasant variegated climbing ivy, it is well suited for covering low walls. Not all present-day stocks agree with the following description which depicts the true plant.

Habit: Vining.
Stems: Green-purple. Internodes 2–3cm (¾–1¼in).
Petioles: Green-purple.
Leaves: 3-lobed, 3–4cm (1¼–1½in) by 3–5cm (1¼–2in). Lobes reduced, sometimes to little more than protrusions. Apices acute, leaf base cuneate. Green, variegated cream-yellow mostly at leaf edge.

Hedera helix 'Marie-Luise'

A mutation from 'Star' discovered around 1976 by Franz Rogmans of Geldern, Germany. The plant circulated in the trade without a name until 1981 when Herr Rogmans named it for his youngest daughter, Marie-Luise.

An excellent house-plant ivy throwing short trails that bear mid-green leaves whose deeply cut lobes are almost linear. AIS Reg No 811882.

Habit: Self-branching.
Stems: Purple-green. Internodes 2–5cm (¾–2in).
Petioles: Green-purple.
Leaves: 5-lobed, 3–5cm (1¼–2in) by 3–5cm (1¼–2in). Centre lobe longer and more prominent than the laterals. The sinuses extend almost to the centre vein thus separating the lobes which are linear and slightly constricted at the base. Apices acute, basal lobes back-pointing, colour mid-green.

Hedera helix 'Mathilde'

Distributed from the Danish nursery industry this is a good, readily branching clone showing a strong affinity with 'Eva' but lacking the cuneate leaf base.

Looking down on a pot-grown specimen the acuminate forward-pointing lobes convey an impression of a 'prickly' plant; naturally this is not so, the leaves are soft to the touch and the blend of light green and cream variegation make this a very pleasing house-plant ivy.

Like others of this type it is less successful out of doors where the elements can mask its attractive features.

Habit: Self-branching.
Stems: Purple-green. Internodes 1–2.5cm (⅓–1in).
Petioles: Green-purple.
Leaves: 3-lobed occasionally 2 vestigial lobes; 2.5–3.5cm (1–1⅓in) by 2–3.5cm (¾–1⅓in). Sinuses narrow, lobes forward-pointing. Apices acute, centre lobe often prolonged; leaf base truncate, rarely slightly cordate. Mid- to dark green with occasional flecks of grey-green, cream-yellow variegation usually at leaf margin.

Hedera helix 'Melanie'

A mutation from 'Parsley Crested' but differing from that clone in that the crested leaf edge shows a narrow strip of violet colour; set against the light green of the leaf blade this forms a striking and interesting contrast. 'Melanie' was discovered in 1980 at the Beth Chatto nursery in Essex as a shoot on 'Parsley Crested' by Melanie Nicholas of Wivenhoe, Essex. Mrs Chatto propagated it and named it in Melanie's honour.

The clone is relatively stable but cuttings rooted can vary in the amount of violet colouring expressed and only the best should be retained. Some ivies, notably *H. helix* 'Tricolor', retain a faint pink-purple leaf rim which colours more deeply in cold weather but the coloured rim of 'Melanie' is not dependent on climatic conditions. Like 'Parsley Crested' it is suitable for covering low walls, similarly it is reasonably hardy, suffering only in extreme weather, but nevertheless is best grown as a pot plant.

The clone has been listed by some nurseries as 'Pink 'n' Curly' an illegitimate name which demeans the English language as well as the nurseryman who coined it.

Habit: Self-branching with trails.

Stems: Purple-green. Internodes 1–3cm (⅓–1¼in).

Petioles: Purple-green.

Leaves: Unlobed or vestigially 3-lobed, 3–4cm (1¼–1½in) by 4–6cm (1½–2⅓in). Shape varying from ovate to almost circular with a bluntly acute apex, leaf base cordate. Leaf margin strongly undulate with a crested edge caused by proliferation of the marginal cells. Colour light green with the crested edge outlined in violet (RHS colour chart 183A). Veins light green and fairly prominent.

Hedera helix 'Merion Beauty'

This clone was described in 1940 by Bates in the American National Horticultural Magazine (Vol 14). It originated with Mr Henry Faust of Merion, Philadelphia, as a mutation from 'Pittsburgh' and was introduced in 1937/8. It has short internodes that make it a compact plant suitable for pot culture or topiary work. Synonyms are 'Hahn Miniature' (recorded by Bates), 'Hites Miniature' and 'Procumbens'. It is possible that over a period of years the original clone lost its characteristic features and that 'Hite's Miniature' was a post-World War II reversion to the original as described by Bates and which of course is the correct name.

'Cascade', a mutation with slightly crimped leaves, was recorded by Leo Swicegood. Yet another has been recorded, 'Baby Merion Beauty', having rounded rather than pointed lobes. The name is invalid but happily it is no longer in cultivation.

'Merion Beauty' propagates easily and has survived -10°C (14°F) in Britain outside but is better suited as a house plant.

Habit: Self-branching and compact.

Stems: Green-purple. Internodes 1–1.5cm (⅓–⅝in).

Petioles: Green.

Leaves: 3-lobed, basal lobes vestigial, 2–3cm (¾–1¼in) by 3–4cm (1¼–1½in). Centre lobe wedge-shaped, lateral lobes obtuse giving a square appearance. Branches readily from every node. Colour mid-green, generally little purple pigment.

Hedera helix 'Microphylla Picta'

The first mention of this very distinctive ivy is in the 1862 catalogue of Haage & Schmidt. There are a couple of subsequent references: Haage & Schmidt of 1875 and Tobler in 1912 and again in 1927, but none of these includes any descriptions and strangely there are no references to the plant or any similar distinctive clone in British catalogues or publications. It was however being grown under the above name in 1966 by Brother Heieck near Heidelberg.

When Mr Terry Jones in 1968 collected in Tenerife an ivy that he could not identify he passed it to the President of the BIS Stephen Taffler who, aware that there was no similar plant in circulation, tentatively called it 'Tenerife'. Subsequently the plant being grown by Heieck came to light.

A check on 'Tenerife' identifies it as a *helix* clone; since *helix* does not occur in the Canaries the name 'Tenerife' is not truly applicable or appropriate. It would appear to be a very old clone that circulated on a limited scale in Germany from as long ago as 1862 but never in Britain, and without a precise published description. It is very distinct by reason of its small green dots: a distinct spotting, not a mottle.

This characteristic suggests that it is the *Hedera helix* 'Microphylla Picta' listed by Haage & Schmidt in 1862 and by Tobler in 1912, a point noted and made by Brother Heieck in his book *Hedera Sorten*. By virtue of priority this is the correct name, with 'Tenerife' a synonym.

Habit: Vining.

Stems: Purple-green. Internodes 1.5–3cm (⅝–1¼in).

Petioles: Purple.

Leaves: Basically 3-lobed but with such shallow sinuses as to give a virtually unlobed leaf that averages 1.5–2cm (⅝–¾in) by 2–3.5cm (¾–1⅓in). Apices bluntly acute, leaf base truncate. Colour dark green irregularly variegated cream-yellow and distinguished by dots of approximately 1mm (1/32in) of green tissue.

Hedera helix 'Midas Touch'

The instability of *helix* and its readiness, particularly the house-plant types, to mutate is well known. In Denmark, where the output of house-plant ivies at present can be reckoned in millions, some unusual and useful clones have appeared and of these 'Midas Touch' is outstanding. A vigorous ivy, the contrast of the unusually bright yellow variegation with the bright-green basic colour is striking.

Imported into Britain among batches labelled *Hedera* it was unnoticed until seen by ivy enthusiast Mr Ken Burkey. Recognizing it as an unusual ivy he made enquiries through the BIS and found it had been raised by the Frode Maegaard Hedera Nursery of Ringe in Denmark, which was listing it as 'Golden Kolibri'. Whilst this name indicated its origins it was not acceptable under ICNCP rules which preclude prefixes to existing names such as 'Kolibri'. Subsequently however the firm accepted Mr Taffler's suggestion of the very appropriate 'Midas Touch'. A variation with slightly curled leaves has been recorded as 'Golden Curl'. In practice it is unstable and prone to revert to the normal type. This is equally true of 'Marylin', a variation having a longer centre lobe and a more regular area of yellow colouration.

The rich green leaves with bold irregular splashes of deep yellow have a flamboyance that is not to everyone's taste but it has won numerous prizes at ivy shows and exhibitions as a pot plant. Outside it is suitable for low walls but a situation away from scorching winds, in good light but not over exposed to sun, is desirable. ♆: 1993.

Habit: Self-branching with short trails.

Stems: Pink-green. Internodes 1–2cm (⅓–¾in).

Petioles: Green-pink.

Leaves: Generally unlobed, deltoid or triangular, 4–5cm (1½–2in) by 4cm (1½in). Apices bluntly acute, leaf base cordate. Basic leaf colour dark green with patches of lighter green. Irregularly variegated with blotches of bright yellow.

Hedera helix 'Milford'

Present in a few old gardens in Surrey this clone is not, as far as I know, available commercially. It has the rather crumpled, wavy, unlobed leaves of 'Conglomerata' and whilst its habit is generally erect, the shoots arise from rather sprawling stems. It appears to be a half-way clone, a form of 'Conglomerata' that has not achieved the completely erect stance of 'Congesta', 'Erecta' or 'Russelliana'. Its existence may well account for past nomenclatural confusion typified by catalogues which listed both 'Conglomerata' and 'Conglomerata Erecta'. All the catalogue entries I have examined are too vague for the acceptance of the name 'Conglomerata Erecta' and since all the specimens I have seen have had some connection with the Milford area of Surrey, I propose the name 'Milford' for this clone. In gardens it can serve a similar purpose to 'Erecta' but its variability and sprawling habit are detracting features.

Habit: Semi-erect.

Stems: Green-purple. Internodes 0.5–2cm (¼–¾in).

Petioles: Green-purple.

Leaves: Unlobed, reniform, 4–6cm (1½–2⅓in) by 4–6cm (1½–2⅓in). Apices obtuse, leaf base truncate. Distichous in arrangement on shoots which are erect but which arise from sprawling shoots upon which the arrangement is normal. Colour mid-green.

Hedera helix 'Miniature Knight'

One of the 'Knight's introduced by Whitehouse Ivies then of Tolleshunt Knights, Essex, this selection from 'Goldcraft' was made in 1985. It is an excellent carpeting ivy for small areas or for low walls.

Habit: Self-branching.

Stems: Green. Internodes 1–2cm (⅓–¾in).

Petioles: Green.

Leaves: 3-lobed, 1.5–2.5cm (⅝–1in) by 2–2.5cm (¾–1in). Centre lobe wedge-shaped and usually folded along the centre vein, lateral lobes overlap. Colour light yellow-green.

Hedera helix 'Minigreen'

The origin of this neat-leaved clone is not known. The AIS had material in its collection in 1979, reputedly received from the Dutch ivy enthusiast Harry van de Laar. A variegated form called 'Frosty' was registered (No 80481) having been received from Howard Van Vleck of Montclair, New Jersey. This had leaves similar to the type, mottled white and green and, as might be expected, not so vigorous.

Habit: Self-branching.

Stems: Green-purple. Internodes 0.5–1.5cm (¼–⅝in).

Petioles: Green-purple.

Leaves: 3-lobed, 2.5cm (1in) by 2–3cm (¾–1¼in). Centre lobe acuminate, lateral lobes acute, sinuses shallow, leaf base truncate. Colour mid-green.

Hedera helix 'Minor Marmorata'

This, the 'salt and pepper' ivy, has had a chequered nomenclatural history. It was first described by William Paul (1822–1905) who in the Gardener's Chronicle of 1867 listed his collection of "some 40 kinds". Among those was "'Minor Marmorata', leaves green, beautifully marbled with white, small, growth rapid, exceedingly pretty."

In 1872 Hibberd described the plant with more detail than Paul, but changed the name to 'Discolor' giving 'Minor Marmorata' and 'Maculata' as synonyms. There seems no reason for this other than possibly a disregard for Paul as a mere nurseryman. Whatever the 19th-century intrigues that led Hibberd to ignore Paul's name, the fact remains that it was properly published by Paul and has priority.

In 1942 Lawrence & Schulze called the plant 'Discolor', in 1970 Nannenga-Bremekamp described it as 'Minor Marmorata'. Other names that have been associated with this clone are 'Howardii', 'Dealbata', 'Maculata', 'Marmorata Elegans', 'Marmorata Elegantissima', 'Richmond Gem' and 'Snowflake'. In 1976 I examined a plant on the Ivy Wall at Kew that had come from Russell in 1927 labelled 'Howardii', it was 'Minor Marmorata' as here described. Similar material received from Holland by the AIS proved equally to be 'Minor Marmorata'.

As the foregoing shows the plant is long established. It is a typical vining ivy with the hardiness associated with *helix*.

The American Leonie Bell in the 1968 Morris Arboretum Bulletin described the leaf as "mottled or coarsely salted – white on deep green" and this well describes the variegation. Essentially a wall ivy and best on a north wall; on south-facing walls it acquires a scruffy look.

Habit: Vining; covering slowly.

Stems: Green-purple. Internodes 2–3cm (¾–1¼in).

Petioles: Purple.

Leaves: 3-lobed, 3–5cm (1¼–2in) by 4–5cm (1½–2in), apices bluntly acute, sinuses shallow, leaf base strongly cordate. Dark green, spotted and splashed with cream-white, often in slightly angular patterns. Variegation so distributed as to cause little or no leaf distortion. Older leaves markedly more green.

Hedera helix 'Minty'

In this clone much of the white of the typical 'Kolibri' mid-green and white is overlaid with a thin layer of chlorophyll-bearing cells giving an unusual soft, slightly olive-green effect, making the clone possibly the most distinct of the many variations of 'Kolibri'. This extremely useful house-plant ivy introduced by the Danish firm of Frode Maegaard in 1986 has circulated in Holland as 'Mint Kolibri'.

Habit: Self-branching with short trails.

Stems: Purple. Internodes 1–2cm (⅓–¾in).

Petioles: Green-purple.

Leaves: 3-lobed, 3–4cm (1¼–1½in) by 2–3cm (¾–1¼in). Centre lobe acute and twice the length of laterals, sinuses shallow. Leaf base slightly cordate to cuneate. Basic colour mid-green flecked with white overlaid in part with light green.

Hedera helix 'Modern Times'

This would appear to be the *H. helix* 'Woodsii' of Pierot (1974). her description and that of 'Modern Times' by Nannenga-Bremekamp (1970) coincide almost exactly, as do the excellent illustrations in both works. The description by Nannenga-Bremekamp pre-dates that of Mrs Pierot and accordingly the plant becomes 'Modern Times'. The clone was selected by Hage & Co, of Boskoop, Holland, in 1951 from 'Curlilocks' which they had imported, presumably from America. This clone was often confused with both 'Parsley Crested' and 'Manda's Crested' so it could have arisen from either.

Both writers have emphasized the blunt apices and the flat appearance of the leaves, Mrs Pierot commenting on the 'velvety' green and the apple-green of the young leaves and the pale veins. I can add two diagnostic points: first the centre veins of the two basal lobes are frequently at compete

right angles to the leaf's centre vein, second the presence of a white 'dot' at the junction of the petiole and leaf blade.

'Modern Times' is reasonably hardy in Britain. Pierot says 'Woodsii' can be grown outdoors as far north as New York City. Under whatever name it is an excellent ivy for low walls and pleasant for any indoor use where a moderately vigorous green ivy is required.

Habit: Vining.

Stems: Green-purple. Internodes 4–5cm (1½–2in).

Petioles: Green-purple.

Leaves: 5-lobed, 5cm (2in) by 5–7cm (2–2¾in). Sinuses shallow giving little length to the near-equal basal and lateral lobes and a 3-lobed impression. Terminal lobe wedge-shaped, as long as broad, laterals blunt and rounded. Colour mid-green, veins light green to white. Centre veins of the basal lobes at right angles to the leaf centre vein. There is often a white 'dot' at the junction of the veins at the petiole/leaf-blade union.

Hedera helix 'Mrs Pollock'

Early catalogue descriptions of this clone suggest that it is the golden variegated form of 'Corrugata'. The name was often quoted as a synonym of 'Palmata Aurea' but the first record of 'Mrs Pollock' is that of Charles Turner of Slough, England, who in 1885 listed both 'Palmata Aurea' and 'Mrs Pollock', unfortunately without descriptions. In 1888 J Backhouse of York listed it as 'Vitifolia Aurea', giving 'Mrs Pollock' as a synonym. The name appeared in many catalogues and horticultural publications and descriptions varied: Barr & Sons (1895) described it as "bright yellow edged green and finely cut". The periodical The Garden of March 1897 said, "variegated well marked foliage somewhat digitate". In a Belgian nursery catalogue of 1910 it is charmingly listed as "'Mistress Pollock', variegated yellow and pink."

The report of the 1888 RHS Ivy Trial indicates some of the confusion of names. "'Chrysophylla Palmata' is a brilliant golden leaved variety of the green leaved 'Palmata'. Contributed by Mr Fraser as 'Palmata Nova Aurea'. Also known in gardens as 'Mrs Pollock' and 'Palmata Aurea'."

Nowadays it is occasionally seen in old gardens and is available from specialist nurseries. Young plants often stay green for a year or so, older plants can colour well.

Habit: Vining.

Stems: Green. Internodes 3–5cm (1¼–2in).

Petioles: Green.

Leaves: 5–7-lobed, 5–6cm (2–2⅓in) by 5–7cm (2–2¾in). Lobes often appear as little more than forward-pointing projections or large teeth at the apex of a leaf whose cuneate base likens it to an inverted triangle

Hedera helix 'Neilson'

with its apex at the petiole junction. The lobes are short and acuminate with narrow sinuses. Medium-green, blotched yellow, sometimes extensively.

Hedera helix 'Mrs Ulin'

This distinctive little ivy was registered in 1995 by Dr Charles Dunham, a distinguished AIS member, to honour the late Mrs Alexander Ulin, a founder member of that Society. An ardent plantswoman, she gardened at Claymont, Delaware and planted this ivy in the late 1940s. She found that it made splendid ground cover, was not invasive and was very hardy.

Material sent for identification to the AIS did not match any plant known to the Society and remained in their collection as 'Mrs Ulin'. It was subsequently lost but not before Ron Whitehouse obtained material and introduced it to Europe. Dr Dunham revisited Mrs Ulin's Claymont garden and obtained material of the original ivy to re-stock the AIS collection and for registration. Small, neat mid- to dark-green leaves and green stems make 'Mrs Ulin' a good house-

plant ivy but perhaps even more useful as a rock-garden ivy underplanted with small bulbs. The leaf is smaller than that of 'Walthamensis'.

Habit: Short-jointed with trails.
Stems: Green. Internodes 1–3cm (⅓–1¼in).
Petioles: Green.
Leaves: Unlobed, occasionally slightly 3-lobed, 2–3cm (¾–1¼in) by 3–4cm (1¼–1½in). Leaf shape deltoid, apices bluntly acute, leaf base slightly cordate. Colour light to mid-green, veins light green, fairly prominent.

Hedera helix 'Natashja'

An unusual ivy from the Danish *Hedera* nursery of Frode Maegaard, named by him and first seen in Britain in 1994, but circulating in Holland in 1990.

Reputedly a self-branching ivy, in practice it appears to be a fairly vigorous vining ivy whose virtue is the attractively shaped leaves. The drawn-out acuminate tip produces a 'Teardrop' figure. An ivy of that name described by Shippy in 1955 and introduced by Terrace View Gardens, Greencastle, Indiana would appear to be very similar. 'Natashja' would appear to be a climbing ivy for outside but in the same

way as 'Persian Carpet' it is initially shy of putting out rootlets. The leaf has some resemblance to that of 'Brokamp' but is neater, more deltoid in shape and with a finer tip.
Habit: Vining.
Stems: Purple. Internodes 2.5–3.5cm (1–1⅓in).
Petioles: Purple-green.
Leaves: Unlobed, very rarely 3-lobed, 4–6cm (1½–2⅓in) by 3–4cm (1¼–1½in). Deltoid, the apex acuminate and extended leaf base truncate. The leaf shape emphasizes the radiation of the veins from the petiole/leaf-blade junction in what appears to be almost parallel fashion to the leaf edge. Colour mid- to dark green.

Hedera helix 'Neilson'

A clone grown extensively for the pot-plant trade but whose origin seems obscure, it appears to have arisen in Denmark, probably in the late 1950s. It is sometimes known as 'Neilsonii' but for a clone distributed after 1959, the date of the implementation of the rules of the ICNCP, this Latinized form would be incorrect. The clone is similar to 'Merion Beauty' and to 'Hahn's Self Branching'; the latter clone, an early mutation from 'Pittsburgh', is now reckoned to be synonymous with it and it seems likely that, along with 'Chicago', they are all fairly similar. In the case of 'Neilson' it is inevitable that a clone grown on a massive scale on a number of nurseries will, with individual selection, produce numerous forms. The following is thought to be reasonably typical of the clone. RHS Ivy Trial 1978/9: HC(T).
Habit: Self-branching and compact.
Stems: Green-purple. Internodes 1–2cm (⅓–¾in).
Petioles: Green-purple.
Leaves: 3-lobed, 3–4cm (1¼–1½in) by 3–4cm (1¼–1½in). Two basal lobes vestigial. Centre lobe wedge-shaped at least twice the length of the laterals. Sinuses shallow, apices acute. Light green, veins lighter green, not pronounced.

Hedera helix 'Nice Guy'

Discovered in 1983 and registered by F Batson of Angelwood Nursery, Woodburn, Oregon (No 830384) and assumed to be a sport from 'Irish Lace', it is best described as an asymmetrical, variegated, 'bird's foot' ivy of irregular outline and an unusual colour combination of chartreuse and grey-green. An excellent pot-plant ivy, the long trails make it a useful clone for hanging baskets.
Habit: Self-branching with trails.
Stems: Green-purple. Internodes 1.5–2cm (⅝–¾in).
Petioles: Green-purple.
Leaves: 3–5-lobed, 2–3cm (¾–1¼in) by 2–3cm (¾–1¼in). The 2 basal lobes often missing or vestigial. Centre lobe acuminate, lateral lobes acute. Asymmetrical, the centre lobe often having a decided lean and slight twist. Colour shades of grey-green with light green, almost cream leaf margins.

Hedera helix 'Nigra'

The earliest description is that of Hibberd (1872) who received the plant from a Mr Wills. This explains subsequent references to *Hedera helix* 'Willseana', described as a dark-leaved form; 'Nigra' however is the older and the correct name. The plant is still occasionally seen and was submitted to the RHS Trial in 1977. Its dark green leaves make a good foil for pale-flowered wall shrubs or climbers.
Habit: Vining.
Stems: Purple. Internodes 3–4cm (1¼–1½in).
Petioles: Purple.
Leaves: 3-lobed, 3–7cm (1¼–2¾in) by 3–5cm (1¼–2in). Lobe apices acute, centre lobe almost twice the length of lateral lobes. Leaf apex slightly down-pointing giving the leaf a convex appearance. Leaf base slightly cordate. Very dark green, veins lighter in young leaves, not prominent in older leaves.

Hedera helix 'Nigra Aurea'

"Distinct colouring of black, gold and red." This catalogue description of an ivy is sufficient to excite any plantsman's interest but, unless some quite extraordinary ivy has been lost to cultivation, it is somewhat exaggerated. The plant under this name today and entered in the RHS Ivy Trial in 1977 is certainly splashed with yellow; its basic colour is dark green, turning almost black in winter and, like many ivies, tinges of purple appear in cold weather, but this hardly adds up to "black, gold and red".

There appear to be no published descriptions other than those in a few British catalogues from about 1908 until the outbreak of World War II. It is possible that the variety 'Flava', described in Haage and Schmidt's catalogue of 1869 as "with small yellow variegates leaves", may have been this plant. This is pure conjecture and in any event the name 'Flava', uncompromisingly yellow, would be as unsuitable a name to describe this plant as the somewhat contradictory 'Nigra Aurea', an interesting clone, similar in leaf to 'Nigra', but as one would expect of a variegated plant, not so vigorous. Suitable light ground cover for border or rock garden.
Habit: Vining.
Stems: Purple. Internodes 3–3.5cm (1¼–1⅓in).
Petioles: Purple-green.
Leaves: 3-lobed, 2.5–3cm (1–1¼in) by 2.5–3.5cm

(1–1⅓in). Apices acute, lateral lobes wedge-shaped, sometimes reduced to protrusions. Leaf base cordate. Basic leaf colour dark green. Young leaves commence green and acquire their dappled, clear butter-yellow mottle with age. Under-surface tends to remain a light green. Veins pale but not prominent.

Hedera helix 'Northington Gold'

In recent years several variegated forms found in the wild have been recorded. 'Northington Gold' is outstanding by reason of the completeness of its yellow-green colouring, which is paler than 'Flavescens' and unlike 'Buttercup', some of whose leaves, particularly in shade, become wholly green. Due to the extent of its non-green tissue 'Northington Gold' is not a strong grower and is of more interest to the ivy enthusiast than to the general plantsman.

It was found as a shoot on wild ivy in woodland at Northington Down House, Alresford, Hants, by the owner, Mrs Marjorie Jackson, in 1978.

Habit: Vining.

Stems: Purple-green. Internodes 1–2cm (⅓–¾in).

Petioles: Purple-green.

Leaves: 3-lobed, 1–3cm (⅓–1¼in) by 2–4cm (¾–1½in). Apices bluntly acute, leaf base cordate. Basic colour yellow-green, many leaves carry a small blotch of green, rarely more than 0.5cm (¼in), between the centre and one of the lateral veins.

Hedera helix 'Obovata'

This clone was first listed by the Lawson Seed and Nursery Co of Edinburgh in their 1874 catalogue and then by various nurserymen until around 1908. The plant was described briefly by that great gardener E A Bowles in *My Garden in Spring* (1914), thereafter the clone appears lost in the general decline of interest in ivies that followed World War I. It is a vigorous grower that clings well and with almost circular, dark green leaves makes an excellent wall-covering ivy. It did not reappear in British gardens until 1988 when material was found by Dr Mark Smith in a garden in Cabrerets, Lot, France. It was grown on in the Bristol University Botanic Garden and distributed by Dr David Gledhill.

Habit: Vining.

Stems: Green-purple. Internodes 2–3.5cm (¾–1⅓in).

Petioles: Green-purple.

Leaves: Unlobed, deltoid to orbicular and obovate, 4–6cm (1½–2⅓in) by 5–7cm (2–2¾in). As the leaves age they tend to become orbicular and concave. Leaf base slightly cordate in young leaves, truncate or cuneate in older leaves. Colour dark green.

Hedera helix 'Olive Rose'

A most unusual ivy, the heavy and extreme cresting of the leaf edges and surface producing a unique plant that, while not a commercial house-plant ivy, is very much a plant for the enthusiast and collector. Grown outside, or if given over-generous pot cultivation, reverted leaves can appear; when grown as a bonsai ivy, for which it is very suitable, this tendency is suppressed. A mutation from 'Très Coupé' it was selected and introduced by Fibrex Nurseries in 1981. Although self-branching its lineage through 'Très Coupé' is that of a vining *helix*. The name honours the wife of the author of *Ivies*.

Habit: Self-branching.

Stems: Purple-green. Internodes 0.5–1.5cm (¼–⅝in).

Petioles: Green-purple.

Leaves: Basically 3-lobed, 1.5–3cm (⅝–1¼in) by 1–3cm (⅓–1¼in). The entire leaf edging heavily cristate with excrescences also showing on the leaf blade surface. Leaves very variable in shape, leaf base truncate. Colour mid- to light green.

Hedera helix 'Ovata'

This came to me labelled *Hedera* 'Ovata', purportedly from Denmark. The leaves were typically deltoid in shape suggesting that it might be a small plant of *H. hibernica* 'Deltoidea': in fact it appears to be the deltoid form of *H. helix*.

References to 'Ovata' are few. In the Kew *Hand List of Trees and Shrubs* (1925) the name appears as a variety (cultivar nowadays) of *H. helix*, as does 'Deltoidea', and some earlier nursery catalogues appear to have used the name in place of and referring to 'Deltoidea'. Various authorities gave it as a synonym of 'Deltoidea' but it is Jenny(1964) who defines the plant. In describing 'Deltoidea' he says, "It is often confused with 'Ovata' whose leaf is rounded at the base and ends in a definite point."

It is unfortunate that recently (1991) the plant has been imported to Britain from continental sources and sold under the name 'Mein Herz' ('My Heart'), an example of the confusion nurserymen and exporters/importers can so easily cause by giving established plants a 'popular' name.

Habit: short-jointed but vining.

Stems: Purple-green.

Petioles: Purple-green. Internodes 1.5–2cm (⅝–¾in).

Leaves: Unlobed and thick, 2–3.5cm (¾–1⅓in) by 2–5cm (¾–2in). Leaf shape variable with some having a much broader base and wedge-shaped apex whereas the typical leaf is acuminate. Leaf base cordate extending out from the petiole junction to form 2 overlapping lobes. Dark green, colouring purple in cold weather.

PLATE VII

All plants are shown at approximately ¾ size

H. helix 'Green Ripple'

H. helix
'Professor Friedrich Tobler'

H. helix 'Luzii'

H. helix 'Ambrosia'

H. helix 'Light Fingers'

H. helix 'Shamrock'

H. helix 'Arran'

H. helix 'Ardingly'

H. helix 'Brokamp'

H. helix 'Cathedral Wall'

H. helix 'Baden-Baden'

Hedera helix 'Palmata'

In the past every tree and shrub nursery appeared to list 'Palmata', albeit with little or no description. Nowadays few nurseries list it and there seems little agreement as to the typical plant.

The first listing I have found is that of Peter Lawson & Son, nurserymen of Edinburgh, who catalogued it without description in 1846. William Paul (1867) described it as "Dark green, medium size, very broad, deeply cleft, veins prominent, vigorous." Over the years it was catalogued, usually as "The five fingered ivy" or, as Jackmans of Woking, Surrey, put it (Catalogue, 1936), "Small leafed with deeply indented foliage". Hibberd (1872) illustrated it, writing of its "medium sized three to five-lobed leaves which tend to a palmate appearance". Thereafter writers seemed to have overlooked this variety until Bean (1973) described it as "Strongly five-lobed, truncate at base, veins prominent beneath." If we combine this with Paul's and Hibberd's writings, we get a picture of this variety which is still found in old gardens and sometimes in the wild. A hardy climbing ivy, useful to plant as an alternative to the common ivy.

Habit: Vining.
Stems: Purple-green. Internodes 3–3.5cm (1¼–1⅓in).
Petioles: Green-purple.
Leaves: 3–5-lobed, 4–6cm (1½–2⅓in) by 3.5–6cm (1⅓–2⅓in). Centre and 2 lateral lobes equally proportioned, wedge-shaped and acute, basal lobes smaller. Sinuses narrow, sometimes convolute at cleft. Leaf base truncate. Dark green, veins light green, prominent on underside of leaf.

Hedera helix 'Parasol'

A mutation from 'Ivalace' having broad, deeply wrinkled and curled leaves held upright on long petioles. It was discovered in the early 1960s by Mr John Huntress and passed to Meadowbrook Farm, Meadowbrook, Pennsylvania, and sold for many years under the name 'Ivacurl'. The possibility that this name, a combination of 'Ivalace' and 'Telecurl' could cause confusion, led to it being registered in 1983 by Charles Cresson of Meadowbrook as 'Parasol' (No 830284). 'Tango', distributed from Germany, appears to be identical.

The glossy green, attractively curled leaves and compact habit of 'Parasol' make it a most useful house-plant ivy.

Habit: Self-branching.
Stems: Purple-green. Internodes 1.5–2.5cm (⅝–1in).
Petioles: Purple-green, twice the length of the leaf blade.
Leaves: 5-lobed, 4–6cm (1½–2⅓in) by 4–6cm (1½–2⅓in). Centre lobe acuminate, lateral lobes acute and downpointing. Leaf margins strongly undulate, sinuses shallow, leaf margins convolute at the sinus, blade held upright on long petioles. Colour glossy dark green.

Hedera helix 'Parsley Crested'

There appear to be no references to this clone until the 1950s although Lawrence in 1956 suggested it might then have been in cultivation for about 25 years. It seems possible that mutations having the same crimped leaf edge may have arisen in several places since the introduction of the 'ramulose' ivy type. This may account for the several names in circulation: 'Crestata', 'Cristata' (Jenny 1964), 'Holly', 'Rokoko', 'Parsley' and 'Pice Lep'. A very similar plant circulated in Belgium in the early 1970s under the name 'Crispa'. Graf in 1963 illustrated it as 'Parsley Crested' and Nannenga-Bremekamp described it under that name. 'Old Lace' is virtually identical.

In addition to its useful self-branching habit it throws trails that make it a suitable ivy for hanging baskets; a measure of root restriction tends to enhance the Parsley effect. Suitable for low walls and excellent for ground cover in small areas. RHS Ivy Trial 1978/91: AM(T).

Habit: Self-branching.
Stems: Green-purple. Internodes 1–3cm (⅓–1¼in).
Petioles: Green-purple.
Leaves: Unlobed or vestigially tri-lobed, 4–6cm (1½–2⅓in) by 4–6cm (1½–2⅓in). Ovate with acute apex to almost circular. Leaf base slightly auriculate. Leaf margin undulate with crimped edge caused by proliferation of the marginal cells. Occasionally this proliferation can occur as eruptions a little way from the margin. Colour a fresh bright green. Veins lighter and fairly prominent. The constricted leaf margin produces some puckering and undulation of the leaf surface.

Hedera helix 'Pedata'

This, the 'bird's foot' ivy, is undoubtedly a natural variant of *H. helix*. In a domesticated landscape such as that of Britain it is difficult to tell that which is wild from a garden escape but it seems certain that 'Pedata', along with other clones such as 'Lobata' and 'Triloba', are variations which have occurred in Britain, particularly in the west, an area very conducive to ivy growth.

Whatever its origins the plant was first known as 'Caenwoodiana', certainly by 1863 when it was listed, without a description, in the catalogue of James & John Fraser of Leebridge Nurseries, Essex. Lacking a description the name is a *nomen nudum* of botanists, a naked name, and so it is Hibberd's name, 'Pedata', that has priority and should be used. The earlier name referred to Caenwood House in

Hampstead, London. This was the seat of the Earls of Mansfield; after 1841 the name of the property was changed to Kenwood House (this incidentally accounts for the reference in the *Handbuch der Laubholz-Benennung, Beissner, Schelle und Zabel* 1903, to *Hedera helix* 'Kenwoodiana'). The name 'Caenwoodiana' survived for many years but in *The Ivy* (1872) Hibberd described the plant in detail as 'Pedata'. Hibberd caused much confusion by changing well known and well used personal names to Latinized descriptive ones. He does not mention 'Caenwoodiana' in his monograph but his description of 'Pedata' indicates the same plant. Other authorities including Bean (1914) and Rehder (*Manual of Cultivated Trees and Shrubs*, 1927) followed Hibberd. The horticultural press from time to time continued to refer to 'Caenwoodiana' and it has appeared in catalogues up to the present time with occasional suggestions that it is a distinct variety. This is not so but it does indicate the confusion that can exist between 'Pedata' and clones such as 'Königer', which have some similarity. A three-lobed form known as 'Arrowhead' has been registered (AIS No 79282).

The report in the RHS Journal of 1889 on the Ivy Trial held at the Society's Chiswick Gardens confirmed the name 'Pedata' as follows:

> *Hedera* 'Pedata' is one of the most distinct and interesting; the leaves are divided like a bird's foot, the grey veins are very distinct. Being rather spare and given to objectionable variations when it has mounted to some height on a wall, it is desirable to cut it down occasionally to keep it well furnished and in proper character. Sent as 'Caenwoodiana' by Fraser and as 'Pedata' by Turner.

Apart from this historical confusion over the name, the plant is a reliable and useful ivy. Its prime use is on walls or pillars where its hardiness, quick growth and attractive leaf pattern are so useful. Leaf coverage is not sufficiently close for ground cover. Synonyms, in addition to those quoted by Hibberd, have included 'Digitata', 'Deltsifolia', 'Caenwoodiana', 'Caenwoodii', 'Combwoodiana', 'Grey Arrow', 'Kenwoodiana' and 'Weinstephan'. 1993: ♛.

Habit: Vining.
Stems: Green. Internodes 2–5cm (¾–2in).
Petioles: Green.
Leaves: 5-lobed, 4–5cm (1½–2in) by 5–6cm (2–2⅓in). Centre lobe prolonged and narrow, about 1cm (⅓in) wide and 1½ times as long as the lateral lobes. Apices acuminate, sinuses wide, lateral lobes almost at right angles to the centre lobe. Basal lobes back-pointing but leaf base truncate. Dark green, veins grey-white giving an impression of grey-green colour to the plant.

Hedera helix 'Pennsylvanica'

The first descriptive record of this clone is in Paul's ivy list in the Gardener's Chronicle of 1867. For an ivy of that period the name is intriguing. Ivy is not indigenous to America although it was one of the first plants introduced from Europe and while it is just feasible that a variation of the introduced plant had occurred in the State of Pennsylvania and made its way to Britain, there is certainly no record of this. We shall probably never know but the name persisted and plants agreeing with Paul's description, "leaves wholly green, large deeply cleft, veins prominent, growth free", were growing and so labelled on the Ivy Wall at the Royal Botanic Gardens, Kew, recently. Material on this wall was planted by George Nicholson (1847–1908) who was Curator from 1886–1901 and it is reasonable to assume that it is authentic.

'Pennsylvanica' and 'Crenata' have both been confused with 'Digitata'; understandably for all three are prone to leaf variation at different periods in their growth. All are useful wall-covering ivies as alternatives to the common ivy.
Habit: Vining.
Stems: Green-purple. Internodes 1.5–2cm (⅝–¾in).
Petioles: Purple-green.
Leaves: Mostly 5-lobed, occasionally 7, 4–6cm (1½–2⅓in) by 5–9cm (2–3½in). Lobes forward-pointing, cleft generally to ⅔ of their length, slight upward ridge at the cleft, sinuses narrow. Apices bluntly acute, leaf base truncate to cuneate. Colour dark green, veins pale grey so as to appear silvery.

Hedera helix 'Perkeo'

This mutation from 'Ralf' was selected by Brother Heieck in 1980. Perkeo was the name of the Court Jester at the Elector's Court in Heidelberg. In 1728 the Elector, Karl Philipp, set Perkeo to act as caretaker of the famously large Heidelberg wine cask. Perkeo, a great drinker, was said to have made inroads on the contents of the vast cask. It was fitting that Brother Heieck should name this very distinctive ivy after Perkeo, who was very much a Heidelberg personage.

'Perkeo' makes an attractive pot plant which few people identify as an ivy. It will persist out of doors but shows to much better effect indoors and benefits from generous cultivation. AIS Reg No 820883.
Habit: Self-branching and upright in growth.
Stems: Green-purple. Internodes 1–1.5cm (⅓–⅝in).
Petioles: Purple-green. 1–3cm (⅓–1¼in) and above-average thickness.
Leaves: Unlobed, 5–7cm (2–2¾in) by 4–6cm (1½–2⅓in). Orbicular to triangular in shape, the latter figuration

Hedera helix 'Perle'

showing the tendency towards a 3-lobed leaf which occasionally appears as a reversion. Leaf base slightly cordate to cuneate. Strongly veined, the veins colouring purple-red when the plant is exposed to cold or stress. Mature leaves medium- to dark green. Leaf surface slightly crumpled.

Hedera helix 'Perle'

A mutation from 'Harald' selected in 1980 by Ingobert Heieck. The small neat leaves, pleasant variegation and trailing habit make it an excellent ivy for hanging baskets. AIS Reg No 826094.
Habit: Short-jointed with long trails.
Stems: Purple-green. Internodes 2–3cm (¾–1¼in).
Petioles: Green, often slightly winged.
Leaves: Unlobed, 2–3cm (¾–1¼in) by 2–3cm (¾–1¼in); ovate, apex acute, leaf base cordate. Mid-green with cream variegation at leaf edge.

Hedera helix 'Persian Carpet'

A good climbing ivy of a particularly fresh light-green colour, vigorous and filling up well. Not suitable for walls because although it puts out the usual aerial rootlets these show little vigour and tend to die away without achieving any grip. The clone is best suited to climb against hurdles or

wire netting where the vigorous shoots gain support by interweaving. It is excellent for making a 'fedge' on chain-link fencing. Found by John Whitehead in 1978 in a park in Tehran. Nobody seemed to know whence it came. Propagated from cuttings which root readily.
Habit: Vining.
Stems: Totally green, internodes 3–4cm (1¼–1½in). Young shoots generously covered with white typically *helix* hairs give an almost tomentose effect.
Petioles: Green.
Leaves: Basically 3-lobed but with sinuses so shallow as to present an entire deltoid shape. Average 4–5cm (1½–2in) by 6–8cm (2⅓–3in). Leaf base generally cordate. Colour light- to mid-green.

Hedera helix 'Peter'

This clone is mainly useful as a house plant where its branching habit makes it more suitable than the more colourful but longer jointed 'Goldheart'. The colours, however, are paler and much less well defined than those of 'Goldheart'. The plant shows little tendency to revert, unlike a similar introduction 'Green Quartz', in which the central yellow splash reverted readily to green so that it is no longer grown or available. Similarly 'Glorious', introduced by Hage of Boskoop, was dropped because of this tendency. A mutation from 'Pittsburgh Variegated' discovered at the Neuburg Monastery in 1978 was recorded in 1982 as 'Serenade'. It is smaller and more self-branching than 'Peter' but again the central blotch of yellow-green is not constant.

'Peter', a mutation from 'Pittsburgh', selected by Brother Heieck and introduced by Gebr Stauss, Möglingen, Germany, won awards at Genoa and Hamburg. Floriade, Amsterdam, 1974: Gold Medal; RHS Ivy Trial 1978/9: C.
Habit: Self-branching.
Stems: Green-pink to purple. Internodes 1.5–2.5cm (⅝–1in).
Petioles: Green-pink.
Leaves: 3-lobed 4–5cm (1½–2in) by 3–6cm (1¼–2⅓in). Centre lobe slightly prolonged and acuminate. Laterals acute, sinuses shallow. Colour light green with pale green-yellow irregular central splash. Veins lighter but not prominent.

Hedera helix 'Pin Oak'

A useful ivy capable of making mounds of small-leaved ground cover or an equally good pot plant. The AIS Checklist of 1975 gave its origin as Merion, Philadelphia, from the nursery of Henry Faust Inc, and stated that it was first marketed in 1941. The same nursery introduced 'Pin Oak

Improved' at the Philadelphia Flower Show of 1942. In June 1976 Henri Schaepman, the then President of the AIS, described 'Itsy Bitsy' in the American Nurseryman and suggested that 'Pin Oak', 'Staghorn' and 'Ferney' were identical to it, citing Pierot's descriptions (1974). In fact as indicated above 'Pin Oak' is the earlier name.

The frequency with which 'Pin Oak' and 'Itsy Bitsy' arise as mutations on plants of 'Königer' suggest that 'Pin Oak', first recorded in 1941, arose from 'Königer' which was in circulation in 1935. 'Erin' is a clone that appears to be identical to 'Pin Oak'. Of the various stocks in circulation the following is probably representative. 1978/9: AM(T).

Habit: Self-branching.

Stems: Red-purple. Internodes 0.5–2cm (¼–¾in).

Petioles: Pink-green.

Leaves: 3-lobed, 1–2.5cm (⅓–1in) by 1–2cm (⅓–¾in). Centre lobe twice the length of lateral lobes. Apices acuminate, sinuses deep, leaf base truncate. Light-almost yellow-green in colour, veins not prominent.

Hedera helix 'Pittsburgh'

This short-jointed, small-leaved ivy was the first of the self-branching ivies. It is said to have originated between 1915–20 as a mutation from *H. helix* 'Hibernica' as it was then termed. It was introduced by Paul S Randolph of Verona, Pennsylvania, who marketed it in 1920.

Hedera helix 'Pittsburgh'

The assumption that it mutated from 'Hibernica' arose because Bates in 1932 showed that the bulk of ivy growing in North America was in fact 'Hibernica'. Since that time it has been shown that 'Hibernica' is a tetraploid which 'Pittsburgh' manifestly is not; I think therefore it more likely to have been a mutation from the ordinary *H. helix*. Mutations from time to time produce shoots that revert to their parents; those produced by 'Pittsburgh' do not resemble 'Hibernica' but are similar to the sharp-leaved-type of common ivy found wild in Britain.

'Pittsburgh' was the forerunner of a whole race of ivies in both America and Europe which Bates termed the 'ramosa' complex, recognized by their branching or ramulose habit and their generally thinner leaves compared with normal *helix* or indeed with other species.

The plant has been grown on a vast scale for the house-plant trade and although largely superseded by short-jointed clones such as 'Neilson' and 'Chicago', it has circulated under many names including 'Hahn Self-branching', 'Emerald Jewel', 'Ray's Supreme', 'Procumbens', 'Spitzberg' and 'Spitsbergii' as well as the Danish 'Sternevedbent'.

A clone called 'Rambler' is quoted as being a reverted form. 'Good's Self-branching' was a clone with slightly blunter and broader lobes.

A lightly variegated form, a very unstable clone, was introduced as 'Chrysanna'. 'Troll', a sport that is like a short-jointed version of 'Green Ripple', was introduced by Frode Maegaard in 1989.

In the RHS Trial of 1978/9 'Pittsburgh' received an HC reflecting its position among present-day cultivars but not the historic position of this clone.
Habit: Self-branching.
Stems: Green-purple. Internodes 1.5–2cm (⅝–¾in).
Petioles: Green-purple.
Leaves: 5-lobed, 3–5cm (1¼–2in) by 5–6cm (2–2⅓in). Apices acute, leaf base cordate, sinuses shallow. Leaf blade held at an angle parallel to the stem, giving a stem taken from the plant an elegant appearance. Medium-green, veins lighter.

Hedera helix 'Pittsburgh Variegated'
The variegated form of 'Pittsburgh', the first of the ramulose or self-branching ivies, arose on the nursery of W A Manda Inc of New Jersey in 1938. According to Bates in the National Horticultural Magazine in 1941 the stock was sold to Carl Hagenburger of West Los Angeles, California, who distributed it.

'Pittsburgh Variegated' became popular both in America and in Europe. Inherently variable and widely grown in both continents, variations soon occurred. Some of these such as 'Eva' and 'Fantasia' became very distinct clones. Other selections included 'Avon', which has large areas of emerald-green within the variegation and was introduced by Fibrex Nurseries in the early 1980s and 'Bodil', described by Mathias Jenny in 1954 as "Small leaves with cream margins, Danish and new". 'Denmark', 'Heise' and 'Heise Denmark No. 2' are all clones that rapidly supplanted the original and it is doubtful if that is still in circulation but the description below is of the plant as originally introduced.
Habit: Self-branching.
Stems: Green-purple. Internodes 1.5–2cm (⅝–¾in).
Petioles: Green-purple.
Leaves: 5-lobed, 2–4cm (¾–1½in) by 4–5cm (1½–2in). Apices sharply acute, leaf base cordate, sinuses shallow. Mid-green with cream-yellow variegation mostly towards the leaf edge.

Hedera helix 'Pixie'
There is something fern-like in this clone with its small, soft green, finely cut leaves. Often linked with the names 'Holly', 'Weber Californian' and 'Margaret'. In my opinion 'Holly' is synonymous with 'Parsley Crested'. 'Weber Californian' and 'Margaret' appear identical to 'Pixie'. The plant is best described as a miniature vining ivy since, although basically self-branching, it is capable of making long trails which, with its small leaves, make it very suitable for hanging baskets or elevated troughs.

A somewhat unstable mutation having curly and interestingly distorted leaves was discovered by Frank Batson of Woodburn, Oregon, in 1982. This miniature edition of 'Pixie' was registered (AIS Reg No 822783) as 'Lilliput'.
Habit: Miniature vining.
Stems: Slender, purple-green. Internodes 2–3.5cm (¾–1⅓in).
Petioles: Slender, purple-green.
Leaves: 5-lobed, often 2 additional but somewhat vestigial basal lobes, 2.5–4cm (1–1½in) by 2–3.5cm (¾–1⅓in). Lobes acuminate, centre lobe prolonged, sinuses narrow, slightly convoluted at the cleft. Leaf margin slightly crimped. Light green, veins lighter.

Hedera helix f. poetarum
Most ivies are grown for the beauty and interest of their juvenile leaves; the merits of this one however lie in its orange-coloured fruits. For this reason it is usually seen as a small shrub or 'tree ivy' having been propagated from adult arborescent growths.

The plant has a long history, for according to the *Natural History* of Pliny (AD 22–79),

> One kind has a black seed and another the colour of saffron, the latter is used by poets for their wreaths and its leaves are not so dark in colour.

As with so many ivies it has suffered name changes. The first description other than that of Pliny is by Richard Weston (1770). He listed five ivies, among them "*Hedera poetica baccis luteis* – yellow archipelagian ivy". In 1753 Linnaeus had published his *Genera Plantarum* initiating the binomial system of naming but the practice, as in this case, of names that were virtually mini-descriptions occasionally persisted. Some 50 years on from Weston the Rev Robert Walsh collected the plant near Constantinople; he gave it species status as *H. chrysocarpa*. In 1835 the Italian botanist Antonii Bertolonii discounted this as well as various older and rather doubtful names and published it in *Flora Italica* as *Hedera poetarum*. Hibberd (1872) maintained Walsh's name, *chrysocarpa*. In 1878 Carl Fredrik Nyman in *Conspectus Florae Europae* recognized it as a sub-species of *Hedera helix*, *H. helix* ssp. *poetarum*.

All these names, as well as 'Lucida', 'Baccifera Lutea' and 'Fructo-luteo', appeared in late-19th-century catalogues and publications. In 1942 Lawrence & Schulze followed Weston, calling it "var. *poetica*". In Bean's 8th Edition (1973) it became "var. *poetica*" in place of the *chrysocarpa* of previous editions and this epithet was adopted by Rose in *Ivies* (1981). In 1993 however, Dr McAllister included it in a note in The Plantsman entitled *New Ivies from the*

Mediterranean Area and Macaronesia, although in fact it is one of our oldest known ivies! Giving a brief description he downgraded it to 'forma', the lowest botanical status. This would seem to be the correct designation since the only differences between it and the common *H. helix* are berry colour and lighter green leaves.

Being accustomed to the black fruits of most arborescent ivies, the orange fruits of *poetarum* are of immediate interest, but some people comparing them with those of pyracantha or cotoneaster will find them dull. Pliny spoke of a "red berried ivy" as well as a "golden fruited ivy"; variations in fruit colour may exist and anyone studying the plant in its Eastern Mediterranean habitat might be able to select forms of varying fruit colour, including perhaps the white *leuco-carpa*, reputed to exist but so far as I can tell, never found.

The Lawson Seed & Nursery Company of Edinburgh and London in their 1871 and 1874/5 catalogues listed, without descriptions, 'Poetica Aurea' and 'Poetica Variegata'. There appears to be no other record of these and I have not seen or heard of a variegated poet's ivy. *Hedera helix* f *poetarum* is seldom seen now but was widely grown in Hibberd's day.

The plant appears to be native to Western Transcaucasia. It is certainly naturalized in Italy and elsewhere due no doubt to its use in mystic rites etc, (see page 12).
Habit: Vining.
Stems: Pink-purple to green. Internodes 4–5cm (1½–2in).
Petioles: Pink-purple to green.
Leaves: 5-lobed, 5–7cm (2–2¾in) by 3–8cm. The 2 basal lobes much reduced giving a rather 'square' leaf. Lobes broadly acute, centre lobe only slightly longer than laterals. Leaf base cordate, leaf has a slight tendency to upward-folding. Colour light- almost yellow-green. Petiole colouring often follows into the veins and is seen both above and below the leaf surface. Fruit as in the species but dull orange in colour.

Hedera helix 'Professor Friedrich Tobler'
This very distinctive clone was selected as a mutation from 'Star' by Hans Schmidt of Bockum-Hövel in Germany and introduced at the BUGA Show in Cologne in 1957. It is fittingly named after Professor Tobler (1879–1957), author and sometime Director of the Botanic Garden, Dresden.

The plant is unusual in that most of the leaves are split into three or five 'part leaves'. The plant is moderately vigorous and will throw long trails which make it very suitable for hanging baskets. It has circulated under various names including 'Dreizehn', 'Green Ripple', 'Pedley's Green Finger', 'Pointer', 'Tobler' and 'Weidenblattrig'.
Habit: Self-branching but throwing vining trails.

Stems: Red-brown. Internodes 1–3cm (⅓–1¼in), extending to 5cm (2in) on trails.
Petioles: Red-brown, up to 1cm (⅓in) but often so short that leaves appear to be sessile.
Leaves: Variably 3–5-lobed, but generally divided into 3 almost linear leaflet-like lobes, each with a minute sub-petiole. Central leaflet 2–4cm (¾–1½in) by 0.5–1cm (¼–⅓in). Subsidiary leaflets 1–3cm (⅓–1¼in) by 0.3–0.5cm (⅛–¼in). Leaflets have a strong centre vein. In some leaves leaflets are joined near the petiole junction making a more normal but deeply cut leaf. Medium-green with lighter green veins some tinged with red toward the petiole/leaf-blade junction.

Hedera helix 'Ralf'
Rounded lobes are the chief feature of this self-branching ivy. The clone was selected by Gebr Stauss. The plant's compact growth and neat foliage make it a useful pot plant. Suitable also for light ground cover it is sometimes incorrectly listed as 'Ralph'. Amsterdam Floriade 1974: Gold Medal.
Habit: Self-branching.
Stems: Purple-green. Internodes 1–2cm (⅓–¾in).
Petioles: Green-purple.
Leaves: Generally 3-lobed with rarely 2 additional small basal lobes; 2.5–4cm (1–1½in) by 3–4cm (1¼–1½in). Lobes rounded, sinuses shallow. Leaf base deeply cordate. Light green; veins not pronounced. In outdoor situations or under stress the primary veins take on a purple colouration.

Hedera helix 'Ritterkreuz'
This clone was a sport from 'Perfection' and arose at the Neuburg Monastery. The leaf lobes are arranged in such a manner as to present a Maltese Cross, to which the German clonal name translates. A suitable climber for low walls. AIS Reg No 81, 1981
Habit: Self-branching with trails.
Stems: Green-purple. Internodes 1–2cm (⅓–¾in).
Petioles: Green-purple.
Leaves: 5-lobed 3–4cm (1¼–1½in) by 3–5cm (1¼–2in). The two basal lobes generally back-pointing, the lobes virtually acuminate triangles, sinuses deep sometimes almost to the mid-rib. The 2 lateral lobes at right angles give the leaf its almost 'Maltese Cross' shape. Colour mid-green.

Hedera helix 'Romanze'
This decorative ivy is an interesting selection from 'Luzii' made by Brother Heieck and named by him in 1979. The

curly leaves resemble 'Manda's Crested' but have a discreet mottle within the apple-green colouring. This combined with the more than usually numerous *helix*-type hairs on the leaf surface give the leaf a velvety appearance.

While 'Romanze' is a first-rate ivy for pot-plant work, it is not suitable for use outside.

Habit: Self-branching.

Stems: Pink-green. Internodes 1.5–2.5cm (⅝–1in).

Petioles: Pink-green. Tend to be long, 5–8cm (2–3in).

Leaves: 5-lobed, 3–5cm (1¼–2in) by 4–5cm (1½–2in). Margin waved, convoluted at the sinus cleft. Centre lobe down-pointing, basal lobes auriculate so that the petiole appears to be at the leaf centre. Leaves so waved and curled that lobing is indistinct. Light apple-green with slightly darker green mottle.

Hedera helix 'Rüsche'

One of several almost bizarre ivies that have appeared in recent years, 'Rüsche' was selected in 1968 from the clone 'Professor Friedrich Tobler' by Brother Heieck. The name has a link with the English 'ruche' meaning a ruffle and the French *'ruche'* or frilling. It well describes the frilled collar effect of the leaves which tend to clasp and surround the stem at the nodes.

The plant is fast growing and throws long trails making it suitable for hanging baskets. It has proved hardy in Britain but is probably seen to best effect indoors.

Habit: Vining, fast growing.

Stems: Green to brown-purple. Extending to make long trails. Internodes 2–5cm (¾–2in).

Petioles: Wine-red, maximum length 2cm (¾in) but often non-existent.

Leaves: Basically 5-lobed, but often tri-sectional because of the deep sinuses that sometimes divide the leaf. Lobes wedge-shaped, the acute tip often down-pointing. The division of the leaf and twist of the lobes often make it appear to clasp the stem. Colour mid-green, veins lighter with a touch of red at the petiole/leaf-blade junction.

Hedera helix 'Russelliana'

Appropriately called the candelabra ivy this erect, non-climbing clone maintains from the cutting stage a single stem for a year or so but when about 60cm (2ft) high, one or more of the lateral buds becomes active and grows upwards to almost equal the leading shoot. This process continues, producing a candelabra effect. Although the stem becomes woody and the plant may achieve 1.5–1.8m (5–6ft) it is unable to stand erect without a supporting stake and left to

itself will flop on the ground, the side branches continuing to grow upwards. It is the ultimate example of the fastigiate non-climbing ivy. The leaves' two-ranked arrangement enhances the curious but interesting aspect of the plant.

I have not been able to trace the origin of this clone but its existence before World War II was confirmed to me by the late Mr John Russell. It was lost until re-discovered by Taffler in a neglected estate garden growing to an extreme height among close undergrowth.

With little or no garden value it is very much, in the words of the old garden books, "for the gardens of the curious".

Habit: Non-climbing, erect and fastigiate.

Stems: Short-jointed. Internodes 0.5–1cm (¼–⅓in).

Petioles: Light green.

Leaves: Unlobed, 3–4cm (1¼–1½in) by 3–6cm (1¼–2⅓in), ovate to reniform, distichous. Leaf margins slightly waved in young leaves. Texture leathery, leaf base cordate. Lateral shoots develop to equal the leading shoot in candelabra fashion. Colour dark green.

Hedera helix 'Russell's Gold'

In leaf colouring this clone is similar to 'Buttercup' but certainly pre-dates it in the literature. It was listed, although not described, in the 1908 catalogue of L R Russell Ltd and was listed thereafter by numerous nurseries.

The 1932 Russell catalogue described it as "small leaf, entirely gold". In the 1920s it had been planted on the Ivy Wall at Kew. In 1949 the late Dr H Eggins, a relative of the Russell family, procured cuttings and established the plant in his garden.

Fortunately it had also been resurrected from another source, Stephen Taffler in the company of Jack Townsend discovered in a neglected garden an ivy which the late Mr John Russell identified as 'Russell's Gold' commenting hat it had similar colouring to 'Buttercup' but a smaller leaf. The clones are certainly similar and bearing in mind that the yellowish leaf colouration is perpetuated by seed it would seem quite possible that 'Buttercup', 'Gold Cloud' and indeed 'Limey', a slight variant recently recorded from the USA, may have common ancestry as seedlings from 'Russell's Gold'.

As a garden plant it is not as good as 'Buttercup', although possibly it serves the same purposes.

Habit: Vining.

Stems: Green-purple. Internodes 2–3cm (¾–1¼in).

Petioles: Green-purple.

Leaves: 5-lobed, 3–6cm (1¼–2⅓in) by 4–7cm. Apices acute, leaf base cordate, sinuses shallow. Young leaves light yellow-green, mature leaves mid-green.

Hedera helix 'Sagittifolia'

This name illustrates the confusion surrounding ivy nomenclature. Hibberd (1872) described a plant which was fairly widely grown at the time as follows:

> Arrow leaved ivy, quite distinct and interesting. In growth free and wiry, running far and filling up slowly. Leaves usually bluntly three-lobed, the centre lobe projecting forward in the form of a letter V. The colour is dull dark green with a few patches of blackish bronze which change in autumn to a rich purple bronze. The principal veins are lighter green in colour and slightly raised above the surface.

A shortened version of this accurate description was repeated by Bean (1914). Confusion has arisen because the same name has been applied, in error, to a small-leaved self-branching ivy. It seems likely that in the late 1940s when this arrowhead ivy made its appearance, nurserymen turned to Bean and without too much thought called it 'Sagittifolia'. The name would have seemed appropriate and this useful ivy is still extensively grown for the pot-plant trade.

The original 'Sagittifolia' is a moderate-growing, rather open plant, a useful darker variation of the common ivy suitable for walls and trees but not as ground cover. It is available from specialist ivy nurseries. Until recently the plant existed only in a few large gardens and public parks where 19th- and early-20th-century plantings have remained undisturbed.

A Swiss clone 'Helvetica' sometimes called 'Helvetia' has been suggested by the Swiss Professor Mathias Jenny and the Dutch Dr Nannenga-Bremekamp as being very near and probably identical to 'Sagittifolia'.

Habit: Vining.
Stems: Dark green-purple. Internodes 3–3.5cm (1¼–1⅓in).
Petioles: Green-purple.
Leaves: Sagittate in outline, 3-lobed, 3–5cm (1¼–2in) by 4–6cm (1½–2⅓in). Centre lobe prolonged, laterals short and blunt forming the wings of the arrow and often overlapping at the base. Basal lobes vestigial, veins not prominent.

Hedera helix 'Sagittifolia Variegata'

An excellent self-branching ivy having small 'bird's foot'-type leaves. It is not, as might be thought, a variegated form of the true 'Sagittifolia'. That name, given by Hibberd (1872), has in recent years been used to describe a self-branching clone more akin to 'Königer' than to the plant of Hibberd. Accordingly, when a variegated form appeared it was understandable that it should be named and described as 'Sagittifolia Variegata'. This name and description was published by van de Laar (1965) and later by Nannenga-Bremekamp (1970). Comparison with 'Königer's Variegated' shows it to be the same plant, however 'Königer's Variegated' has not been published as a name, and certainly not prior to 1965; accordingly 'Sagittifolia Variegata' stands, although the plant bears no resemblance to the true 'Sagittifolia' (see above).

This ivy is a charmer and a fine plant for troughs, hanging baskets and as a pot plant. Outside it will drop some leaves in a hard British winter but seems to survive frost better than many variegated clones and can be used on low walls and as gentle ground cover on rock gardens. RHS Ivy Trial 1978/9: HC(T). A particularly good variation named 'Blodwen' arose in 1984 on the nursery of Whitehouse Ivies. In 1985 Conifers Nursery of Woking, Surrey, introduced a clone with a substantial amount of yellow leafage that in 1986 received an RHS PC as 'Light Fingers'.

Habit: Self-branching and close growing.
Stems: Green-purple. Internodes 0.25–1cm (⅒–⅓in).
Petioles: Green-purple, generally short.
Leaves: 3-lobed and small: 2–2.5cm (¾–1in) by 2–3cm (¾–1¼in). 2 basal lobes vestigial or, where present, back-pointing. Lobes acuminate, centre lobe prolonged to twice the length of lateral lobes. Central portion grey-green, irregular border of cream-white. Veins light green, those of the lateral lobes often make a right angle with the centre vein.

Hedera helix 'Sally'

This clone originated on Whitehouse Nurseries in 1980; the name honours the wife of the owner, Ron Whitehouse. It is very similar to both 'Sinclair Silverleaf' and 'Trinity'; generally however 'Sally' is a better grower than either of the others and with a higher proportion of truly variegated leaves is a more attractive plant. It is at its best as a house-plant ivy.

Habit: Self-branching.
Stems: Purple-green. Internodes 1–2cm (⅓–¾in).
Petioles: Green-purple.
Leaves: 3-lobed, 3–5cm (1¼–2in) by 4–6cm (1½–2⅓in). Leaf base strongly cordate creating the impression of a 5-lobed leaf. Centre lobe apex acute, lateral lobes bluntly acute. Basic colour mid-green, some leaves with suffused cream variegation, others flecked and splashed cream, yet others wholly green. A proportion of leaves all cream, the veins remaining green.

Hedera helix 'Sark'

Vigour, completely green stems and glossy dark green leaves make 'Sark' a useful wall covering ivy. The material circulating in Britain is from an introduction from the island by Mr and Mrs W Roxburgh: they passed material to the ivy enthusiast Miss Alison Rutherford who recognized its potential and ensured its distribution.

Habit: Vining.

Stems: Green. Internodes 2–4cm (¾–1½in).

Petioles: Green.

Leaves: 3-lobed, sinuses so shallow as to make an unlobed deltoid 6–10cm (2⅓–4in) by 8–10cm (3–4in). Leaf base strongly cordate, lobes sometimes overlapping. Dark green, the upper surface glossy, under surface mid-green and matt. Veins light but not prominent.

Hedera helix 'Schäfer Three'

This clone had its genesis in 1949 when the German nurseryman Emil Schäfer of Stuttgart-Vaihingen noted and propagated a mutation on a plant of 'Merion Beauty'. He sold it, largely within the trade, as 'Typ. Schäfer I'. A short-jointed clone, the five-lobed leaves were grey-green with broken white variegation. In 1960 he selected an improved

Hedera helix 'Schäfer Three'

version, 'Typ. Schäfer II'. This had more irregular lobing, a leaf base that was cordate tending to truncate, the basal lobes vestigial or missing, the variegation similar to Typ. I but with a noticeably prominent centre vein. In 1974 this was totally eclipsed by his introduction of 'Typ. Schäfer III'. This has similar but more sharply defined green areas. More importantly for the trade it was vigorous and propagated well. The wholesale house-plant trade has little use for names and it became universally known as 'Typ. Schäfer III'. From a taxonomic point of view this was unsatisfactory so the widely used name was given official sanction as 'Schäfer Three' and published with an appropriate description in the BIS Journal (Vol 5, No 2, 1982).

In 1981 Stephen Taffler spotted in Jerusalem an ivy that was new to him. He brought a piece home and named it 'Jerusalem', under this name it was sold by various nurseries until its subsequent identification as 'Schäfer Three'.

Although widely grown in Europe it was not known to have circulated in America and it was perhaps unfortunate that an identical plant was registered by the AIS in 1984 (No 820384) as 'Calico'. The American plant first appeared as 'Vick's Variegated' and 'Vick's Hybrid' and was reported to

have been found in 1975. This suggests that it may have been a sport from a plant of 'Typ. Schäfer III' brought into the country in the early 1970s. Authorities in America compared 'Calico' with 'Kolibri'. Certainly all the Schäfer clones are similar to 'Kolibri' which was a mutation from 'Ingrid', itself a break from 'Merion Beauty', so both clones have a common source.

A clone having a prolonged centre lobe and sometimes known as 'Blank Elise' has been registered as 'Lady Frances'. A sport named 'Schimmer' having bluish dark-green leaves was selected from 'Schäfer I' by Brother Heieck in Heidelberg in 1980.

The inherent instability of Schäfer mutations has led to the emergence of slightly different clones. These differ mainly in the amount of white variegation present. A 'Typ. Schäfer IV' has circulated, a clone of lighter green, slightly broader leaves but similar variegation.

Habit: Short-jointed.
Stems: Purple-green. Internodes 1–1.5cm (⅓–⅝in).
Petioles: Purple-green.
Leaves: Basically 3-lobed, 2–4cm (¾–1½in) by 3–4cm (1¼–1½in). Sinuses non-existent or so shallow as to give a high proportion of unlobed triangular leaves. Apices acute, leaf base truncate to slightly cordate. Basic colour dark green with areas of grey-green irregularly splashed cream-white variegation.

Hedera helix 'Scutifolia'

The first record of this clone is in Hibberd's *The Ivy* (1872) where it is described as having rounded, triangular, sometimes three-lobed leaves; he gave 'Cordata' as a synonym.

From 1872 onwards it was catalogued, described usually as shield-shaped, by many nurseries. In 1942 Lawrence and Schulze recorded it as three- to five-lobed, ovate, lobes not prominent, leaf base strongly cordate.

In America Shippy (1950) noted it as three- to five-lobed, shield-shaped, dull green sometimes listed as 'Lucida'. Leonie Bell (Morris Arboretum Bulletin, September 1968 in *The Beauty of Hardy Ivy* illustrated both 'Scutifolia' and 'Sagittifolia'; they are not dissimilar but the former has a more rounded and broader leaf.

In habit and indeed in use 'Scutifolia' is similar to ordinary *helix*. It is now seldom offered in Britain.

Habit: Vining.
Stems: Purple. Internodes 4–5cm (1½–2in).
Petioles: Green-purple.
Leaves: Basically 3-lobed but lobes more usually missing to give a roundish triangular leaf 4–6cm (1½–2⅓in) by 7–8cm (2¾–3in). Colour dark green.

Hedera helix 'Shamrock'

This, the clover leaf ivy, may well have been a mutation from 'Green Feather' to which it bears some resemblance. Indeed Nannenga-Bremekamp (1970) places it in the 'Green Feather' group. Very distinct in leaf form, it was introduced from the USA into Holland in 1954 and thence to the rest of Europe, becoming a popular house plant for which purpose it is excellent. Sufficiently self-branching to be used for topiary, it throws short trails making it suitable for hanging baskets or moss-sticks. Reasonably hardy but best as an indoor plant. A form with slightly broader leaves was recorded as 'Shannon' by Pierot (1974). A variation with slightly asymmetrical leaves was introduced as 'Wichtel' by Heieck in 1982, from this he had earlier selected a miniature form 'Kobold'. A variegated form 'Tussie Mussie' arose in the USA and was named in 1984. A lime-green-leaved mutation was introduced by Maegaard in 1983 as 'Golden Shamrock' but later named as 'Golden Envoy'. 'Emerald Globe' has been quoted as being a fasciated form of 'Shamrock'. RHS 1978/9: HC(T); 1993: ♀.

Habit: Self-branching with short trails.
Stems: Green-purple. Internodes 1cm (⅓in).
Petioles: Green-purple.
Leaves: 3-lobed, centre lobe broad wedge-shaped. 2.5–3.5cm (1–1⅓in) by 2–3cm (¾–1¼in). Apices blunt, often rounded. Sinuses shallow but in some leaves split to the centre vein giving a 3-leaved effect. Lateral lobes sometimes folded in pleated fashion alongside the centre lobe. Colour dark green with a trace of lighter green along the veins. The purple of the petiole often extending 0.5–1cm (¼–⅓in) into the lower part of the centre and/or lateral veins on the upper side.

Hedera helix 'Sinclair Silverleaf'

Reputedly a sport of 'Merion Beauty' this is a short-jointed clone whose small leaves display a range of variegation. The young leaves emerge pale cream-yellow; some remain that colour, others gradually become light green while yet others assume a faint green mottle, so fine that it is like a green smudge. A compact, colourful and useful pot ivy. Not recommended for outside.

Habit: Self-branching, compact.
Stems: Purple-pink. Internodes 0.25–1cm (⅒–⅓in).
Petioles: Green.
Leaves: 3-lobed, 1.5–3cm (⅝–1¼in) by 2–3cm (¾–1¼in). Centre lobe wedge-shaped. Sinuses shallow, leaf base truncate to slightly cordate. Colour cream-yellow, mottled light green in varying degrees, some leaves entirely green. Veins cream to light green, not pronounced.

Hedera helix 'Spear Point'

Hedera helix 'Spear Point'

This mutation seems to have been in circulation for some years before 1965 when described by van de Laar. He recorded that it came from the Morris Arboretum in 1960. It seems probable that it was an improved version of the clone 'Long Point' which originated on the nursery of W A Manda inc, South Orange, New Jersey and was named, described and illustrated by Bates in his series on ivies in the American National Horticultural Magazine 1932–42. Bates' description was of a three-lobed ivy, centre lobe twice as long as the laterals, leaf base cuneate. The description of 'Spear Point' is similar: it bears some resemblance to 'Green Feather' from which it may have mutated. 'Spear Point' has also circulated under the synonyms 'Green Spear' and 'Pencil Point'.

A useful, quick growing house-plant ivy, often showing considerable variation.

Habit: Short-jointed.

Stems: Green-purple. Internodes 1.5–2cm (⅝–¾in).

Petioles: Green-purple.

Leaves: 3-lobed, 4–6cm (1½–2⅓in) by 4–5cm (1½–2in). Centre lobe prolonged, apices acuminate, leaf base cuneate, colour mid-green.

Hedera helix 'Spectre'

Aptly named, this clone with its long, almost claw-like leaves with streaked yellow variegation has an almost spectral appearance. Its origin is uncertain but its introduction to Britain is attributed to Taffler. It does not appear to have been named until listed as 'The Spectre' by Hazel Key in the Fibrex Nurseries' 1979 catalogue. The ICNCP proscribes the use of 'A' and 'The' so the name properly becomes 'Spectre'.

It is the mildly variegated form of 'Triton' and whilst essentially an indoor ivy can, like that clone, provide interesting ground cover for small areas.

Habit: Branching and sprawling with no climbing characteristics.

Stems: Purple-green, twisting and slightly zig-zag, non-climbing, hairs few and scattered. Internodes 1–2cm (⅓–¾in).

Petioles: Wine-red, often twisted.

Leaves: 3–5-lobed, 5–7cm (2–2¾in) by 2–4cm (¾–1½in). Sinuses deep and narrow, some leaves divided almost to the petiole. Lobes curled and twisted with the acuminate tips curling downward. Mid-green streaked with faint yellow. Veins prominent, fanning in parallel fashion from the petiole/leaf-blade junction.

Hedera helix 'Spetchley'

The botanical epithets minor and minima, had they not been applied in the past, mostly incorrectly, to various ivies, would certainly fit this plant whose leaves can justly claim to be the smallest. Because of this past confusion it seems better to adopt a purely vernacular name. The plant's origin is obscure; it was certainly growing in 1962 in the gardens of Spetchley Park, near Evesham in Worcestershire. Although subsequently lost, material originating from Spetchley worked its way into a limited circulation. Material was passed to America in the 1970s when it became known as 'Gnome', but prior to the publication of this name investigation in Britain had revealed the plant's long association with Spetchley Park and the Spetchley name published.

I have been unable to ascertain the origin of 'Spetchley' but various collections of H. helix made on the island of Crete are similar, such as 'Cretan Gorge' collected by D B Roxburgh in 1980. Various small-leaved clones appear from time to time, one such is that collected in 1974 by N & J Rutherford in the Province of Huelva, Spain. McAllister, Rutherford & Mill (The Plantsman, Vol 15, pt 2, 1993) proposed it as a helix sub-species, rhizomatifera, but it is very doubtful if it deserves anything more than forma status.

An interesting and very useful plant with age it sometimes throws a few normal-sized leaves. These should be removed, almost in the fashion of bonsai gardening, to preserve its miniature character. An excellent ivy for small rock gardens as rock cover, limited ground cover or indeed as a bonsai ivy. 1993: ♛.

Habit: Dwarf vining.
Stems: Purple. Internodes 0.5–1.5cm (¼–⅝in).
Petioles: Purple.
Leaves: Remotely 3-lobed, 0.5–2cm (¼–¾in) by 0.5–1.5cm (¼–⅝in). Variable from 3-lobed with the centre lobe prolonged to just a single elliptic or triangular lobe. Blade slightly canaliculate. Dark green; due to the small leaf size the centre vein seems prominent and the leaf texture thicker than it is. Occasional 'off-type' shoots have internodes 1.5–2cm (⅝–¾in) and leaves 2–3cm (¾–1¼in) by 2.5–3cm (1–1¼in).

Hedera helix 'Spinozia'

A self-branching ivy not dissimilar to 'Alt Heidelberg'. The first reference to the name is Pierot's in 1974. It would appear to have been the same plant as that listed by Whitehouse Nurseries in 1989 and by the American Nursery, Hedera Etc, in 1995 as 'Spinosa'. In her description Pierot pointed out that it looked more like a bonsai shrub than an ivy. It certainly has a shrubby habit and leaves that are variable in size and shape. It is not widely grown in Europe.
Habit: Self-branching and slightly upright.
Stems: Green-purple. Internodes 0.5–2cm (¼–¾in).
Petioles: Green-purple.
Leaves: Unlobed, older leaves occasionally show a 3-lobed pattern, 0.5–2cm (¼–¾in) by 0.5–2cm (¼–¾in). Bluntly acute, leaf base cuneate, leaves sometimes fan-shaped. Colour light green.

Hedera helix 'Star'

First recorded by Shippy in the American Flower Grower Vol 38, 1951. She recorded it as having come from Louis Hahn & Son of Pittsburgh, Pennsylvania and noted its slender growth and five-lobed star-like leaves.

It appears to have been imported into Europe by Hage & Co of Boskoop in 1950, presumably from Hahn & Son and before it was noted by Shippy. Since that time it seems to have merged into what might be termed the 'Königer' group and is no longer seen as a distinct clone. But it has given numerous interesting mutations, among them 'Gavotte', 'Goldstern', 'Green Finger' and 'Professor Friedrich Tobler'. 'Galaxy' is a form of 'Star' reputed in the USA to be hardier.
Habit: Self-branching.
Stems: Green-purple. Internodes 2–4cm (¾–1½in).
Petioles: Green-purple.
Leaves: 5-lobed, 4–6cm (1½–2⅓in) by 6–8cm (2⅓–3in). Basal lobes slightly back-pointing giving a modified 'bird's foot' effect. Apices acute, leaf base cordate, dark green.

Hedera helix 'Stift Neuburg'

This fascinating ivy was selected by Brother Ingobert Heieck at Neuburg Monastery, Heidelberg, Germany in 1962 from the clone 'Bruder Ingobert', also raised there.

Essentially a house-plant ivy, it has proved hardy outside in Britain, surviving -9°C (16°F). It is an interesting variety for the enthusiast with its sharply variegated white and light-green, crinkled, round leaves and pink stems. Too slow growing for commercial use it is also prone to infestation by Red Spider Mite. When grown outside the leaves become a much darker green but the clone is not a good outside ivy.
Habit: Short-jointed with trails.
Stems: Pink to red-purple. Stiff, initially elevated from the plant until extended growth brings them to soil level.
Petioles: Pink-purple.
Leaves: Orbiculate, 2–3cm (¾–1¼in) by 4–5cm (1½–2in). Leaf margin irregularly undulated, the vestigial lobes showing as indentations. Leaf blade wrinkled and undulating, leaf base cordate. Colour bright green with

PLATE VIII

All plants are shown at approximately ³/₄ size

H. helix 'Duckfoot'

H. helix 'Ursula'

H. helix 'Perle'

H. helix 'Perkeo'

H. helix 'Telecurl'

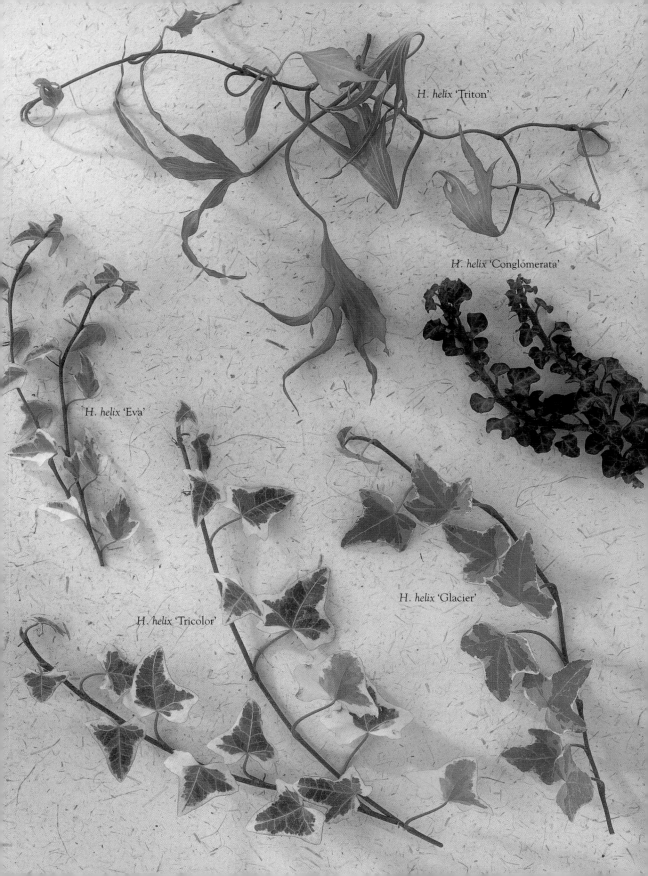

H. helix 'Triton'

H. helix 'Conglomerata'

H. helix 'Eva'

H. helix 'Glacier'

H. helix 'Tricolor'

substantial areas of clear white, mostly at leaf centre. Veins white or light green, slightly pink in winter.

Hedera helix 'Sub-marginata'

Nursery catalogues of the 19th century show something like 24 clones of 'Marginata' to have been in circulation. It is not easy to reconcile some of those we have today with those of the past but this clone is readily identified by Hibberd's description (1872) of the spoon-like leaves of bluish-green, irregularly variegated at the margin.

Hibberd listed five synonyms, 'Marginata Major', 'Rhombea Variegata', 'Rhomboidea Japonica', 'Japonica Variegata' and 'New Japanese'; the last four applicable to the Japanese ivy but indicative of the confusion then prevailing over that plant (see p134).

Slow growing, 'Sub-marginata' is occasionally seen as an old plant but if more widely available it might be appreciated for the quiet singularity of the modest wall coverage achieved by its small, pendent, spoon-shaped leaves. A possible choice for the larger rock garden, either to clad rocks or to act as ground cover beneath small bulbs.

Habit: Vining.
Stems: Green. Internodes 1.5–2cm (⅝–¾in).
Petioles: Green.
Leaves: Unlobed, 2–4cm (¾–1½in) by 2–4cm (¾–1½in). Occasional vestigial lobes. Deltoid-elliptical, sometimes showing an apex reduced to a small acuminate protrusion. Leaf base cuneate, colour a bluish grey-green with grey-cream variegation and a barely discernible variegated leaf edge on most but not all leaves, this causing the typical spoon-like concavity.

Hedera helix 'Succinata'

Described by Hibberd (1872) and catalogued by various nurserymen including in 1885 Turner of Slough, *H. helix* 'Succinata' disappeared from lists and apparently from cultivation in the post-1914 era. There is however evidence that it persisted on the nursery of L R Russell Ltd, although not catalogued by them, and also in Holland where it may on some nurseries have become confused with 'Buttercup'.

Hibberd described the clone as "richly mottled with amber and pale green". The mottled variegation is similar to that of 'Angularis Aurea' and 'Mrs Pollock'. It is less striking than either of those clones and like those clones requires full sun for development of its variegation. RHS Ivy Trial 1888: Award.

Habit: Vining.
Stems: Purple. Internodes 4–6cm (1½–2⅓in).
Petioles: Purple.
Leaves: 3-lobed, 3.5–4cm (1⅓–1½in) 4–5cm (1½–2in). Sinuses generally so shallow as to present an almost triangular leaf. Apices bluntly acute, leaf base cordate. Dark green, individual leaves mottled pale yellow, in some cases this colours the entire leaf.

Hedera helix 'Sylvanian'

This clone is reported to have arisen in the USA, imported into Holland in 1935 and subsequently back into the USA where it was grown by Sylvan Hahn of Pittsburgh, Pennsylvania, initially as 'Sylvan Beauty' but in 1940 Plant Patented by him as 'Sylvanian' (No 430).

With 'Brokamp' and 'Gavotte' this clone completes a trio of what have been termed 'willow-leaved' ivies. In any of these three, slim willow-like leaves are occasionally formed but 'Sylvanian' is perhaps more noteworthy for its asymmetrical leaves which often have a single lateral lobe protruding as it were at right angles to the centre lobe.

Its favourite use is for hanging baskets.

Habit: Vining with trails, occasionally self-branching.
Stems: Green-purple. Internodes 1–2.5cm (⅓–1in).
Petioles: Green; long at 4–6cm (1½–2⅓in).
Leaves: Unlobed, 6–8cm (2⅓–3in) by 5–6cm (2–2⅓in). Asymmetrical with often a broad basal lobe to the left or right, rarely 3-lobed. Apices bluntly acute, leaf base cordate. Colour mid-green.

Hedera helix 'Symmetry'

At a distance this appears to be an ordinary green ivy, closer examination reveals the very elegant and symmetrical outline of the leaves and the minute teeth on the leaf edge of young leaves.

More suited as a house-plant ivy where the leaf shape can be appreciated, it does however throw out sufficient trails to make it suitable as ground cover. The leaves readily adopt a coppery tint with the onset of cold weather. It was selected from 'Pittsburgh' at the Whitehouse Ivy Nursery in 1989.

Habit: Self-branching with trails.
Stems: Green-purple. Internodes 2–3cm (¾–1¼in).
Petioles: Green-purple.
Leaves: 5-lobed, 4–5cm (1½–2in) by 5–6cm (2–2⅓in). Apex of the centre lobe acuminate, those of the lateral lobes acute. Sinuses shallow with a slight curl at the cleft, leaf base cordate. Leaf edges of young leaves bear fine, almost hair-like teeth. Colour mid-green.

Hedera helix 'Tanja'

Sometimes listed as a clone of *H. caucasigena*, a species described in Vol 16 of the *Flora of the USSR* (1950), this species has been 'sunk' into *H. helix* by many botanists. The hair structure is identical to that of *helix*, indeed the description in the Flora shows that only slight flower details such as the size of the umbels could separate it from *helix*.

The clone recorded here was collected by Mr Zwijnenburg of the Dutch nursery company P G Zwijnenburg in 1979 in the Sukhoms district of the Caucasus and named to honour the Russian guide of the trip. It is hardy and a good ground-cover ivy.

Habit: Vining.

Stems: Purple-green.

Petioles: Purple-green.

Leaves: 3-lobed. 7–9cm (2¾–3½in) by 4–6cm (1½–2⅓in). Centre lobe extended, the two lateral lobes about ¼ the length of the centre lobe. Colour dark green.

Hedera helix 'Telecurl'

This appears to be similar to 'Little Picture' described and figured by van de Laar in 1965 as derived from 'Curlilocks' but it is sometimes distributed under the invalid name of 'Nana'.

Shippy in the American Flower Grower (37-11, 1950) stated that 'Telecurl' was discovered as a sport of 'Ideal' and introduced by the wholesale florist Keith E Williams of Springfield, Ohio, in 1950. 'Telecurl' was noted by Lawrence in 1956, the name therefore pre-dates that of van de Laar and becomes the correct name.

The convolute and deeply folded bright-green leaves make this an excellent pot plant and it throws out sufficient trails to be suitable for hanging baskets. Pierot (1974) says that it can be grown outdoors south of New York.

Habit: Self-branching with short trails.

Stems: Green-purple. Internodes 1.5–2.5cm (⅝–1in).

Petioles: Green-purple.

Leaves: 5-lobed, acuminate, 2–3cm (¾–1¼in) by 3.5–4cm (1⅓–1½in). Sinuses narrow, leaf blade curling upwards at the cleft. Apex of centre lobe often down-pointing. Leaf blade folded upwards from mid rib. Bright green, veins fairly pronounced with some red colouration in winter at petiole/leaf-blade junction.

Hedera helix 'Tess'

From time to time ivies have appeared that have veins lighter in colour than is normal. People acquiring such ivies and casting around for a name have, perhaps not unreasonably, alighted on *H. helix* 'Tesselata' (RHS, 1895: AM). This was a strongly veined ivy found by a Victorian gardener Miss Browning-Hall in 1892 in Algiers. The Garden in its 1894 issue said "This is a distinct and prettily variegated ivy whose three-lobed leaves are reticulated with yellow after the manner of the Japanese *Lonicera brachypoda aurea-reticulata*. In appearance a form of the common ivy." Despite the fact that it had received a prestigious award, nothing more was heard of it. The answer probably lies in the repeated comparisons made at the time with the variegated Japanese Honeysuckle whose variegation is of virus origin and it is virtually certain that the Committee was looking at an ivy temporarily infected with virus.

Of the clones to which the name 'Tesselata' has been ascribed this one, found by Taffler in a garden in southern France, is particularly distinct. It was being marketed in the USA and Britain as 'Tesselata' but comparison with the early descriptions of that clone, the illustration and the herbarium specimen at Kew showed it was not the original. When the Whitehouse Ivies of Essex, UK, were persuaded of this they hit on the happy idea of naming it 'Tess'.

Virus-induced vein clearing as seen in the honeysuckle, *Lonicera brachypoda aurea-reticulata* affects the complete network of leaf veins so that they stand out brightly yellow. The vein clearing in 'Tess' is less dramatic: highly visible in the younger stages of growth it tends to lessen on older growth and in shade.

The plant's habit of growth and vigour is the same as *H. helix* and for the garden it can be recommended as a more decorative form for situations where the ordinary ivy was intended.

Habit: Vining.

Stems: Purple-brown. Internodes 2–3cm (¾–1¼in).

Petioles: Purple-brown.

Leaves: 3-lobed, 4–6cm (1½–2⅓in) by 4–7cm. Sinuses shallow, apices bluntly acute, leaf base slightly cordate. Dark green with veins distinctly white and yellow in young growth.

Hedera helix 'Thorndale'

The much-lauded trait of this clone is its hardiness. Introduced by Thorndale Farm Nursery of Woodstock, Illinois in the late 1940s it was reported by William Weers, the owner, to have survived a temperature drop of "31°F below zero (-17°C) here in Woodstock." The firm catalogued the clone as 'Thorndale Sub Zero' and recorded that it was a descendant of a remarkable parent plant that had withstood 25 Chicago winters (since around 1929) without protection.

It is a favourite ground-cover ivy in the mid-west. Thorndale Farm Nursery is no longer in existence but the ivy was described by the AIS Registrar in the Society's Journal (Vol 18, 1992). Another clone occasionally distributed, 'Alaska',

Hedera helix 'Tricolor'

Hedera helix 'Trinity'

is identical; 'Edison', circulating in the early 1970s, was a similar clone with slightly larger leaves and reputedly hardy.
Habit: Vining.
Stems: Purple-green. Internodes 5–7cm (2–2¾in).
Petioles: Purple-green.
Leaves: 5-lobed, 5–7cm (2–2¾in) by 6–8cm (2⅓–3in), basal lobes often vestigial giving a triangular-shaped leaf, apices bluntly acute, leaf base cordate. Veins light coloured becoming white in winter. Colour dark green.

Hedera helix 'Treetop'

Arborescent forms of 'Pittsburgh' have occurred from time but this one is unique in that it roots extremely easily. This is unusual: most arborescent ivies are slow and difficult to root.

The clone originated from an English ivy climbing a large pine tree near North Carolina State University. Cuttings were taken and provided stock plants at Johnson Nursery Corp, Williard, North Carolina. A description by Davis, Bilderback and Fantz was published in Horticultural Science 27(3) pp279–80, 1992. The article gives the impression of the clone being an arborescent form of *helix* in which case the name 'Treetop' would be invalid because the

arborescent form of *helix* was published as *H. helix* 'Arborescens' as long ago as 1838. However when the clone was presented to the AIS for registration (No 910292) Dr Sulgrove recognized it as an adult form of 'Pittsburgh' for which the name 'Treetop' is valid.

The clone easily makes a small, flowering, pot ivy.
Habit: Shrubby.
Stems: Green. Internodes 2–3cm (¾–1¼in).
Petioles: Green.
Leaves: Unlobed, ovate or elliptic, apices acute, leaf base truncate or slightly cuneate, 5–6cm (2–2⅓in) by 4–6cm (1½–2⅓in), medium green. Flowers borne on a panicle of small globose umbels.

Hedera helix 'Très Coupé'

This clone was introduced into Britain from France. The story goes that the plantsman Mr Maurice Mason, in company with the French nurseryman Roger de Vilmorin, called in the early 1960s at the Windlesham nursery of L R Russell Ltd. Discussing plants with Mr John Russell, M Vilmorin gave him an ivy plant which he said was popular in France. Accepting the generously offered plant Mr Russell asked its name, "*Je ne sais pas*," replied M Vilmorin, "*il est très coupé*," and 'Très Coupé' it became. It was introduced to the trade by L R Russell in 1968.

The name describes the clone well, but care is essential in selecting material for propagation if the short-jointed, cut-leaved characteristics are to be maintained. Although self-branching, its origin and nature suggest it to be a mutation from vining *helix*.

An excellent house-plant ivy for pots, baskets or topiary, it is also suitable for low walls and moderate ground cover.

Habit: Self-branching.

Stems: Purple-green. Internodes 0.5–1cm (¼–⅓in).

Petioles: Green-purple.

Leaves: 3 lobes, 1–4cm by 1.5–3cm (⅝–1¼in). Very variable, some leaves show 2 reduced basal lobes, making a 5-lobed leaf, others may be reduced to 1 or 2 attenuated lobes. In the average leaf sinuses are wide, centre lobe twice the length of laterals, apices acuminate, leaf base truncate. Colour mid- to dark green. Veins lighter and prominent.

Hedera helix 'Tricolor'

Many ivies take on red or purple colouration under conditions of low temperature. This phenomenon was mentioned by Paul in 1867 and was investigated in 1912 on a scientific basis by Tobler, who identified various clones that coloured more readily than most. Of the variegated ivies only this one, as far as I know, consistently retains some pink colour; even in summer the cream-yellow and grey-green leaves have a pink edge whose colour intensifies in winter.

A small-leaved ivy of rather wiry slow growth, it is a colourful plant for low walls or situations where vigorous growth is not required.

The plant was known as 'Tricolor' as long ago as 1866 when Munro Nursery, Essex, and Sunningdale Nursery, Surrey, were among those who listed it. From then to the turn of the century and later many nurseries in Britain and on the continent catalogued it as 'Tricolor' although with sketchy or non-existent descriptions. Hibberd in 1872 confused the issue by listing the plant as 'Marginata Rubra' with 'Tricolor' as a synonym. Lawrence and Schulz (Gentes Herbarum 1942) following the rule of priority published the name 'Tricolour' with a proper and detailed description. Other synonyms included 'Argentea Rubra', 'Latifolia Elegans', 'Microphylla Variegata' and 'Silver Queen'.

The descriptions varied and one must assume the existence of a number of different stocks of a clone no longer grown but most likely to be what we know as 'Tricolor'. A clone circulating in 1909–38 as 'Sheen Silver' may well have been one of these stocks. Stocks of 'Tricolor' are not consistent but the following may be taken as the standard.

Habit: Vining, slow growing.

Stems: Green-purple to dull brown. Internodes 1–2cm (⅓–¾in).

Petioles: Purple.

Leaves: Small, 2–4cm (¾–1½in) by 2–3cm (¾–1¼in). Triangular, unlobed or with only vestigial basal lobes. Colour grey-green centre with irregular cream-yellow edge. Leaf margin generally with a thin pink edge, the colour intensifying and spreading in winter.

Hedera helix 'Trinity'

This has been commercially available in Britain since 1969 but its origin is not known.It can be confused with only one other clone, 'Sinclair Silverleaf', but may be identified by its whiter leaf and sharper, slightly more elongated centre lobe.

The non-green leaves of 'Sinclair Silverleaf' are of a honey-coloured cream, those of 'Trinity' creamy-white with the primary veins tending to retain green colour; as with some other clones this is more noticeable in shade conditions. An excellent and colourful ivy for indoor use, it will succeed outside only in favourable sheltered conditions.

Habit: Self-branching.

Stems: Green-purple. Internodes 2cm (¾in).

Petioles: Green-purple.

Leaves: 5-lobed, 3–5cm (1¼–2in) by 5–6cm (2–2⅓in). Basal lobes cordate, tending to overlap. Centre lobe 1½ times the length of laterals, apex acuminate, apices of laterals acute. Leaf colour variable, some light green others suffused cream variegation, others cream-white.

Hedera helix 'Tristram'

The very distinct cuneate leaf base betrays this clone as being a mutation from 'Eva'. It differs by being very short-jointed and by the leaf variation that extends from the three-lobed leaf to those that appear to be just a single lobe.

The extensive cream-white variegation and short-jointed habit make it a good house-plant ivy, outside its graceful style is less apparent. A sport of 'Tristram' having unlobed, small linear leaves with cream-white variegation was introduced by Whitehouse Ivies in 1984 and named 'Guenevere'.

Habit: Self-branching, short-jointed with trails.

Stems: Green-purple. Internodes 1–2cm (⅓–¾in).

Leaves: 3-lobed, 2–3cm (¾–1¼in) by 2–3cm (¾–1¼in). Central lobe long and acuminate, the 2 laterals short and less acute. Some leaves attenuated to a single lobe. Light green; cream-yellow variegation mostly at leaf margin but variable in its spread. Leaf base cuneate.

Hedera helix 'Triton'

A most unusual ivy, 'Tristram' has been grown in Britain from around 1970 and listed by several nurseries as 'Green Feather', an invalid name because it was used and properly published by Bates in the American National Horticultural Magazine in 1940 to describe a totally different plant. In 1965 the name 'Triton' without any description appeard in a list of collector's ivies quoted by Harry van de Laar in a Dutch horticultural magazine.

Nannenga-Bremekamp (1970) gives it as a synonym of 'Green Spear'. It has also been known as 'Macbeth' and 'Trident' but 'Triton' would seem to be the prior and proper name.

This ivy is a fine subject as a specimen plant or for use in hanging baskets. It is hardy in Britain and because of its sprawling habit can be used as ground cover for small areas. The leaf colour and prominent veins suggest that it might be a mutation from 'Green Ripple' but Sulgrove (AIS Journal Vol 10, No 3, 1984) records that 'Triton'-type shoots have arisen on plants of 'Spear Point' in the Society's collection. Apart from this nothing seems to be known of its origin or introducer save that it came from America.

A clone named 'Neptune' was introduced by the American ivy nurseryman Frank Batson in the early 1980s. Slightly thickened leaves and a readiness to revert to 'Triton' suggest it to be but a fasciated form of that clone.

Habit: Branching and sprawling without any climbing characteristics.

Stems: Purple-green, twisting and slightly zig-zag, non-climbing, hairs few and scattered. Internodes 1–2cm (⅓–¾in).

Petioles: Wine-red, often twisted.

Leaves: 5-lobed, 5–8cm (2–3in) by 3–5cm (1¼–2in). Sinuses deep and narrow, some leaves divided almost to the petiole. The 5 lobes are slender and acuminate with the 3 centre lobes often longer and twisted to their points. Colour bright deep green. Veins prominent, fanning in parallel fashion from the petiole/leaf-blade junction.

Hedera helix 'Trustee'

Introduced by Mr Wally Freeland of Columbia, South Carolina and reputedly found in a garden in Savannah, Georgia, known as the 'Trustee's Garden'. According to Freeland writing in 1971, it was the first experimental garden station in America. 'Trustee' was selected from an ivy branch found growing over the old walls made of English stone which had come to America as ballast in the days of sailing ships, as Freeland put it, "under bulging white sails".

Freeland thought it approximated to the 'Scutifolia' described by Hibberd and it may well be that it was one of the numerous forms of *helix* taken from the wild in the 19th century and given garden status. It is an attractively leaved ivy for a situation demanding a vigorous climbing *helix*.

Habit: Vining.

Stems: Purple-green. Internodes 5–7cm (2–2¾in).

Petioles: Purple-green.

Leaves: Unlobed, 9–13cm (3½–5in) by 9–13cm (3½–5in). Apex acute, leaf base cordate giving a deltoid shape. Colour light- to mid-green.

Hedera helix '238th Street'

The rather unusual name of this clone stems from its discovery in 1935 by Mr T H Everett, a former Director of Horticulture at the New York Botanical Garden, who found it growing in a church garden by Matilda Avenue and 238th Street in the Bronx, New York. He named it accordingly.

It appears to be semi-arborescent, all descriptions record the stiffness of its shoots; Pierot in 1974 stated that it produces trailing shoots directly from flowering and fruiting branches. Ron Whitehouse of Whitehouse Ivies recorded the zig-zag progression of shoots on the ground. It appears to fruit readily and early in the plant's development.

A strong grower, its near-arborescent nature makes it a difficult ivy to place in the garden, suitable neither as a climber nor as a shrub.

Habit: Vining and stiff.

Stems: Purple-green. Internodes 2–3cm (¾–1¼in).

Petioles: Purple-green.

Leaves: 3-lobed but sinuses so shallow as to present a virtually unlobed leaf, 2.5–3.5cm (1–1⅓in) by the same in breadth. Apex acute, leaf base slightly cordate, colour light green.

Hedera helix 'Ursula'

Ivy mutations often occur spontaneously in different areas or even different countries and this has been the case with 'Shamrock'.

In 1985 Mrs Ursula Key-Davis noted a variegated mutation in a plant on Fibrex Nurseries, Worcester and not long afterwards identical plants were being exported from Denmark as 'Golden Shamrock', a similar mutation having occurred on a Danish nursery. The name 'Golden Shamrock' is not acceptable under the ICNCP rules because such a name could be confused with a totally different plant, ie shamrock a kind of clover. The original 'Shamrock' was given the name before the rules came into being. The Danish exporting nurseries accordingly changed the name

to 'Golden Carpet', but the Fibrex Nurseries plant was the first to be described. The clone retains the habit of the parent; in spring and strong light the yellow tends to dominate, in duller conditions the green part shows up to make an attractive contrast. RHS Floral 'B' Committee, 1988: PC.
Habit: Self-branching with short trails.
Stems: Green-purple. Internodes 1–1.5cm (⅓–⅝in).
Petioles: Green-purple.
Leaves: 3-lobed, 3–4cm (1¼–1½in) by 2–3cm (¾–1¼in). Centre lobe broad wedge-shaped. Apices bluntly acute. Sinuses shallow, occasionally split to the centre vein giving a 3-leaved effect. Lateral lobes sometimes folded in pleated fashion alongside the centre lobe. Colour a soft yellow-green.

Hedera helix 'Walthamensis'

This was one of the ivies listed by the nurseryman William Paul in 1867 in his ivy collection "of more than 40 sorts". Paul was writing from his nursery in Waltham Cross and doubtless the name he bestowed recorded the origin of the clone.

It seems strange that 'Walthamensis', a useful small-leaved ivy, figured only in Paul's list and not, so far as I can find, in any nurseryman's catalogue until comparatively recently. A possible reason may be the fact that Paul was essentially a modest man, extremely capable but unlikely to 'promote' a variety he had introduced and in any event, as time went on he concentrated on various other plants.

The following description by the American Leonie Bell in the Morris Arboretum Bulletin of September 1968 summarizes very well the quiet charm of the plant.

> An isolated runner of 'Walthamensis' is all stem, little leaf, yet once established on the ground it makes an even blanket four inches deep, stems invisible, a lovely fabric of sooty green, white threaded, no leaf larger than a single inch."

The plant is available in America as 'Walthamensis' but has also circulated under the invalid names of 'Transit Road' and 'Peacock'. It is not widely grown in Britain and is presently available from only one specialist nursery.

A similar clone has circulated as 'F.C. Coates' with a suggestion that it emanated from Kew. If so it is likely that it bore the name of C F Coates who was Foreman Propagator in the Arboretum Nursery in the early 1950s. As a clone it has no distinction however.

'Walthamensis' can be found in the grounds of one or two of Britain's stately homes and probably in the wild in Wales. A very similar form has been noted in the wild near Heidelberg in Germany.

Habit: Vining.
Stems: Purple. Internodes 3–5cm (1¼–2in).
Petioles: Purple, thin.
Leaves: 3-lobed, 2–3cm (¾–1¼in) by 3–5cm (1¼–2in). Sinuses shallow, sometimes non-existent giving a triangular leaf. Apices bluntly acute, leaf base truncate. Dark dull green, veins lighter.

Hedera helix 'White Knight'

This attractive clone is a selection from the well known 'Kolibri'. This particular selection, which has a high proportion of white colouration, arose in Denmark and had been exported as 'Silver Kolibri'. The name had not been published and indeed would not comply with the rules of the ICNCP which does not look kindly upon appendages to established names.

During 1989 Whitehouse Nurseries secured material of the selection and by increased selectivity and with the agreement of the exporters named and catalogued it as 'White Knight'. The plant is distinctive by the very large area in the leaves of clear white; the extent of variegation leads to attractive puckering of the leaf surface.
Habit: Self-branching.
Stems: Pink-green. Internodes 1.5–2cm (⅝–¾in).
Petioles: Pink-green.
Leaves: 3-lobed, occasionally unlobed, 3–4cm (1¼–1½in) by 4–5cm (1½–2in). Sinuses shallow, apices bluntly acute, leaf base generally cordate. Colour mid-green with irregular, mostly central, white variegation, leaf surface slightly puckered.

Hedera helix 'William Kennedy'

One of the most popular small-leaved, cream variegated ivies, this clone was selected in 1965 by Charles Bond in the Borough of Brent's Parks and Gardens, London.

The clone was selected from a batch of 'Little Diamond' for its compact and slow-growing habit. Ivy enthusiast Fred Kennedy purchased a plant from the Park and he and Stephen Taffler registered it as 'William Kennedy' to honour Mr Kennedy's son who died tragically young from leukaemia. AIS Reg No 811582.

A compact and attractive clone, it propagates sufficiently easily to make it a good commercial house-plant ivy.
Habit: Self-branching.
Stems: Purple-green. Internodes 1–1.5cm (⅓–⅝in).
Petioles: Green.
Leaves: 3-lobed, lateral lobes sometimes much reduced to give a single-lobed leaf, 1.5–3cm (⅝–1¼in) by 1–2.5cm (⅓–1in). Leaf base truncate or slightly cordate, apex

Hedera helix 'William Kennedy'

sometimes acute but usually rounded. Sinuses very shallow. Short shoots 1–2cm (1/3–3/4in) long and bearing from 4–10 leaves appear readily from the leaf nodes giving the trails an almost fern-like appearance. Colour grey-green with slight cream-yellow variegation mostly at the leaf margins.

Hedera helix 'Williamsiana'

This clone has good, clear, almost white variegation and delicately curled leaves. A sport from 'Glacier', it was found and introduced by Keith E Williams of Springfield, Ohio, and first described by Shippy (1955). Since 1959, Latinized cultivar names have not been permissible under the rules of the ICNCP: the Latinization of Mr Williams' name reminds us therefore of how long this excellent house-plant ivy has been in circulation.

Habit: Self-branching with short trails.
Stems: Green-purple. Internodes 1–3cm (1/3–1 1/4in).
Petioles: Green Purple.
Leaves: 3-lobed, 3–4cm (1 1/4–1 1/2in) by 3–5cm (1 1/4–2in). Sinuses shallow, lobes ovate, leaf base strongly cordate. Leaf blade slightly puckered, margin wavy. Apices acute, often down-pointing and curled. Grey-green with a generous leaf margin of cream-white.

Hedera helix 'Wingertsberg'

Among ivies in the wild there are individual plants that, with the onset of cold weather, take on a more intense purple tint than their fellows. This clone is one such but has the added virtue of considerable vigour, making it an excellent ground-cover plant for large areas.

It was found in 1980 growing in woods near the Neuburg Monastery, Heidelberg, in an area that once formed a vineyard, a connection retained in the name 'Wingertsberg'. Although turning a pleasant purple it never colours as deeply as 'Atropurpurea' or 'Glymii'. AIS Reg No 812082.

Habit: Vining.
Stems: Purple-green. Internodes 2–3cm (3/4–1 1/4in).
Petioles: Purple-green.
Leaves: 5-lobed, 3–5cm (1 1/4–2in) by 4–5cm (1 1/2–2in). Basal lobes often show only as extensions of the cordate leaf base. Centre lobe bluntly acute, lateral lobes wedge-shaped and less prominent in the older leaves. Colour dark-green, purple-green in cold weather.

Hedera helix 'Woerneri'

This clone can share with 'Atropurpurea' and 'Glymii' the epithet 'purple'. Actually no ivy is purple in leaf colour but many clones take on pink or purple shades in cold weather, a phenomenon noted by Paul in 1867 and investigated scientifically by Tobler (1912). These three clones however can be relied upon for good purple colour in most winters, in severe weather they turn to deepest purple.

The clone was described by Jenny (1964) as 'Woerneri' but the Ivy Registrar has suggested that he was in error in using the Latinized version, such use being proscribed for names published after 1959, and that the name should be 'Woerner'. There exists however an earlier description by H Schenk in the Swiss gardening magazine Scheizerische Gartnerzeitung of December 1956 praising in particular the clone's hardiness compared to that of *H. hibernica*. The date of this article validates Jenny's use of the Latinized version.

An ivy called 'Remscheid' found by G Frahm on a church in the place of that name in 1949 was listed by his firm Timm & Co. Sometimes quoted as a synonym of 'Woerneri', it does not appear to have been in circulation for some time.

Habit: Vining.
Stems: Purple-green. Internodes 4–5cm (1 1/2–2in).
Petioles: Purple-green.
Leaves: 3-lobed, 3–5cm (1 1/4–2in) by 5–6cm (2–2 1/3in). Sinuses shallow or non-existent. Centre lobe broadly wedge-shaped, leaf base slightly cordate. Lobes often have a minute white tip at the apices. Dark green turning purple in cold weather.

Hedera helix 'Yalta'

Collected by Dr J L Creech in damp wooded hills at approximately 366m (1,200ft) above Yalta in the Crimea, USSR this clone was introduced to the USA under the Government Plant Introduction No 293883.

As an ivy it has no horticultural significance but Yalta was the city where the very significant meeting of the World War II leaders, Churchill, Roosevelt and Stalin, took place so the name is perhaps of greater interest than the plant!

Helix clones that are of more significance by virtue of association than by merit include 'Mount Vernon' from the home of General George Washington at Mount Vernon, Virginia and 'Rubáiyát', reputed to have come from a plant on the grave of Edward Fitzgerald (1809–83) author/translator of the *Rubáiyát* of Omar Khayyam.

Both are interesting associations but the ivies are ordinary *helix* forms. As a recorded introduction 'Yalta' merits the following description.

Habit: Vining.
Stems: Purple-green.
Petioles: Purple-green.
Leaves: 3-lobed, 6–7cm (2⅓–2¾in) by the same broad. Sinuses so shallow as to present an almost triangular leaf. Apices acute, leaf base cordate. Dark dull green.

Hedera helix 'Zebra'

This introduction from Gebr Stauss was placed on the market during 1978. A mutation from the clone 'Harald', the name aptly describes the almost striped effect of the broken cream-yellow variegation enhanced by the way in which the primary veins radiate from the petiole/leaf-blade junction. The leaf in general is less lobed than 'Harald' with a tendency to be cupped. 'Zebra' makes an interesting and attractive pot plant. It has a tendency to revert and care is needed in selecting propagating material.

In 1984 Brother Heieck introduced an improved form under the name 'Reef Shell'. This has small long unlobed slightly cockle-shaped leaves, 1.5–2.5cm (⅝–1in) by some 1–1.5cm (⅓–⅝in). It has well marked cream-yellow stripes on a green ground but is slightly less robust than 'Zebra'.

Habit: Self-branching.
Stems: Pink-purple. Internodes 1.5–2cm (⅝–¾in).
Petioles: Green-pink.
Leaves: Remotely 5-lobed, but lobes often vestigial, 2–3cm (¾–1¼in) by 3–4cm (1¼–1½in). Colour grey-green splashed with cream-yellow often longitudinally from the petiole junction but sometimes at the leaf edge. Primary veins light yellow radiating from the petiole/leaf-blade junction in almost parallel fashion.

Hedera hibernica Carr

Botanical taxonomy has not been kind to what nurseryman Robert Furber in his catalogue of 1727 listed as "ivy the broad-leaved kind". Probably the most widely planted of all ivies, controversy as to its origin and identity has continued for something like 150 years.

It was first recorded as a name by George Lindley, a nurseryman of Catton near Norwich, England, who in 1815 listed three varieties in his catalogue: common ivy, the striped ivy and *hibernica*, but unhappily without descriptions. George Lindley was the father of the scientist Dr John Lindley (1799–1865), Professor of Botany at University College, London, from 1829–60 and Secretary to the RHS from 1858–63. At his death his extensive horticultural library was purchased by the Society and became the nucleus of the world famous Lindley Library. It is tempting to think that in his younger days (he was only 23 when appointed Assistant Secretary) he may have helped in the preparation of his father's catalogue and been instrumental in naming as *hibernica* what had previously been called the Irish ivy. This is speculation but it was well before 1836 when Mackay wrote in his *Flora Hibernica*, "A variety called the Irish ivy is much cultivated on account of its very large leaves and quick growth".

Uncertainty attended the plant's name for many years: in 1864 the botanists Petzold & Kirchin recorded the plant as *H. helix hibernica*. A year later Seeman in the Journal of Botany described it under the name *H. hibernica scotica*. Hibberd (1872) proposed *H. grandiflora*. In 1890 Carrière in the Revue Horticole returned to Lindley's name, *H. hibernica*, but it was the earlier name *H. helix* var. *hibernica* that was repeated in catalogues and horticultural dictionaries until 1981.

It was then that Dr H McAllister, writing in the International Dendrology Society Year Book proposed a return to species status as published by Carrière. He based his proposal on the plant's tetraploid chromosome number, 2N=96, (*helix* is 2N=48), its geographic distribution (the west of England and the Atlantic seaboard of France) and also the tendency of the leaf hairs to lie in parallel fashion rather than in the irregular manner of *helix*. The proposal was challenged by the American botanist Laurence Hatch who contended that tetraploidy and a geographical locus of origin do not warrant species rank and that the hair arrangement was trivial and like the geographic evidence warranted nothing more than varietal status. While accepting the above I feel the balance is marginally in favour of species status. I have no doubt that the argument will surface again when future botanists examine the genus.

If we accept *hibernica* as a species it is reasonable to assume that a number of large-leaved, vigorous clones, 'Deltoidea' is an example, previously appended to *helix* should be transferred to *hibernica*. This acceptance resolves the puzzle of 'Ovata' which has always seemed to be a small form of 'Deltoidea' but would appear to be the deltoid form of *helix* in the same way that 'Deltoidea' is the deltoid form of *hibernica*.

Occasionally *hibernica* has circulated in the USA as 'Four Square' a fanciful comment on its robust leaf. The appendage 'Arborescens' was ascribed to the adult form by Hibberd under the species name he had bestowed, ie *grandiflora*. The plant is now correctly *H. hibernica* 'Arborescens'.

In 1912 the botanist Dr G C Druce described an ivy from the Petit Bot area of Guernsey as having broad, scarcely angled, deep-green leaves, calling it *H. helix* var. *sarniensis*. It is now generally agreed to be a geographical variant of *H. hibernica* and thus becomes *H. hibernica* var. *sarniensis*.

The origin of the Irish ivy may be doubtful but its value in the garden is certain. As long ago as 1868 M Delchevalerie, Chef de Culture au Fleuriste de la Ville de Paris, wrote on the virtues of "le lierre d'Irlande" for use in the squares and beds of Paris. His recommendation can be seen to this day on Parisian boulevards, squares and cemeteries. In the celebrated Cimetière du Père-Lachaise, the élite of France from Chopin and Maréchal Ney to Edith Piaf rest surrounded by stone and *hibernica*. Many other European cities and towns contain examples of its value as an unobtrusive background to architectural splendours or follies and its wide use in eastern USA, although ivy is not an indigenous plant, demonstrates its versatility.

In its adult form it can make an effective hedge and in Britain there can be few churchyards, parks or gardens of stately homes where its large, slightly upward-folded, green leaves do not provide cover or background. It is also one of the parents of the useful bi-generic x *Fatshedera lizei*, the other parent being *Fatsia japonica*.

The description by Carrière (1890) is not very detailed. The appended description is of the plant seen in the wild in Britain and as offered by nurserymen. 1993: ♔.
Habit: Vining and vigorous.
Stems: Green, browning with age. Internodes 5–7cm (2–2¾in).
Petioles: Green-purple.
Leaves: 5-lobed, 5–9cm (2–3½in) by 8–14cm (3–5½in). Lobes triangular and bluntly acute, centre lobe large and more prominent, sinuses shallow. Leaf base cordate, colour mid-green sometimes glossy but often matt green. Hairs stellate tending to lie in parallel fashion. Adult leaves unlobed and ovate and not narrowed to

the same extent as *helix*. Umbels of flowers on often solitary peduncles, fruit a purple-black berry but never so numerous as in *helix*, possibly because it is a tetraploid. Chromosome number 2n=96.

Hedera hibernica var. *aracena*

From a botanical point of view this is an interesting variety since it is probably the eastern limit geographically of the species. At first sight it looks like a lobed form of *pastuchovii*.

Collected by D & B Roxburgh in 1973 in the Sierra de Aracena, north of Huelva, Spain. In Britain it proves to be a hardy and vigorous vining ivy. Like the species it is a tetraploid; 2n=96. In winter the stems darken almost to black.
Habit: Vining.
Stems: Purple-green. Internodes 2–3cm (¾–1¼in).
Petioles: Purple-green.
Leaves: Unlobed, occasionally 3-lobed, 4–6cm (1½–2⅓in) by 3–8cm (1¼–3in). Ovate-elliptic, apices bluntly acute, sinuses when present, shallow. Leaf base cuneate or truncate. Dark matt green, veins slightly outlined grey-white. Hairs 5–9 rays.

Hedera hibernica 'Deltoidea'

Described and figured by Hibberd (1872) as "the blunt triangular ivy" and noted by him as "a dull unattractive plant, strikingly interesting to an amateur of ivies". It is known generally as the shield ivy because of the shape of the leaves but in America as the sweetheart ivy from the supposedly heart-shaped leaves. A distinct variety it was a favourite of the late E A Bowles, a noted British horticulturist, and is sometimes called Bowles shield ivy. Synonyms have included *Hedera hastata*, *H. helix* 'Cordata' and *H. helix* 'Sweetheart'; the plant has often been confused with *H. helix* 'Scutifolia' and *H. helix* 'Ovata'.

As 'Deltoidea' it has usually been listed as a clone of *H. helix* but current research suggests that it is a deltoid-leaf variation of the large-leaved Irish ivy *hibernica*. There is no reversion to the normal 'ivy' leaf but the plant achieves arborescence and the more simple, rounded leaves fairly rapidly. Essentially a wall ivy, the plant has a quiet appeal. RHS Ivy Trial 1978/9 (as *H. helix* 'Deltoidea'): HC.
Habit: Vining.
Stems: Green, stout. Internodes 2–3cm (¾–1¼in).
Petioles: Green.
Leaves: In outline 3-lobed but sinuses absent or so shallow as to make an unlobed deltoid, 6–10cm (2⅓–4in) by 8–10cm (3–4in). Leaf base strongly cordate with overlapping basal lobes. Leaf blade thick with smooth well defined edge. Dark green with purple tones in autumn.

Hedera hibernica 'Hamilton'

Of the sundry variations of *H. hibernica*, this one approaches very closely to the typical species.

In essence it has the same slightly 'fluted' leaf as *hibernica* and certainly the same vigour but differs in having cuspid lobes and a slightly thickened leaf edge giving the leaf a 'sculptural' appearance with almost the solidity of a *Fatshedera*. The petioles are very light green, lacking the slight tinge of red usually present in *hibernica*. It is hardy and will thrive in the same situations as *hibernica*.

'Hamilton' was introduced by Hazel Key of Fibrex Nurseries, the name being that of premises upon which it was found. It is hardy, a vigorous climbing and ground-cover ivy whose leaf variation makes it a useful alternative. RHS Ivy Trial 1978/9 (as *H. helix* var. *hibernica* 'Hamilton'): HC.
Habit: Vining.
Stems: Green. Internodes 3–5cm (1¼–2in).
Petioles: Light green.
Leaves: 5-lobed, 6–7cm (2⅓–2¾in) by 9–10cm (3½–4in).
Lobes cuspid, centre lobe only slightly longer than laterals. The 2 basal lobes reduced to about ⅓ of laterals. Sinuses deep with convolution at the cleft. Distinctive thickened leaf edge giving a 'rimmed' appearance to the leaf. Fresh mid-green, veins light green.

Hedera hibernica 'Helford River'

Large leaves, vigorous growth and a west-of-England origin suggest that this may be a clone of *H. hibernica* rather than of *helix* where it was previously placed.

The following description appears in Bean (8th Ed,1973). A large-leaved ivy found growing wild near the Helford Estuary by George Nicholson, Curator of Kew, in 1890 and introduced by him to the collection where it still grows. The leaves are conspicuously white-veined, variable in shape but mostly with a long central lobe and two backward spreading laterals.

The variety was recorded as 'Helfordiensis' in the Kew Hand List (1925). The name has been associated with the purple-leaved clones 'Woerneri' and 'Purpurea' but this variety does not colour at all.

Bean's description appears to be the first published and 'Helford River' to be the correct name. A vigorous climber, the grey-veined leaves provide contrast to other ivies. Can be used for ground cover.
Habit: Vining.
Stems: Green-purple. Internodes 2–3cm (¾–1¼in).
Petioles: Green-purple.
Leaves: 5-lobed, 6–10cm (2⅓–4in) by 7–11cm (2¾–4⅓in).

Centre lobe prolonged and acuminate, lateral lobes wedge-shaped and acute, basal lobes back-pointing. Sinuses shallow. Medium-green, veins show up strongly grey-white giving the impression of a greyish leaf.

Hedera hibernica 'Lobata Major'

The names 'Lobata' and 'Triloba' have been applied and misapplied over the years. It is likely that both types arose in the west of the British Isles where the native *hibernica* shows variations from time to time. The following description is based on plants at the Royal Botanic Gardens, Kew, and which broadly coincide with Hibberd's (1872) description of 'Lobata Major'. Lawrence & Schulze (1942) were correct in saying that this is not a very distinguished clone. It is now seldom offered by nurserymen but may be found in old gardens and in the wild in areas colonized by *hibernica*.
Habit: Vining.
Stems: Green-purple. Internodes 5–6cm (2–2⅓in).
Petioles: Green-purple.
Leaves: 3-lobed, 4–8cm (1½–3in) by 5–11cm (2–4⅓in).
Two basal lobes always present to a greater or lesser degree. The lateral lobes at right angles to the long acuminate centre lobe. Similar in leaf shape to 'Pedata' but the leaf is larger, dark green and the lighter green veins much less prominent than in 'Pedata'.

Hedera hibernica 'Maculata'

The first reference to a silver-variegated form of *hibernica* is in the 1862 catalogue of Francis and Arthur Dixon of Upton Nurseries, Chester, who listed "*Hedera hibernica* (New silver striped) – Very attractive." By 1868 however their ivy entries had been reduced and *hibernica* excluded altogether.

During the latter half of the 19th century *H. hibernica*, the Irish ivy, became confused in horticultural writings and catalogues with *H. canariensis* the Canary Island ivy. This was largely because Hibberd (1872) referred to *H. canariensis* as the Irish ivy, as a result many nurserymen adopted that name for what was *hibernica*. Variegated forms of both species were in circulation and became equally confused.

It was W J Bean (1914) who brought order into chaos. He followed the French botanist Carrière in listing the Irish ivy as *H. hibernica* and listed its silver variegated form as var. *maculata*. His succinct description; "a form of *hibernica* with leaves three- or five-lobed and streaked with creamy-white" easily distinguished it from the sharply defined, more generous cream-yellow variegation of *H. hibernica* 'Variegata'.

Like 'Variegata' this clone is apt to produce an extent of green leaf that can overwhelm the variegation which in any event is not particularly striking. It is not surprising therefore that the plant seemed to disappear during the period between the wars when interest in ivies had declined.

Habit: Vining and vigorous.

Stems: Green, browning with age. Internodes 5–7cm (2–2¾in).

Petioles: Green-purple.

Leaves: 5-lobed, 5–9cm (2–3½in) by 8–14cm (3–5½in). Lobes triangular and bluntly acute, centre lobe large and more prominent, sinuses shallow, leaf base cordate. Colour dark green streaked with often faint cream-white. In some leaves it can increase into a slight cream-white variegation.

Hedera hibernica 'Rona'

This clone came from a plant found in 1975 by Mrs Schaepman, wife of the then President of the AIS, Henri Schaepman. Found in a bed of ordinary *H. hibernica* , the single shoot was propagated and selected by Mr Schaepman who named it for his wife and published a description in the Flower and Garden in November 1980.

'Rona' is freckled and diffused yellow on green as opposed to the sharply defined yellow variegation of 'Variegata' and the slight and wispy white variegation of 'Maculata'.

Habit: Vining.

Stems: Green. Internodes 5–6cm (2–2⅓in).

Petioles: Green-purple.

Leaves: 5-lobed, 4–8cm (1½–3in) by 8–12cm (3–4¾in). Lobes triangular and bluntly acute, centre lobe larger and more prominent, sinuses shallow. Leaf base cordate, colour mid-green with freckled and diffused variegation, occasionally more substantial patches.

Hedera hibernica 'Rottingdean'

This clone was introduced in 1964 by G Jackman & Sons Ltd, of Woking, Surrey. It originated from a plant noted by Mr Roland Jackman on a wall in Rottingdean, a suburb of Brighton. Its vigorous growth, ease of propagation and handsome 'fingered' leafage have made it very popular.

Originally assumed to be a *helix* clone, recent investigation suggests that it is a clone of the large-leaved and vigorous *H. hibernica* and may well be the original 'Digitata' described by Dr Mackay (*Flora Hibernica*, 1836). William Paul (1867) listed 'Digitata' and also a smaller-leaved fingered ivy which he called 'Digitata Nova'. It may be that in the nursery trade 'Digitata Nova' gradually superseded and was sold as 'Digitata', especially since after Paul few nurserymen appear to have listed 'Nova'. Still in the realms of speculation it is possible that the plant spotted in Rottingdean was in fact a specimen of the original 'Digitata'.

Habit: Vining.

Stems: Green-purple. Internodes 3–5cm (1¼–2in).

Petioles: Green-purple.

Leaves: 5-lobed 7–9cm (2¾–3½in) by 7–10cm (2¾–4in). Digitate, centre lobe a little longer than the two laterals. Apices acute, the 2 basal lobes reduced, leaf base truncate or very slightly cordate. Sinuses narrow, convolute at the clefts. Leaves can show variation in which the sinuses are broad and the lobes consequently less cleft. Dark green, veins light but not prominent.

Hedera hibernica 'Sulphurea'

This very useful clone was described as a variety of *helix* by Hibberd in 1872 and also in his commentary in the RHS Journal of 1890 on its Chiswick Ivy Trial. It was listed in catalogues of the day but not after World War I and seemed lost until the discovery by staff from the Pershore Agricultural College of a plant at Spetchley House near Evesham, Worcestershire. The gardens, planted largely at the turn of the century, bear the influence of the redoubtable Ellen Willmott, a relative of the owning Berkeley family.

The plant was distributed from Pershore initially as 'Spetchley Variegated', later its true name was realized and it was described and pictured in the RHS Journal of February 1975. Unlike the other variegated *hibernica* clones it rarely reverts to green. Since its re-introduction it has proved to be a good clone for ground cover and a good wall ivy. It is as hardy as the species, standing up well to frost and cold winds. RHS Ivy Trial of 1977/9: C, but merited higher.

Habit: Vining.

Stems: Purple-green. Internodes 2.5–3cm (1–1¼in).

Petioles: Purple-green.

Leaves: 3-lobed, 4–7cm (1½–2¾in) by 6–8cm (2⅓–3in), sinuses shallow, sometimes non-existent so as to give an unlobed leaf. Leaf base truncate to slightly cordate. Colour grey-green with some darker patches, becoming greyer and more sulphury in older leaves. Yellow areas of indefinite shape almost always at the leaf margins. This variegation causes a certain amount of leaf puckering and concavity which, with the lack of distinctive lobing, gives a somewhat misshapen leaf. An ear-like protrusion is often present, mostly on the right of the leaf-base as seen from the petioles. This was observed by Hibberd and is diagnostic of the clone.

Hedera hibernica 'Triloba'

Like 'Lobata Major' this is a variation of the Irish ivy native to the west of Britain. The clonal name was first used by Hibberd (1872) and illustrations of two types of leaf appear in his book. Subsequently it appeared in one or two 19th-century catalogues and was listed by one British nursery as recently as 1927, but in all cases with little description other than 'three-lobed'. Lawrence & Schulze (1942) seem to describe a much smaller-leaved plant, as did Graf (1963) and Pierot (1974); indeed the illustration in the last book is certainly not the plant described by Hibberd and which is still to be found in old gardens and collections. It is correct to retain Hibberd's name for this large-leaved vigorous variety; the smaller-leaved plant illustrated by Pierot (it may well have been a *helix* clone) warrants a different name.

Habit: Vining.

Stems: Purple-green. Internodes 4cm (1½in).

Petioles: Purple-green.

Leaves: 3-lobed, 3–6cm (1¼–2⅓in) by 5–9cm (2–3½in). Lobes usually wedge-shaped and acute, this is variable and sometimes apices are rounded, leaf base cordate. Colour dark green.

Hedera hibernica 'Variegata'

The species *hibernica* has produced fewer variegated forms than *helix*; however a variegated form was in existence as early as 1859, for the catalogue of Henderson & Sons of St John's Wood, London, listed "*H. hibernica* foliis *elegans variegata*".

Further references are found as *hibernica variegata* in the 1860 catalogue of Peter Lawson of Edinburgh; in the 1867 catalogue of Haage & Schmidt; the 1868 catalogue of Charles Turner of Slough, Buckinghamshire and that of 1877 of Thomas Warre of Tottenham, London.

All these indicated the clone as 'variegated' but the first detailed description is that of Hibberd(1872), given under the name *Hedera grandifolia pallida* as follows.

The pallid large-leaved ivy (syn. 'Golden Blotched', *Hibernica* fol. var., 'Aurea Maculata', *canariensis* var. *aurea*, golden-blotched Irish ivy). This is well known, and deservedly so, for its beauty. It differs from the type only in its variegation which occurs irregularly in 'splashes', some parts of the plant being superbly coloured, while others are green, and differ in no respect from the common 'Irish ivy'. The variegation consists of a pale yellowish or primrose colour, with which some leaves are entirely overspread, while others are half green and half yellow, the mid-rib marking the division sharply; others again are blotched and patched with variegation. This never acquires a rich variegation except when planted out, and then it is usually a noble plant though irregularly coloured.

The line illustration in Hibberd's book certainly depicts the plant we have today with its fairly sharp colour definitions. Not all nurseries followed Hibberd's nomenclature and the names he showed as synonyms have persisted for years.

The plant in circulation today fulfils Hibberd's description. When it throws variegated shoots it can be a striking plant but often the variegated shoots are rare. Just as vigorous as the type it is worth planting on a wall or as ground cover but not where consistent variegation is required.

Habit: Vining, vigorous.

Stems: Green-purple. Internodes 5–7cm (2–2¾in).

Petioles: Green-purple. Green-yellow when supporting semi- or entirely yellow leaves.

Leaves: 5-lobed, 5–9cm (2–3½in) by 8–14cm (3–5½in). Lobes triangular and bluntly acute. Centre lobe larger and more prominent, sinuses shallow, leaf base cordate. Colour matt green, some leaves entirely yellow or particoloured often defined by veins, some leaves with slight broken variegation. Generally a predominance of all-green leaves.

Hedera maroccana McAllister

The type material was collected by the International Dendrology Expedition of 1974 from the Middle Atlas Mountains in Morocco. Plants from this collection are seldom seen other than in the gardens of ivy specialists. Large-leaved forms, presumed by McAllister (The Plantsman Vol 15, pt 2, 1993) to be of this species, have long been grown in southern France and Spain and latterly in Britain under such names as 'Morocco' and 'Spanish Canary'.

Habit: Vining.

Stems: Purple – briefly green when young. Internodes 3–5cm (1¼–2in).

Petioles: Purple-red.

Leaves: 3-, mostly 5-lobed, 7–9cm (2¾–3½in) by 7–9cm (2¾–3½in). Centre lobes twice as long as laterals, sinuses shallow, apices bluntly acute, leaf base truncate or slightly cordate. Glossy dark green, veins fairly prominent. The few scale-like hairs have 6–9 rays. Chromosome number 2n=48.

Hedera maroccana 'Spanish Canary'

This large-leaved ivy of luxuriant growth has been so widely grown over a long period in southern France and Spain as to appear as a naturalized plant. It is reasonably hardy in Britain, certainly in hard winters it seems to suffer less than the var. *algeriensis* clones. Vigorous and of rapid growth, large and apparently aged plants can be established in a matter of a few years. A glossy-leaved decorative climber

PLATE IX

All plants are shown at approximately ³/₄ size

H. helix 'California'

H. helix 'Pittsburgh'

H. helix 'Cheste

H. helix 'Bodil'

H. helix 'Lemon Swirl'

H. helix 'Spectre'

H. helix 'Little Diamond'

H. helix 'Parsley Crested'

H. helix 'Merion Beauty'

H. helix 'Très Coupé'

H. helix 'Thorndale'

H. helix 'Glymii'

for large wall areas which it will take over. The plant is occasionally confused with the smaller, broader-leaved 'Montgomery'.

Habit: Vining.

Stems: Purple. Internodes 5–7cm (2–2¾in).

Petioles: Green-purple, up to 20cm (8–in).

Leaves: 3-lobed when young but developing to 5 lobes, 8–12cm (3–4¾in) by 10–14cm (4–5½in). Centre lobe acuminate, lateral lobes acute and ½ the length of the centre lobe. Leaf base cordate. Dark glossy green.

Hedera nepalensis K Koch

This, the Himalayan ivy, was described as *Hedera helix* by Wallich in Roxburgh's *Flora of India* (1824). De Candolle in 1830, noting differences between it and *helix*, described it as a variety, *chrysocarpa*, a name already used by Walsh (1826) to describe what we know as var. *poetica*. The German botanist Karl Koch in 1853 named it a distinct species, *H. nepalensis*. Hibberd (*The Floral World*, 1864) called it *H. himalaica* but in 1872 referred to it as *H. helix cinerea*. Neither name had justification although *himalaica* was adopted by Tobler (1912), who rather strangely overlooked Koch's earlier name. In an article in 1927 he accepted the earlier name, uncovered it seems by Rehder and reported in the Arnold Arboretum Journal 4. 250 (1923). Hibberd's name of *cinerea* was used by Bean (1st Ed, 1914) but was suitably amended in subsequent editions.

Considered to be one of the older *Hedera* species, *nepalensis* is more stable than the younger and very variable *helix*, nevertheless further exploration or possibly propagation in quantity might bring different varieties or clones. A variegated form has not been recorded, indeed it has been suggested that the accepted type with its shallow-lobed leaves with their 'stepped' or 'oak-leaf' appearance may in fact be a variation. Roy Lancaster reports the more widely seen plant as having entire unlobed leaves and suggests the type plant may have been from Kashmir.

Essentially a wall ivy it is particularly attractive for a north wall. Less hardy in Britain than *colchica* and *helix*, probably hardy in USA Zone 7.

The fruit is orange and in this connection it is interesting to note the coloured plate that appeared in the Revue Horticole of 1884 with a description by M André of the "Scarlet fruited ivy" grown in Cannes by M Besson, a nurseryman of Nice. M André named his plant *Hedera helix aurantiaca* but no one else seemed to get scarlet fruits from material of this or other plants and discussion on the subject continued for some years in the horticultural press of the period. The illustration is certainly of *H. nepalensis* which in my experience

does not fruit in Britain but may do so in southern Europe and clonal variations in berry colour could well be possible. The plant's geographical range has been given as Afghanistan to Kashmir, Nepal and Assam.

Habit: Vining.

Stems: Red-brown when young to green with age. Internodes 2–4cm (¾–1½in).

Petioles: Light-green.

Leaves: Ovate to lanceolate, 6–10cm (2⅓–4in) by 3.5–4.5cm (1⅓–1¾in). Obscurely lobed, lobes little more than rounded projections 3–6 in number. Apices acute, leaf base truncate. The veins, running almost parallel with the centre vein, appear as pale areas on the mid- to light-green leaf blade. Adult leaves elliptic-lanceolate and unlobed. Hairs scale-like, 12–15 rays and orange brown. Fruit not seen but reported dull orange, 1cm (⅓in) in diameter. Chromosome number 2n=48.

Hedera nepalensis var. sinensis

The Chinese ivy had been noted by botanists during the 19th century and assumed to be *H. helix* until Professor Tobler studied the plant in detail. He realized that it had little in common with *H. helix* but resembled the Himalayan ivy, *H. himalaica* as he then termed it. Although inclined to consider it a distinct species, Tobler felt that not enough was known of it and named it *H. himalaica* var. *sinensis*. Later, in 1927, he maintained this varietal status but followed Rehder who had reinstated for the Himalayan ivy the name established by K Koch, *H. nepalensis*.

Other botanists had different views. Handel-Mazzetti, the Austrian who travelled in south-west and central China and saw the local ivy under varying conditions, raised it in *Symbolae Sinicae* (1933) to the specific rank of *H. sinensis*. A paper published by A I Pojarkova, V L Komarov Botanical Institute (Vol XIV, 1951) supported this view. She qualified it slightly by pointing out the difficulties of defining the northern and eastern boundaries of the plant's range and felt that other species might be involved.

More recently the Chinese *Flora Yunnanica* Tomus 2, pp424–6 (1979) gives a detailed description of the plant as *H. nepalensis* var. *sinensis* with illustrations of leaves, hairs, flowers and fruit. The distribution is given as the southern part of Yunnan below 3,500m (1067ft), middle, eastern, southern and south-western parts of China and more specifically in Shanxi, Ganshu and Xizan. It is used in Chinese medicine in treating wounds and for hepatitis. There have been a number of recent introductions of the plant; Roy Lancaster who collected it on the Sacred Mountain, Emei

Hedera nepalensis

Shan and Sichuan (L.555), records in *Travels in China* seeing it and stated that lobed and unlobed forms were encountered. He commented also on the 'chocolate' colour of the young leaves. The plant was also collected by Keith Rushforth (KR.236) at 2,000 m (610 ft) in the same area. Material from these introductions as well as that by Chris Brickell (CB.3577) collected in Hangchow, eastern China, is in circulation in a number of gardens.

The Brickell collection differs in leaf outline from those of Lancaster and Rushforth. The juvenile leaves are triangular, indeed more typical of the illustration in *Flora Yunnanica*. It could agree with the description by Pojarkova of the plant she named as *H. shensiensis* (Pojark sp. nova in *Flora USSR* XVI, 1950) but she gave its distribution as central China, Shensi and Szechuan, a long way from Hangchow. In a country as large as China there will be differences within the species but to my mind these are varieties or forms that do not merit the status of species.

A variation of var. *sinensis* having grey-green veined leaves and termed 'Marble Dragon' has been in circulation since 1979. I have been unable to find any details of its origin but it is assumed to be a *sinensis* clone. All the recent var. *sinensis* introductions grow well in Britain.

Habit: Vining

Stems: Red-brown when young, green with age. Internodes 4–6cm (1½–2⅓in). Hairs scale-like, 12–15 rays.

Petioles: Light green.

Leaves: Ovate to lanceolate, 7–9cm (2¾–3½in) by 5–7cm (2–2¾in), Unlobed but occasionally 3-lobed, acuminate, leaf base cuneate. Thick and matt mid-green, veins light-green, the emerging leaves deep maroon. Adult leaves similar shape but 8–12cm (3–4¾in) by 4–6cm (1½–2⅓in).

Hedera nepalensis 'Suzanne'

This clone of the Himalayan ivy was collected in 1975 by the USDA Plant Introduction Expedition in Nepal. It was growing on oak trees and on moist rocks at an altitude of 2,680m (8,000ft). Collection number PI.285496, its name honours Suzanne Pierot, founder of the AIS.

It is distinct from the species by reason of its 5-lobed leaves that give it a 'bird's foot' appearance similar to that of *H. helix* 'Pedata'. Reputedly hardy in USA Zone 7, the deep purple young growth can be damaged by late frosts.

Habit: Vining.

Stems: Purple-green. Internodes 3–5cm (1¼–5in).

Petioles: Purple.

Leaves: 5-lobed, 5–7cm (2–2¾in) by 6–8cm (2⅓–3in).

Sinuses deep, centre lobe rarely more than 1cm (⅓in) wide, often with vestigial lobes in its length. Lateral lobes ⅓ of centre lobe length and equally narrow. The two short basal lobes back-pointing to give a 'bird's foot' effect. Colour matt dark green, veins fairly pronounced and outlined grey-green. Hairs scale-like, 16–20 rays. Flowers and fruit not seen.

Hedera pastuchovii G Woron

This species was first published as *H. pastuchowii*, (spelt with a 'w') by the botanist G N Woronow with a three-line diagnosis in Russian in *Grossheim's Flora*, 1c, 111 p108, 1932. Because this appeared before January 1st 1935, after which a Latin description became obligatory, it was a valid publication.

In the following year however, a detailed Latin description by Worrow was published in *Flora Systematica Plantae Vasculares* of the *Acta Instituti Botanici Academiae Scientiarum*, Fasc 1, 1933. In this the 'w' is substituted by 'v' and I am advised on good authority that this should be accepted as an emendation, ie a correction of his earlier and Latinistically incorrect *pastuchowii*.

Found in Western Trans-Caucasia and Northern Persia *pastuchovii* like all ivies is variable in its juvenile leaf forms. The form depicted in *Flora Iranica* (1973) has deeply lobed leaves very different from those described in *Flora USSR* (1950) and the material currently grown in Britain.

Reference to the plant was made in the RHS Journal of 1934 but there is no evidence of introduction to Britain until that made by Lancaster in December 1972 from the Caspian Forest area, Khair Rud Forest in Iran (A&L No 26).

Although it has a resemblance to *H. nepalensis* its garden value is probably less than that species. It seems to be one of several species described by Russian botanists that may comprise a 'bridge' as it were between *nepalensis* of the East and *colchica* and *helix* of the West.

The species is hardy in Britain and its place of origin suggests hardiness in USA as far as Zone 4.

Habit: Vining.

Stems: Green-brown. Internodes 3–4cm (1¼–1½in). Hairs sparse, scale-like; 8–12 rayed.

Petioles: Green-brown.

Leaves: Juvenile leaves narrowly ovate, 4–9cm (1½–3½in) by 3–4cm (1¼–1½in). Unlobed apex acute to acuminate. Blade slightly cupped, margin entire, base slightly cordate. Dark glossy green, texture slightly leathery. Veins grey-green and not noticeable. Adult leaves ovate rhomboid, flowers in erect umbels of 10–20, fruit black. Chromosome number 2n=144.

Hedera pastuchovii var. cypria

Although fairly distinctive, this ivy has only recently come into circulation. It is unlikely that experienced botanists would have confused it with *H. helix*, the ivy listed by R D Meikle in *The Flora of Cyprus*, and one can only assume that the very limited stand of the plant lay undiscovered. During the 1970s however plants of this endemic of the Troödos mountains were collected by visitors to the island including Mr Ron Whitehouse; meanwhile at the University of Liverpool Botanic Garden, seed from a 1970 collection produced material for a study by Dr H McAllister from which he initially recorded the plant as "Cyprus *taxon* aff. *pastuchovii*".

The plant closely resembles *H. pastuchovii* and has the same chromosome No and hair type but in a note in The Plantsman (Vol 15, pt 2, 1993) McAllister and the botanists Rutherford and Mill postulated that it warranted species status. The grounds for such elevation are slender for the only difference between this plant and *pastuchovii* is the presence of grey-green areas around the veins of the juvenile leaves and a certain greater vigour. Other leaf variations of *pastuchovii* are recorded; the plant figured in *Flora Iranica* from material collected in the Elburze mountains by the botanist Erwin Gauba shows deeply juvenile leaves; similar plants are listed in American ivy plant catalogues.

The locus of *pastuchovii* is the Caucasus, east Transcaucasia and the northern Iranian areas of Astrabad and Mazanderand. It seems reasonable to assume that the Cyprus plant is a relict form clinging to the mountainous area whilst the remainder of the island was colonized by *helix*.

For the garden, var. *cypria* is a good climbing ivy for north or east walls, it is a rapid grower whose overhanging leaves make attractive coverage.

Habit: Vining.

Stems: Purple-green. Internodes 4–5cm (1½–2in).

Petioles: Purple-green.

Leaves: Unlobed, 7–9cm (2¾–3½in) by 5–6cm (2–2⅓in), occasional vestigial lateral lobes. Lanceolate and ovate, apices acuminate and prolonged, leaf base truncate to slightly cordate. Dark green, veins of younger leaves surrounded by areas of grey-green giving a dappled appearance. Scale-type hairs of 10–12 short, brown rays. Adult leaves, flowers and fruit not seen.

Hedera rhombea Miq

This, the Japanese ivy, has had a more than usually chequered nomenclatural career which is perhaps best encapsulated in chronological style.

1784 Thunberg (1743–1822) published *Flora Japonica* in which he described the plant using the name bestowed by Linnaeus on the common European ivy, *H. helix*. Thunberg commented that it grew near Nagasaki and had unlobed leaves.

1863 The Dutch botanist Miquel recorded it in *Annales Musei Botanici Lugduno Batavi* (Bat 1, p13) as *H. rhombea* with the required Latin description as follows. "Juvenile leaves three to five-lobed, ovate acuminate; adult leaves rhomboid-lanceolate. Adult shoots terminate in panicles of umbels of flowers. Stellate scales scattered on stems. Fruit probably black." He gave its origin as southern Japan, Kyushu island.

1912 Tobler described the Japanese ivy as a new species under the name of *H. japonica*, presumably unaware of the earlier valid publication by Miquel.

1924 The botanist Nakai in the Journal of the Arnold Arboretum (V.24–27), rejecting *rhombea*, coined the name *H. tobleri*.

1965 In the *Flora of Japan* Ohwi listed the Japanese ivy as *H. rhombea* and noted a form, *pedunculata* from Kyushu, as having peduncles and pedicels longer than normal, the latter from 2–4cm (¾–1½in).

Thus between 1784 and 1942 the plant attracted four names and one must have considerable sympathy with the nurserymen, uncertain as to where their loyalties lay between *helix*, *rhombea*, *japonica* or *tobleri*, an uncertainty manifest in catalogues of the period.

The plant is found in Japan from Kyushu north to the centre islands but excluding Hokkiado, then west through the southern portion of the Korean peninsula. It is not in general cultivation, it is the variegated clone, *H. rhombea* 'Variegata' that has been most frequently planted. Sundry 19th-century references to 'Rhomboidea' may refer to what we know as 'Deltoidea' or possibly to *helix* forms with slightly rhomboid leaves.

Habit: Vining.

Stems: Green-purple. Internodes 2–2.5cm (¾–1in). Scale hairs 10–18 rays.

Petioles: Green-purple.

Leaves: Generally unlobed, ovate to triangular, 2–4cm (¾–1½in) by 4–5cm (1½–2in). Texture thick, apex acute, leaf base truncate or slightly cordate. Medium green, veins recessed in the leaf blade tend to give a milky-veined appearance to the leaf. Chromosome number 2n=48.

Hedera rhombea 'Variegata'

The first reference I have been able to find to a variegated form of the Japanese ivy is that in La Belgique Horticole of 1865 where it is described as "A distinct green leafed variety, leaves edged with a silver band." In 1866 the nursery firm Dillistone & Woodthorp of Sible Hedingham, Essex, catalogued "*Hedera rhombea variegata*, the new Japanese ivy," but also listed "*H. japonica argentea*, neatly edged with silver". It was included by the nurseryman William Paul in 1867 in the *colchica* section of the varieties he grew as, "Leaves dark green, slightly but regularly margined with silver, broad and smooth. Very distinct and elegant." In the same section he listed also '*Hedera japonica*, leaves green, clearly and regularly margined with white, small. Very pretty, producing dense masses of foliage."

It is strange that two very similar ivies appear to have been in circulation, however the 1865 catalogue of E G Henderson & Sons of London sheds some light on the puzzle. It listed "*Japonica argentea* (New Japanese). Silver margined Japan ivy, introduced by Mr Fortune, distinct."

One of the most successful of plant introducers, Robert Fortune (1812–80) visited Japan from 1860–62. Much of his collecting comprised buying plants from local nurseries, plants long cultivated in the East but new to Western gardens and presumably in that manner he collected the variegated Japanese ivy. It is understandable that he would name it *H. japonica argenta* for due to the long periods he spent away from Europe he would be unaware of the parent species as *H. rhombea*. It is extremely probable that those already familiar with the Japanese ivy as *H. rhombea* would, when presented with a variegated form, tack 'Variegata' onto that name as did the writer in La Belgique Horticole leading to two names in circulation for the same plant. There is so little difference in the descriptions of the two plants listed by Paul that we can assume that a small difference in individual plants led to two stocks being built up and listed as separate kinds. The plant appeared in many catalogues thereafter under both names as well as *H. japonica* 'Variegata'.

The Japanese variegated ivy, easily separated from any *helix* clones by virtue of its scale-like hairs, has particularly delicate variegation and is a good garden plant that would merit presentation for some horticultural award.

Habit: Vining.

Stems: Green-purple. Internodes 2–2.5cm (¾–1in). Scale hairs of 10–18 rays.

Petioles: Green-purple.

Leaves: Generally unlobed, ovate to triangular, 2–3cm (¾–1¼in) by 2.5–3cm (1–1¼in), texture thick, apex acute, leaf blade tending to concavity. Medium- to dark green with a narrow, regular rim of white at the leaf edge. Veins recessed in the leaf blade. Adult shoots short and delicate with ovate to circular leaves 3cm (1¼in) by 3cm (1¼in). Flowers not seen.

6

IVIES FOR GARDEN, HOUSE & LANDSCAPE

Above: The unique golden colouring of *Hedera helix* 'Buttercup' makes it a superbly decorative climbing ivy

Left: *Hedera colchica* 'Dentata Variegata' adds colour and interest to these garden steps

HOUSE AND GARDEN WALLS

It is a fact, though often disputed, that ivies will not harm any building or wall that is in good repair. The museum buildings of the Royal Botanical Gardens at Kew, Surrey, have supported ivies for almost 100 years with no sign of trouble and old buildings covered with ivy often retain a freedom from damp which they lose if deprived of their leafy insulation.

Vigorous ivies that have reached the top of walls or houses benefit from a biennial or sometimes annual clip with shears to remove old leaves and insect harbourage; it is also advisable to keep ivy growth well below the gutter line so that it does not grow into loft spaces.

Clipping is best done in high summer when not only is there no danger of disturbing nesting birds but the new growth will be sufficiently restricted to provide neat over-winter coverage without the leafy exuberance that can occur if ivy is clipped in early spring. Large-leaved kinds such as *H. colchica* should be pruned with secateurs to avoid the eyesore of half-cut leaves.

If there are borders in front of the wall against which ivy is grown, consideration should be given both to the variety of ivy and to the plants that may grow in front of it. For example yellow-leaved 'Buttercup' with a front planting of caryopteris, the blue spiraea, in its several kinds or the blue-flowered *Ceratostigma plumbaginoides* can make a splendid picture. Alternatively a blue-flowered clematis such as 'Perle d'Azure' may be planted to scramble over the ivy making the same colour contrast. The winter leafage and stems of the clematis will be cut down to some 45cm (18in) revealing the lovely lime-green and yellow of the ivy; 'Buttercup' also makes a superb backing for purple-leaved shrubs such as *Cotinus coggygria* 'Royal Purple'. If it is a south-facing situation the clone 'Angularis Aurea' can be used instead, its particular type of yellow variegation is less apt to suffer the sun scorch which sometimes affects 'Buttercup'.

The so called 'purple' ivies, 'Atropurpurea', 'Glymii' and 'Woeneri', make good backgrounds for yellow-flowered shrubs such as forsythia, coryopsis or the grey-leaved *Senecio* 'Sunshine'. Another attractive combination can be made by planting *H. helix* 'Glacier' to climb up and through *Cotoneaster horizontalis*: the silvery grey-green leaves make a delightful foil for the red berries.

The soft cream-grey of *H. hibernica* 'Sulphurea' makes it an ideal background for scarlet or blue flowers such as phlox, red roses or delphiniums. If a climbing red rose would not show to advantage against a red brick wall owing to the clash of colour, a 'curtain' of 'Sulphurea' could be interposed. It would make an admirable background for the rose, which would not suffer by being trained against the ivy. In the same way *Clematis jackmanii*, lovely against a white wall, loses much of its attraction when seen against red brick. If allowed to climb against an ivy such as 'Glacier', 'Sulphurea' or *H. colchica* 'Dentata Variegata', the deep-purple flowers show to advantage. The clematis will need to be cut almost to the ground in autumn but the variegated ivy will remain to colour the wall area through winter.

Turning from colour combination and thinking only in terms of wall coverage, the ivy chosen should bear some relation to the height and breadth of wall to be covered. While the normal-sized *helix*-type leaves adapt to any wall space, the large-leaved kinds look out of place on short stretches of low wall.

In planting for wall coverage it should be borne in mind that while the green kinds will be 'absorbed' in the general scene, the eye will be drawn to the more brightly variegated kinds, thus one can choose whether to attract or deflect the eye from a particular point or area.

IN THE LANDSCAPE

For the landscape architect ivy provides the ideal background plant: hardy, uncomplaining as to soil or situation and reasonably cheap. It is small wonder that tens of thousands are used each year. Ivy is resilient to the kinds of abuse often sustained in areas such as town centres, motorway service stations, roundabouts, open spaces in housing developments and so on.

Ivy's value is mainly as ground cover, for good reasons architects are reluctant to use ivy or indeed other climbers on walls of public buildings. Climbers can give rise to maintenance problems and also require more care than the average public authority can give. An ivy-covered town hall is, unhappily, not likely to be seen in Britain!

Since as far back as 1868 *H. hibernica* has been favoured as ground cover but more recently advantage has been taken of the wide range of ivy clones available as regards colour and leaf shape. For example a ground-cover 'base' of *hibernica* is attractive with, at intervals, arborescent plants of variegated clones such as 'Goldheart' or 'Angularis Aurea'. Particularly suitable for a large area, overshadowed perhaps by tall

Above and far left: *Hedera helix* 'Angularis Aurea', bright green and glossy leaved, is the perhaps the most reliable of all the yellow-variegated ivies. It makes superb cover for walls and buildings in shade or sun

Left: The 'Ivy Wall' surrounding the Palm House at Kew Botanical Gardens is often assumed to be an ivy-clad wall but is in fact a planting, made at the turn of the century, of clipped 'tree' ivies. These were extremely popular in Victorian times but are less often seen today

buildings, is a ground cover of the large-leaved *H. colchica* 'Dentata' with specimens of the arborescent variegated form planted at intervals. To give an illusion of height, variegated ground cover can have arborescent specimens of the same clone planted at intervals.

Reverse planting, that is to say a ground cover of variegated clone with arborescent green kinds at intervals, is also effective. The use of 'pillar' ivies (juvenile-state ivies trained on wood pillars) placed at intervals in a ground cover of a contrasting variety is feasible but necessitates more maintenance.

For small areas, enclosures of about 3 x 3m (10 x 10ft), a ground cover of variegated ivy can have a single plant of *H. helix* 'Erecta' in the centre. For immediate effect three plants may be better but it should be borne in mind that the ultimate spread of 'Erecta' is about m (3ft). For even smaller areas the thin-stemmed and weaker-growing 'Congesta' can be used. This arrangement can be very effective if *H. helix* 'Buttercup' is used as ground-cover. It does not colour as well as it does on a wall but the soft yellow-green that it adopts in such a situation can be quietly pleasing.

An occasional landscape problem is that of tree stumps in situations where their removal is difficult or undesirable but some form of screening is required. Ivy's evergreen nature makes it ideal for this purpose. If the stump is to merge into the background, select a green kind, *H. hibernica* or *H. helix*; if it is in any way a focal point, a variegated kind, large or small leaved according to the size of the stump. Since soil in such a situation may not be of the best, suitable planting holes should be made.

A landscape effect that harks back to a more leisured era is the 'wall' made of closely planted 'tree' ivies. A most striking example of this is that surrounding the Palm House Terrace at Kew Gardens in Surrey. Many people assume it to be an ivy-covered wall but it is in fact a low-clipped hedge of arborescent *H. hibernica* 'tree' plants.

A 'fedge' is defined as a cross between a fence and a hedge. It can be a useful feature and usually implies climbing plants on a fence of wire, wattle-hurdle, spaced-board or chestnut fencing. Climbing ivies are excellent for the purpose. Initially they may need a little tying in as an encouragement to climb but kinds such as 'Deltoidea', 'Sulphurea', 'Digitata',

'Palmata' or even common ivy quickly provide an evergreen face to what may be an uninviting prospect. A fedge can be worthwhile in a narrow garden where a hedge would take up much-needed ground; it can even make a chain-link fence a thing of beauty.

Victorian gardening books often show ivy-covered arbours; a sitting place of fairly rough and basic wood outline can be made attractive when covered with ivy. On both fedge and arbour, clipping will be necessary and care should be taken to check adult growth which may bunch out at the top and make the structure top-heavy.

COVER FOR SHEDS, GARAGES AND OTHER BUILDINGS

One assumes that house and garden walls have at least some architectural merit, but this is not always so with garages or garden sheds. A quick-growing evergreen climber is often needed and nothing excels ivy for this purpose. Obtrusive concrete and inappropriately coloured brick can become most attractive and quickly assume an established air.

For larger structures two kinds reign supreme, the large-leaved *H. colchica* 'Dentata' and the slighter smaller *H. hibernica*. Among a number of kinds suitable for smaller structures, the bright-green leaves of *H. helix* 'Angularis' or the more sculptured leaves of 'Digitata' and 'Pedata' make pleasant cover. 'Obovata' with its rather kidney-shaped leaves is quick growing and gives good dark-green cover. As with ivies for walls, variegated kinds can make excellent cover (although they are slower growing) but this can of course draw attention to the feature. If there is no objection *H. colchica* 'Dentata Variegata' is superb as a large-leaved ivy, of the smaller-leaved kinds the variegated clone of 'Angularis' supplies brilliant yellow variegation.

GROUND COVER

The term 'ground cover' is applied to plants which by their spreading and close habit of growth cover the ground to the exclusion of weeds. When established, ground cover will preclude the establishment of seed-borne weeds but it is essential to eliminate all perennial weeds before planting.

Ivies are very suitable plants for ground cover and increasingly used in these days of high-cost garden labour. The idea is not new; ivy-clad banks and beds were often a feature of large gardens in Victorian times. Interestingly M Delchevalerie, Chef de Culture au Fleuriste of the City of Paris, writing in La Belgique Horticole in 1868 recommended "La Lierre d'Irlande" *H. hibernica*, for this purpose in towns. His advice was indeed followed as can be seen to this day in Paris and many other European cities.

Hedera colchica 'Dentata Variegata', a spectacular hardy ivy suitable for walls, buildings and ground cover for large areas

The characteristics required of ground-cover ivies are close leafage, a spreading habit, resistance to frost and general toughness. A walk through almost any wood in Britain and northern Europe shows the suitability of the common ivy *H. helix* for the purpose.

There are however more interesting kinds for garden situations. First is *H. hibernica*, that mentioned by M Delchevalerie. Seldom affected by frost in Britain and Europe and widely grown in America, its five-lobed, matt-green leaves are close enough to make good cover whilst its vigour ensures spread. Tolerant of town conditions and shade it has been used to screen many an eyesore.

For reasonably large areas the striking elephant's ears of *H. colchica* 'Dentata' make interesting and effective ground cover. The plant runs more widely but less thickly than *H. hibernica* and needs rather better soil. It is frost hardy as is its variegated clone 'Dentata Variegata', which will bring light to any dull corner. For smaller areas there is plenty of choice: the grey-green and sulphur-yellow *H. hibernica* 'Sulphurea' is less vigorous than other *hibernica* clones, underplanted with blue spring-flowering bulbs such as *Chionodoxa luciliae*, *Muscari* or *Scilla* it can present a very attractive picture.

Clones with varying leaf shapes such as *H. helix* 'Maple Leaf', 'Königer' and 'Parsley Crested' and the wavy-leaved 'Manda's Crested', whose leaves turn a pleasant coppery shade in winter, can produce interesting cover. Daffodils are often planted in mown grass but if an area has been given over to ground-cover ivies, bright-green leaved clones such as 'Angularis' and 'Pittsburgh' or the darker-leaved 'Walthamensis' make an attractive and trouble-free background for this spring favourite. This same ivy is undoubtedly the best one to serve as a background for snowdrops: the dark green leaves show off the white flowers to perfection. Later in the year ivy can provide first-class protection for the autumn crocus – *Colchicum* sp.. These lovely autumn-flowering corms are not always easy to place in the garden. In open ground the flowers become mud-spattered by autumn rains and in spring their substantial foliage can overpower smaller plants. Planted to grow up through ivy ground cover, preferably large-leaved variegated clones (*H. colchica* 'Dentata Variegata' is ideal) the flowers have protection and their lilac colours are enhanced by the cream-yellow variegation of the ivy. *H. hibernica* 'Sulphurea' is another very suitable clone for this purpose.

Planting distances for ground-cover ivies are to an extent governed by the speed with which cover is required. One plant will cover 8.5m^2 (10yd^2) over a period of say five years. Most people require more rapid cover and it is realistic to plant at 60cm- (2ft-) intervals to gain adequate cover in a couple of years.

In countries where grass is expensive to maintain or difficult to keep alive use can be made of ivy for carpeting the ground. In this capacity it is sometimes planted beside freeways in California and elsewhere in the USA. The kinds used are usually *H. hibernica* or *H. canariensis* 'Ravensholst' at four plants per square metre or yard. The ground cover can be kept trim by rotary mowing, in which case the mower should be fitted with a pick-up box and the work done in spring. Leaves that have died or become discoloured during the winter will then be collected and a pleasant green carpet will soon result. This system can be adopted for any large area of ivy ground cover.

ROCK GARDENS

Rock gardens tend to be of two kinds. The first and most acceptable is that built after the tradition of Reginald Farrer: a garden of alpine flowers based on nature's own rock gardens, providing suitable habitats for true alpine plants. The other may be termed public or municipal, where attractive and often natural rock and water effects, although planted primarily with alpines, are filled in with non-alpines, even bedding plants, to provide colour and display for as long as possible.

Certain ivies can be useful in both kinds of garden. For the first, the truly alpine garden, the only ivies to be admitted are the small-leaved clones of *helix* that make ground cover for small bulbs, particularly those such as early crocus species or the delicate flowers of *Leucojum autumnale* that benefit from protection from mud-splash. Small-leaved ivies such as 'Mrs Ulin', 'Walthamensis' or the minute-leaved 'Spetchley' are excellent for this purpose.

Three ivies, *H. helix* 'Conglomerata', 'Erecta' and 'Congesta' are often seen on rock gardens, even those of the alpine purist; 'Conglomerata' will cover a rock attractively with its wavy leaves and stubby little stems while the erect, self-supporting stems of 'Erecta' and 'Congesta', the latter of finer growth and narrower leaves, are very effective as spot plants. They are more easily controlled and cut back than the conifers often used as focal points.

While the purist's rock garden should not admit variegated ivies, the more showy 'public' type of garden need have no such inhibitions. On big rock gardens backgrounds may be needed or a drift of evergreen to link the rock garden into surrounding features. For such purposes few ivies can equal *H. colchica* 'Sulphur Heart', large-leaved and with enough variegation to provide interest. On rocks or in alpine pockets, small-leaved clones such as the glossy green 'Ivalace' with its distinct crimped leaves or variegated clones such as 'Eva', 'Harald' or 'Midas Touch' provide colour and a good background to bright-coloured annuals or flowering bulbs.

TOWN GARDENS

When smoke-belching chimneys added soot and sulphur to even a slightly foggy day, evergreens, including ivy, fared badly. Deciduous trees and shrubs drop their soot-clogged leaves in autumn; ivy, whose leaves may persist for three or four years, presented in common with other evergreens a sorry sight. The decline of coal fires and the Clean Air Act released ivy from that handicap and presented those gardening in heavily shaded town gardens with a most effective all-purpose plant.

Walls enclosing town gardens are seldom of great beauty, they cry out to be covered with living green and for this nothing can surpass ivy for year-round coverage. There is a wide choice of varieties but for small areas it is advisable to avoid large-leaved kinds that can swamp the picture.

For plain green coverage it is hard to beat *H. pastuchovii*, particularly in its quick-growing Cyprus variety. The shield-shaped leaves naturally hang downwards and produce a striking curtain of glossy dark-green leafage. As a contrast in leaf shapes there are the finger-leaved kinds such as the light-green *H. azorica* and the dark-green 'Pedata'; 'Asterisk' and 'Lalla Rookh' have yellowish-green, finely cut leaves. Dark corners can be brightened with yellow variegated kinds such as 'Goldheart', 'Goldchild' and 'Midas Touch'. The more modest white variegated kinds such as 'Glacier' and the speckled salt-and-pepper ivy 'Minor Marmorata' all add to the overall interest. The variegated form of the Japanese ivy, *H. rhombea* 'Variegata', is slow growing but its silver-edged leaves have great charm.

If in addition to wall coverage surface ivies are planned, there is ample choice. There are contrasting types such as 'Manda's Crested' whose wavy leaves turn a pleasant copper shade in winter and 'Parsley Crested' whose light green leaves have crested and curled edges. Both are fairly vigorous growers. Others to give interest include 'Curvaceous' with wavy cream-variegated leaves and the several small-leaved variegated kinds such as 'Schäfer Three', 'Bruder Ingobert' and 'Spectre'. Variation in the form of height can be provided by the erect ivies 'Erecta' and 'Congesta' planted in situations that will draw the eye. A similar role can be played by 'standard' ivies. These can be grown in large pots and set out patio style. Standard ivies can be grafted (see page 150) but if grown (a process that can take from three to five years) or procured as trained specimens, they can give an impression of age and dignity. Standards of the poet's ivy *H. helix* f. *poetarum*, which has orange berries, always excite interest.

IVIES AS HOUSE PLANTS

The virtue of ivy as a house plant is so well established that, not unreasonably, many people think of the plant in only that capacity. Its suitability for indoor cultivation in pots, glass cases and special window cases was recognized and popular in Victorian times in Britain, America and several European countries.

Between the wars ivy lost its Victorian popularity but after World War II an upsurge of interest in house plants generally led to recognition of its merits and its present popularity as a decorative plant for home, office or restaurant. This popularity depends in part on the plant's acceptance of shaded situations and, perhaps regrettably, its acceptance of rather indifferent care. Reasonable attention to watering, occasional feeding with a balanced fertilizer and re-potting when the plant has outgrown its original container will result in a healthy plant and a pleasure to the eye. Unhappily the reverse is all too often seen: ivies sitting in a south-facing window where they quickly dry out, become under-watered and fall victim to red spider mite.

While ivies look attractive as individual pot specimens a useful alternative is to plant several kinds in a plant trough. Short-jointed kinds such as 'Eva', 'Harald', 'Luzii', 'Ivalace', 'Midas Touch' and 'William Kennedy' can be planted so as to contrast with one another. If required as a room divider the trough may be set against a lattice screen of wood or metal and some plants set to climb. Varieties such as *canariensis* var. *algeriensis* 'Gloire de Marengo', 'Manda's Crested', 'Green Ripple' and 'Goldchild' may be tried in this situation. Because of its comparative permanence the lattice must be in a reasonably good light situation since poor light will lead to pale, attenuated growth.

There are many clones whose unusual leaf shapes or variegation show to good effect as pot plants. A full list is given in the Index of Ivies (pages 153–6) but the following are particularly noteworthy: 'Bruder Ingobert', 'Caecilia', 'Lalla Rookh', 'Olive Rose', 'Melanie', 'Professor Friedrich Tobler', 'Sally' and 'Triton'.

PILLAR IVIES

Elegant ivy pillars, suitable as decorative features in the home and also for large displays in hotel foyers and the like may be built around moss-sticks. Previously these were based on bamboo canes but nowadays rigid plastic tubing of the kind used for water pipes is used. The length may vary from 0.9–1.8m (3–6ft) according to requirements and the diameter should be about 4cm (1½in). Sphagnum moss is bound with twine to encase the pipe. The lower part of the stick is then inserted into a compost-filled pot of between 15–25cm (6–10in) in diameter according to the stick length.

One or two ivies are planted and trained, preferably in a twisting fashion, up the moss-stick which they eventually clothe completely. The stick should be kept moist and indeed a fairly warm and moist growing atmosphere is best to get the plants going.

A variation on this is the familiar pyramid made by inserting three or four canes down the side of a compost-filled pot and tying the cane tips at the top. Hoops of stout wire can also be used. All these erect types of support require climbing kinds of ivy. The following have been used with success: *H. canariensis* var. *algeriensis* 'Gloire de Marengo' and 'Margino-Maculata' and the *helix* clones, 'Green Feather', 'Shamrock', 'Glacier', 'Parsley Crested' and 'Green Ripple'. 'Goldheart' may be used but needs to be grown up quickly.

Of them all 'Gloire de Marengo' is the most widely used and from the number grown one would imagine it to be in every house, office and public building throughout the ivy-growing world. It is a good-tempered plant for the purpose with bright variegation and glossy leaf.

HANGING BASKETS

These are an interesting form of floral decoration for verandas and patios and often become cherished features. For good effect they require brightly coloured flowers but these do not always trail and hang down as quickly as required. Small-leaved ivies can fulfil this purpose very well. Grown in house or greenhouse in 8–10cm- (3–4in-) pots and then planted three or four to a basket, they hang down giving pleasant backing to pelargoniums and fuchsias until lobelia, *lysimachia* or similar flowering plants trail and blend their flowers with the ivy.

It is possible, of course, to make an all-ivy hanging basket, supplementing the trailing kinds with short-jointed variegated kinds for the basket centre. The clone 'Professor Friedrich Tobler' is unsurpassed for trailing, its deeply split foliage is most unusual and readily provokes comment and query. 'Mrs Ulin' is another good clone, small leaved and with quite good trails. For the centre clones such as 'Ardingly', 'Eva', 'Luzii' and 'Midas Touch' are very suitable; 'Melanie' with its purple-edged, curly leaves also throws commendable trails. Ivies will persist and over-winter in such baskets but this is not advisable: even if they survive they eventually look very unhappy.

BOTTLE GARDENS AND TERRARIA

The fact that a virtually enclosed glass vessel will support plant life for long periods with minimum attention has been known for well over a century. The principle was used in the form of the botanical 'Wardian Case' that was extensively used for the long-distance conveyance of plants before the advent of rapid air transport.

The more recent vogue for bottle gardens makes use of the same principle. Broad-based glass bottles of some 30cm (12in) diameter at the base and about the same height taper to an 8cm- (3in-) open neck. A layer of moist soilless compost is placed in the bottom and, using long tweezers, three or four plants of a suitable selection are planted in the compost and lightly watered in. Plants often used are the smaller *dracaenas*, *cryptanthus*, leaf begonias and of course *Hedera*, usually a variegated clone such as 'Harald'.

It is possible to make a very attractive bottle garden with the same technique but using only ivies. Suitable clones are 'Bruder Ingobert', 'Ardingly', 'Harald', 'Eva', 'Midas Touch'

and 'Spetchley'. As with all bottle gardens, overcrowding problems will arise. These may be controlled initially by careful trimming, but a re-plant will eventually be required.

Terraria are glass cases similar to household aquaria and indeed like the original Wardian Case. Planting and growing techniques are the same as for bottle gardens but as the top is open, or has a removable lid, access is easier and a more extensive range can be grown.

TOPIARY

Topiary usually conjures pictures such as the ancient yews of Levens Hall Gardens, Kendal, Cumbria, UK planted in 1698 and clipped into fantastic shapes over the centuries. The same art is alive and well today: plants of yew, box and bay, clipped into spirals, globes or peacocks still enhance various garden situations. Most of those on sale in Britain originate in Belgium which has a long tradition of producing these trees.

Ivy was used in topiary in a small way in Victorian Britain but it is in America that the practice has really taken off. It is used to make three-dimensional figures similar to those sometimes created by public park departments in connection with summer bedding, but on a truly fantastic scale.

The procedure involves wire forms of various shapes that are stuffed tightly with sphagnum moss or sometimes a mixture of moss and coarse peat, this having first been soaked in a dilute fertilizer solution. The whole is then planted up with rooted cuttings or small plants of suitably short-jointed clones such as 'Chicago', 'Direktor Badke', 'Goldchild', 'Ivalace', 'Merion Beauty', 'Needlepoint', 'Schäfer Three', 'Shamrock' or 'Wichtel'.

This bald account of the modus operandi does not convey the height which the art has achieved in America. The pages of the American Ivy Society's journal depict entire animal zoos as well as prehistoric animals, all life-size, as well as a pony and trap which can accommodate driver and passengers. Much of the enthusiasm for these fascinating productions has been engendered by *The New Topiary* by Pat Hamer, a remarkable book by an expert topiarist with, happily, a penchant for ivy.

Like its bedding-plant counterpart however this three-dimensional topiary does not have the staying power of the Levens Hall topiary. Housed under large glass-covered areas it will persist given the constant clipping and water-spraying needed. It might over-winter in the mildest areas of Britain but to date there has been no enthusiasm for large set pieces. Occasionally one sees small figures, cats or dogs for example, carried out in the manner described above and usually kept indoors or under glass.

PLATE X

All plants are shown at approximately ³/₄ size

H. helix 'Mathilde'

H. helix 'Adam'

H. helix 'Filigran'

H. helix 'Hazel'

H. helix 'Manda's Crested'

H. helix 'Pedata'

H. helix 'Lalla Rookh'

H. helix 'Ritterkreuz'

H. helix 'California Gold'

H. helix 'Romanze'

H. helix 'Leo Swicegood'

7

THE CULTIVATION OF IVY

PROPAGATION

Anyone who has gardened will have come across ivy seedlings when weeding. They appear in awkward places, in paving cracks or with choice plants on the rock garden. Their frequency often correlates to the amount of adult ivy in the vicinity; birds, particularly blackbirds, feed on the berries, the seeds pass through the bird and are dropped where they rest or feed. For anyone wishing to raise ivies from seed, the clues are there – imitate nature! Fresh seeds should be taken from ripe berries, cleaned of pulp and sown on the surface of damp sand, compost or even blotting paper kept moist in a petri dish. In a temperature of 5–10°C (40–50°F) germination takes from four to six weeks.

Few however will wish or need to undertake this procedure. Ivies root extremely easily from cuttings, furthermore most people are interested in ivy clones that have particular leaf characteristics or variegation; such characteristics are not usually transmitted by seed. A notable exception here is 'Buttercup'; this is probably because its variegation is genetic rather than chimaeric as most variegated ivies are (see page 30).

Fortunately most ivies are easy to propagate, producing trails which root at the nodes when lying on the soil. Sections of these trails when cut off will root easily and may be planted where they are required to grow or, as a refinement, first planted in a frame of sandy soil.

For the commercial grower, or where large quantities are required, this method is hardly sufficient and in any event is not suitable for tree ivies or for *canariensis* or *colchica* varieties or non-trailing *helix* clones. For these and for situations where quantities are required, nodal cuttings are taken.

Nodal cuttings are made from trails or from shoots and are sections of stem cut so that the node is the base of the cutting. They should have one or two leaves at or above the next node. In taking material it should be remembered that cuttings from adult shoots, that is flowering shoots or shoots high up on a plant that has produced flowers, will produce 'tree' or shrub ivies. They are more difficult to root and it may well be necessary to use hormone rooting powder if a good-percentage 'take' is necessary.

Nodal cuttings may be inserted in a cold frame from mid- to late autumn when 12cm- (5in-) cuttings should be made of the previous season's growth. Alternatively, cuttings made in midsummer may be placed on a warm bench in a shaded glasshouse; they should be 7–10 cm (3–4 in) and of semi-hard shoots. A sand/peat compost is suitable. Cuttings taken in autumn should be ready to be lifted and potted the following mid-spring; summer cuttings after only about six weeks.

The pot-plant trade depends on a full-looking pot of ivy, produced as quickly as possible in order to economize on heat and provide a quick turnover. To this end five, six or seven small nodal cuttings are inserted in a 7.5cm- (3in-) pot filled with a normal potting compost, usually a sand/peat mix with nutrients. The pots are stood closely together often under polythene tents within a glasshouse and an average temperature of 18–21°C (65–70°F) maintained. The cuttings are kept moist with a watering can or an automatic spray. When the cuttings have rooted the pots are moved to a cooler house or the temperature is dropped to 15–18°C (60–65°F) for growing on.

This method is effective with all *helix* clones, but clones of other species do not respond readily to high temperatures and are best rooted by nodal cuttings inserted in boxes or directly in sand beds on a mist bench in a glasshouse.

When propagating clones with distinctive features or leaf vegetation, care should be taken to use only material typical of the clone. The inclusion of only slightly off-type material can result in batches of uneven plants that are not only less acceptable to buyers but also less easily identified as the clone being purchased.

COMPOSTS

Apart from topiary and outside planting, some form of compost is required for all other growing methods. In the past, potting soil was made using loam or garden soil, leaf mould and sand with the addition of bone-meal, sulphate of potash and lime according to the type of plant. In addition some gardeners favoured additions of organic materials bordering on the curious. Results were sometimes good but not consistently so. Working at the John Innes Research Institute in England, W J C Lawrence discovered that consistent growth and prevention of soil-borne diseases were effected by partial sterilization of the loam, substitution of the leafmould by peat and the addition of small amounts of fertilizers. The resulting compost was called 'John Innes' and although devised for experimental work it became extensively used in commercial and domestic horticulture.

Loams vary however and, seeking an even more standardized growing medium, the University of California in the 1950s produced the 'UC' composts of peat, sand and balanced nutrients. These, with few modifications, were widely adopted and although loam-based composts are still used for certain subjects the bulk of the pot plants produced in America, Britain and Europe are grown in peat/sand mixes. For domestic horticulture loam-based composts are preferable; fear of letting plants dry out in peat mixes, which are difficult to wet once dried out, can often lead to over-watering – fatal to ivies! Concern for the diminishing peat reserves is leading to great efforts to find suitable substitutes and whenever possible these should be sought out and used.

Ivies are tolerant of a wide range of soil types, they are basically calciphilous (chalk-loving) and grow better in conditions where the pH level, the acidity/alkalinity, is slightly above the neutral point of pH7. Commercial growers have the means to adjust the level and on a domestic scale it is readily achieved by adding something like a handful of mortar-rubble or crushed chalk to a 50kg (1cwt) bag of compost, unless of course it has been already adjusted in favour of calciphilous plants.

PLANTING

Ivies are remarkably adaptable but generally do best on alkaline soil. Garden or house walls often provide alkalinity by the lime or mortar in their foundations. If the support is not a wall, or the planting is for ground cover or rock work and the soil is acid, it may be worthwhile adding lime in some form, preferably old mortar rubble or crushed chalk. This should not be done if the border is designed to receive acidloving plants such as heathers or rhododendrons; ivies will tolerate the acid soil and still grow well enough.

Planting should be as for other shrubs or climbers with a hole dug out somewhat larger than the root-ball of the plant, the roots gently spread in the hole with the neck of the plant at soil surface level, the hole filled and the soil firmed around the roots. Spring and autumn are the best planting seasons, but pot-grown ivies can be planted at any time. In dry conditions the planting hole should be filled with water prior to planting and care taken to ensure that the plant does not dry out in its early days.

Plants for wall coverage should be planted as near to the wall as is practicable with the leading shoot directed to it. If the shoot is long it may be fixed with loose ties to wall-nails or a similar fixing. Given this gentle guidance the plant's climbing characteristics soon take over. Ivy can take a little while to establish but in spring and in favourable circumstances the rate of growth can be impressive. I have measured a young shoot of *H. hibernica* growing 10cm (4in) in 14 days, a rate of 1.4cm (⅗in) a day – useful if you have an ugly shed to cover!

PESTS AND DISEASES

From the gardener's point of view one of the virtues of ivy is its ease of cultivation. Whether outside or indoors it will survive treatment which would kill many other plants. In some respects this is unfortunate as it can result in the plants' either lingering in unsuitable situations or being riddled with pest or disease to which a lesser plant would have succumbed.

Advances in pest and disease control are rapid and continuous and specific recommendations can easily be outdated or invalidated by the increasing legislation to which poisonous sprays are subject. Having identified the problem it is fairly easy to find the means for its control. The Royal Horticultural Society will readily advise its members as will the British Ivy Society; in addition there are the services of horticultural sundriesmen. The USA, in addition to its university-based advisory organizations, has its own Ivy Society which gives specialized, locally based advice.

The pests and diseases detailed below are those most likely to occur in Britain; with one or two local variations they are mirrored in other countries and continents where ivy is grown.

PESTS

Mites

Ivy on walls, particularly dry sunny walls, can become infested with various species of mite. Most destructive is the red spider mite, the two-spotted mite of North America,

Hedera helix 'Erecta'. Ivies of this type are particularly suitable as front shrubs in woodland settings

Tetranychus urticae. There are various biological types of this and other mites but the kind of damage is common to all. It is first seen on the leaf surface as a light-yellow fine spotting, commencing in small patches but as the pest increases, covering the whole leaf. The effect is not unlike the suffused type of variegation seen on certain ivy clones. A check is easily made by turning the leaf over and examining it closely, preferably with a hand-lens, when the yellowish mites, eight legged and about 1mm (⅒in) long, are easily seen; in bad infestations the leaves may be covered with fine webbing among which the mites will move.

The term 'red spider' refers to the resting stage and the brownish-red colour the mites assume when lurking in crevices of plant tissue or glasshouse woodwork. They should not be confused with the harmless large active scarlet spider that is occasionally seen. Acaracides in various forms have been developed to control the pest but have been banned in many countries because of their harmful effect on the environment.

For the protection of greenhouse or conservatory ivies there is fortunately excellent biological control in the form of a predatory mite, *Phytoseiulus persimilis*. This can be purchased from specialist pest-control firms and will clear attacks, but inevitably when the red spider is killed off the predator is starved and may well have to be re-introduced the following year.

It is not possible to use the predator on outside ivies. Red spider flourishes in hot and dry conditions and the first practical measure is to avoid planting ivies in such situations. Sometimes however the pest will attack ivies even on a northern aspect. When faced with an infestation it is a good plan to clip the plant over in the summer as this removes the mature leaves and the mites with them. The clippings should be burnt. Spraying the plant occasionally with water will deter the pest and also promote the young growth with which, by autumn, the plant will be furnished.

Scale insects

Those likely to infest ivy are soft scale, *Coccus hesperidum*, brown scale, *Parthenolecanium corni*, oleander scale, *Aspidiotus hederae*, and cushion scale, *Chloropulvinaria floccifera*. Often the first sign of the pest to the casual observer is a sooty deposit on leaf surfaces. This in fact is a mould growing upon the sticky secretions made by the insects as they suck the plant sap. Scale insects all have similar features: the female is round, oval or flat, dark to light brown and about 3–4mm (⅛in)long. The cushion scale takes the form of a white 'cushion' about 5mm (³⁄₁₆in) long by 3mm (⅛in) wide. Beneath the shield of the female scale which adheres tightly to the leaf surfaces, the young scales are nurtured, eventually emerging as 'crawlers' who move on to other leaves or stems and settle. Losing the power of movement they develop their protective covering and in turn produce more crawlers. All scale insects are most vulnerable to sprays when in this crawler stage, usually between late spring and late summer on ivies outside.

Closely related to scale insects, mealy bugs, particularly *Pseudoccus gahani*, will sometimes infest greenhouse ivies. They differ from scale insects in that they are protected by a white waxy secretion. This protection is difficult to penetrate by sprays, particularly as the bugs often lurk in leaf axils, sheaths or similar secure places. A stiff-bristled 6–12mm (¼–½in) paintbrush dipped in methylated spirit can be used to tease them out: an old but well tried remedy appropriate to individual plants.

Aphids

Several kinds will on occasion colonize the young shoot tips of ivies outside, but little long-term damage is done. On house-plant ivies they can be more damaging but there are a number of recommended and safe sprays which should be used as soon as – or preferably before – the tell-tale 'sooty mould' is seen.

Vine weevil

As regards ivies, vine weevil *Otiorhynchus sulcatus* is a pest of pot-grown ivies rather than of those outside. It is a considerable nuisance to nurserymen for it is possible unwittingly to sell a plant whose root ball contains the immature grubs of this pernicious pest. The adults feed on leaves and seem to have a predilection for rhododendrons where cut out and frayed leaf edges are typical of weevil damage. This is unsightly but greater damage is done in the larval stage. The weevil lays its eggs close to the stems of the young plant, the emerging larvae burrow into the root system upon which they feed, gradually debilitating the plant. The larvae are creamy white, legless, wrinkled and lie in the soil in a curved position. They feed from early summer to late winter by which time they are about 15mm (⅝in) long and ready to pupate and emerge as adult weevils. They can occur in large numbers in potted ivies and it is sometimes worthwhile re-potting ivies that do not appear to be growing well – a surprising catch of larvae can occur.

When it was possible to use Aldrin the nursery trade had the pest completely under control. Added to the potting compost Aldrin kills the larvae as soon as they hatch. Very properly however, Aldrin was withdrawn from sale because of its persistence in the food chain. The vine weevil flourished again but happily a recent introduction of biological control in the form of a predatory eelworm, *Heterorhabditis*, has shown great promise. Obtainable from specialist pest-control outlets it is increasingly used by nurserymen.

DISEASES

Ivies growing on walls are less prone to attack by fungi or bacteria than are ground-cover or house-plant ivies. Moist conditions on the ground or in the greenhouse can occasionally predispose ivies to the comparatively few diseases that may assail the genus. These can be summarized as follows.

Bacterial leaf spot
(Xanthomonas hederae)

In Britain this occurs occasionally on glasshouse ivies but very rarely outside. It is seen as black spots, usually angular in outline, on the leaf surface. Bacteria are not easily controlled by sprays. If a rare or favoured plant is affected, picking off and immediately burning leaves may halt the spread, otherwise destruction of the plant by burning is the only course of action.

Ivy leaf spot
(Colletotrichum trichellum)

This appears as soft brown leaf spots up to 1cm (⅜in) in diameter: in bad cases they join up to cause the collapse of the whole leaf. It is spread mainly by water splash and if ivies are grown in wet, humid conditions it can be troublesome. It can be destructive outside, particularly on young growth in moist autumn periods. Fungicidal sprays to check the disease are often routine practice in commercial glass-houses. On a house or garden scale preventive sprays may be worthwhile if the disease is seen.

Black leaf spot
(Phyllosticta hedericola)

This is infrequently seen in Britain and then principally on *H. colchica* and its clones. The spots are large, 5–15mm (³⁄₁₆–⅝in)across, circular, deep black and with a slightly 'crusty' appearance. It can be unsightly and, if extensive, advice as to spraying should be sought.

Powdery mildew
(Oidium sp.)

This occasionally occurs under glass in Britain but appears to affect only the glossy-leaved *H. canariensis* and then only on large established pot plants. It is possibly caused by irregular watering.

Honey fungus
(Armillaria mellea)

This is a saprophytic fungus living on dead woody matter but unfortunately it can readily become parasitic. In maturity it appears as a cluster of brownish-yellow toadstools at the base of dead or dying trees or shrubs. Vast quantities of spores are dispersed from the toadstools but it can also spread through the soil by means of boot-lace-like growths of compacted mycelium. These extend through the soil until they encounter tree or shrub roots which they then invade. Although honey fungus is mainly of concern to arboriculturists, instances have occurred of ivies planted to cover dead trees becoming infected and dying.

VIRUSES

Many plants propagated by vegetative means are plagued by virus problems but there are no records of crippling virus diseases affecting ivies. It has been suggested that the more bizarre variegation patterns in some house-plant ivies, *H. helix* 'Fantasia' for example, may be virus induced. This is doubtful: that clone among others has been tested by both sap inoculation and electron-microscope examination and found to be virus free.

The type of 'suffused' variegation seen in *H. helix* 'Angularis Aurea' and others is more suspect. Arabis Mosaic Virus (AMV) and Strawberry Latent Ringspot Virus (SLRV) have been identified in ivies with this type of variegation but it is fair to say that samples examined subsequently have failed to show the virus. This suggests that viruses in ivies may be of a somewhat transient nature and it may explain

the curious episode of *H. helix* 'Tessellata' (see page 118) where a very striking 'vein clearing' type of variegation disappeared within two years. The possibility of virus-induced variegation is discussed in more detail on page 31. A theory that fasciation in ivies or indeed the erect forms themselves may be virus manifestations has been disproved by the work of Witz and others.

GRAFTING

Ivies as standards were grown in Victorian gardens: in Shirley Hibberd's *The Ivy* (1872) there is an illustration and description of the training process. Cuttings of the common ivy, or indeed any preferred variety, were pot grown, cane tied and topped at 0.6–0.9m (2–3ft) according to requirements. Lower-side shoots were consistently removed so that a 'head' eventually developed. Hibberd does not mention the possibility of grafting and strangely, having regard to the long history of grafting, there seems no written reference to the grafting of ivy until very recently.

Standards produced as described above can look very effective growing in large ornamental pots. It is a process that will take anything from four to ten years; the plants acquire a suitably aged appearance and ten-year-old plants will possess stems sufficiently thick to support the head unaided. If four years seems too long standards can be

A standard *Hedera helix* 'Glacier' with *Hedera helix* 'Kolibri' (right) and *Hedera helix* 'Chicago' (left) in a formal situation

The novel appearance of standard ivies and their presentation of variegated foliage at eye level make them ideal plants for focal points as in this example of *Hedera helix* 'Adam' with a pot of *Hedera helix* 'Trinity' at its foot

produced in a much shorter time by grafting onto stocks of *Fatshedera* x *Fatshedera lizei*. This quick-growing vigorous plant was the result of a chance cross between *Fatsia japonica* and *H. hibernica* that occurred in 1910 on the nursery of Lizé Frères and was first seen at a flower show in Nantes, France, in 1912. Cuttings of this rapidly produce pot-grown plants that can be easily grafted. The procedure needs to be carried out in a greenhouse or indoors. The stock should be vigorous and preferably no more than 12 months old. The height is determined by personal preference.

The stock should be kept dry for two weeks prior to grafting in order to prevent any burst of sap pushing the graft away. The tip of the stock is cut off just above a node at the required height and the leaves removed from the top 15–22cm (6–9in) leaving an area devoid of foliage upon which to work. Personal choice will govern the clones used as scions, clones that produce long trails can be impressive on tall stocks but more compact kinds make an interesting rounded head. It is desirable to insert four grafts, which need not necessarily be of the same kind but should be of a similar growth habit. The scion material chosen should be vigorous. The scion is prepared by removing the lower two leaves and making a sloping 15mm (¾in) cut on each side so as to give a wedge-shaped base. On the stock, cut down the middle of

the stem about 15mm (¾in) using a sharp knife and, leaving the knife in the cut, insert the ends of the wedged-shaped scion in the opened cut. The scion should be placed so that the cambium, the growth area just under the skin, is against that of the stock and pushed down so that the cut surface is just visible on top of the stock. Withdraw the knife so that the cut closes to grasp the scion.

Using clear adhesive tape bind the graft fairly tightly and cover all the cut surfaces. To achieve a voluminous head it is a good plan to insert two more scions by grafting them on the side of the stock about 5–8cm(2–3in) from the top. For this side graft make a sloping cut 15mm (¾in) long in the side of the stem, prepare a scion as before, insert into the cut and bind in place with tape. The final stage is to place a clear polythene bag enclosing the grafts over the top of the plant to prevent them from drying out before a union is made.

The best time for grafting is early spring when plants are active and temperatures rarely reach harmful levels. After grafting the plant should be kept dry, watered perhaps once a week. Four weeks after grafting the polythene bag should be untied, so as to ventilate the grafts gradually, and finally removed completely. The plant will of course need to be cane supported.

In the USA *Schefflera arboricola* is often used as a stock. Possibly it is more readily available as young plants there than it is in the UK, certainly it is likely to make a more sturdy stem and American experience indicates that it grafts perfectly well.

BUDDING

It is possible to bud ivies in rather the same manner as roses and fruit trees are budded. A leaf with its incipient bud is carefully sliced off and a 'T'-shaped cut is made in the stem, the stem having been prepared as for grafting. The bud is inserted and carefully bound so as to hold the leaf in place but leaving the bud itself exposed. Unless the scion variety is very small leaved it is a good plan to reduce the size of the leaf by about half. The top of the stock is not cut off until the bud or buds have 'taken'.

Due to the soft nature of both stock and scion it is a more fiddly procedure and the success rate always seems lower. In view of the ease with which grafts can be made and the high rate of success there seems little point in pursuing the more difficult technique.

GLOSSARY

Acuminate Tapering to a fine point.

Acute Sharply pointed.

Adventitious Normally all roots other than those produced from a seedling. In the ivy context often refers to the roots or rootlets produced on climbing stems.

Apex (pl **apices**) Leaf or lobe tip.

Auriculate Ear-shaped extensions at the base of the leaf.

Basal lobes The two lower lobes adjacent to the petiole.

Canaliculate Having a longitudinal groove or channel.

Cleft The bottom or lower part of the sinus.

Clone Any number of plants arising originally by vegetative propagation from one plant or portion of a plant.

Convolute Rolled with two edges towards each other.

Cordate Heart-shaped, when the base of the leaf curves back from each side of the petiole.

Cultivar (abb **cv.**) A clearly distinguishable cultivated plant which when propagated retains its distinctive characteristics. Can apply to seed-raised plants unlike 'clone' which presumes vegetative propagation only.

Cuneate Wedge-shaped at leaf base tapering to the petiole.

Cuspidate Abruptly sharp-pointed.

Deltoid Irregularly triangular.

Distichous Arranged in two opposite rows.

Entire A description usually applied to the leaf edge meaning plain or untoothed.

Forma (abb **f.**) The lowest category of taxonomic rank, often applied to little more than differences in berry colour.

Genus (pl **Genera**) A group name comprising related species. *Hedera* is the genus to which all ivies belong.

Indumentation The occurrence of hairs or down on a plant.

Internodes The spaces between the nodes or joints of the stem.

Lanceolate Shaped like a spear blade.

Lateral lobes In ivies, the lobes immediately below the centre lobe.

Leaf blade The flat part of the leaf.

Leaf base Where the leaf blade joins the petiole.

Linear Long and narrow with almost parallel sides.

Lobes Divisions of a leaf which do not go as far as the mid-rib.

Mid-rib The central vein running from the petiole to the leaf tip or furthermost leaf part.

Moss-sticks Stout bamboo sticks or plastic tubes 1½in (3.7cm) diameter to which sphagnum moss is tightly bound to make a moss-covered stick. If kept moist, house plants including ivy will root into and cling to it.

Mutation Changes in plant habit, leaf shape or colour caused by breakdowns or divergences in the cell system. Most ivy clones are the result of mutations. See also **Sport**.

Node The point of union between petiole and stem.

Obtuse A blunt leaf tip.

Orbiculate Almost circular in outline.

Ovate Egg-shaped in outline.

Petiole The leaf stalk from stem to leaf blade.

Ramulose *See* **Self-branching**.

Reniform Kidney shaped.

Rhomboidal Similar to two triangles joined base to base.

Rootlets The adventitious roots by which ivy clings.

Sagittate Like an arrow head with two equal basal lobes directed downwards.

Scale hairs Hairs arising from epidermal cells having from 7 to 20 rays and so closely adpressed to the surface as to appear like scales.

Self-branching Shoots arising from every node. Ivies with this characteristic are sometimes termed ramulose or belonging to the ramosa group.

Sessile Not stalked; without a petiole.

Sinus The gap or division between any two lobes. A narrow sinus indicates a deep cleft with the lobes near to one another, a shallow sinus implies a broad gap with lobes widely separated.

Species Plants within a genus that have natural common characteristics that define them from other species within that genus.

Sport An alternative name for mutation.

Stellate hairs Star-like hairs arising from epidermal cells and having from 3 to 5 comparatively long rays.

Sub-species (abb **ssp.**) Usually used to define a distinct geographic race or variation within a species.

Synonym (abb **Syn**) A superseded name.

Trails Lengthened stems.

Trichome Technical term for scale and stellate hairs.

Truncate Cut across, almost straight.

Varietas Correctly written as **var..** A variation or form of a species found in the wild. Both the botanical varietas and the term cultivar is sometimes incorrectly referred to as 'variety'.

Vestigial Little more than a trace of what is normally present.

Vining Describing a plant whose shoots elongate to form long 'vines' usually with few branching shoots.

INDEX OF IVIES

Ivies can be roughly divided into the 12 types shown below (and as indicated in the following index). In order to identify an unknown clone, carefully examine average leaves from an average shoot to assess the type into which the unknown fits. If the descriptions of clones of that type are then consulted, a process of elimination should produce the answer.

A   Large (10–20cm, 4–8in) leaved, green
B   Large leaved variegated
C   Medium (5–10cm, 2–4in) leaved, green
D   Medium leaved variegated
E   Small (2–5cm, ¾–2in) green
F   Small leaved variegated
G   'Bird's foot' types, green
H   Bird's foot' types, variegated
J   Leaves markedly curled, crested or waved, green
K   Leaves markedly curled, crested or waved, variegated
L   Leaves unusually divided – linear or very small leaved
M   Naturally non-climbing, erect ivies

Ivy is a versatile plant but some kinds are better for certain purposes than others. A few that can be specially recommended are marked with the following numbers.

1   Green coverage for walls and buildings
2   Variegated coverage for walls and buildings
3   Green ground cover for large areas
4   Variegated ground cover for large areas
5   Green ground cover for small areas
6   Variegated ground cover for small areas
7   Green ground cover for rock gardens & small bulbs
8   Green house-plant kinds
9   Variegated house-plant kinds
10   Green & variegated for hanging baskets
11   Green & variegated for topiary work

WHERE TO SEE IVIES

UNITED KINGDOM

The premier National Collection is at Erddig, a National Trust property near Wrexham, Clwyd. North-facing walls carry many vining-type ivies. The recently formed National Collection at Fibrex Nurseries Ltd, Pebworth, near Stratford-upon-Avon, is rich in house-plant types and also boasts some interesting standard grown ivies. The National Collection at Kirkley Hall, Ponteland, Newcastle-upon-Tyne, the home of the Northumberland College of Agriculture, comprises material planted out in the College grounds.

Many gardens of stately homes and of National Trust properties contain ivies as part of their plantings as do most botanic gardens. Kew has the Ivy Wall established by the then Curator, George Nicholson in the 1920s; this carries some interesting mature specimens, supplementing the various plantings in the garden. Oxford Botanic Garden has a small interesting collection, noteworthy for the presence of the ivy parasite *Orobanche hederae*. Cambridge Botanic Garden has amongst its ivies probably the oldest specimen of *H. pastuchovii* in Britain. The work undertaken on ivies by Dr McAllister at the Liverpool University Botanic Garden at Ness on the South Wirral has resulted in a very complete collection of ivy species, grown mostly upon trees. The RHS Garden at Wisley was the scene of the 1979/80 Ivy Trial, much of the resulting material was planted in the garden.

UNITED STATES OF AMERICA

The AIS provides contact numbers for the following collections, some of which may be viewed by appointment only.

California: Mendocino Coast Botanical Gardens. 18220 North Highway One, Fort Bragg, California 95437.

Florida: Sugar Mill Botanic Gardens, 950 Old Sugar Mill Road, Port Orange, Florida 32124.

Maryland: Brookside Gardens, 1500 Glenallan Avenue, Wheaton, Maryland 20902.

Illinois: Chicago Botanic Gardens Hardiness Trials, PO Box 400, Lake Cook Road, Glencoe, Illinois 60022.

Ohio: American Ivy Society Hardiness Trials, C/o Gillia & Don Hawke, 205 Summit Street, Lebanon, Ohio 45036.

Tennessee: University of Tennessee, Dept of Ornamental Horticulture, Display Collection and Hardiness Trials, PO Box 1071, Knoxville, Tennessee 37901.

Virginia: Lewis Ginter Botanical Garden Display Collection, 1800 Lakeside Avenue, Richmond, Virginia 23228 and River Farm, Headquarters of the American Horticulture Society, Ivy Display Collection, 7931 East Boulevard Drive, Alexandria, Virginia 22308.

WHERE TO BUY IVIES

UNITED KINGDOM

Most garden centres and nurseries carry the more common kinds but for those of particular interest one has to turn to the specialist ivy nurseries, in alphabetical order these are:

Fibrex Nurseries Ltd, Honeybourne Rd, Pebworth, Nr Stratford-upon-Avon, CV37 8XT. (For catalogue, enclose three first-class stamps.)

Green's Leaves (Paul Green), Leba Orchard, Lea Baily, Nr Ross-on-Wye, Herefordshire HR9 5TY. (For catalogue enclose two second-class stamps; minimum order £10.)

Whitehouse Ivies, previously at Fordham near Colchester now incorporated as a separate entity within the Eggesford Gardens Group, Eggesford, Chumleigh, Devon EX18 7QU. (Full descriptive catalogue £1, refunded against purchase.)

UNITED STATES OF AMERICA

Ivies exported to the UK or Europe have to carry a USA Federal Plant Health Certificate obtainable by the exporting nursery. Of the many ivy nurseries in the USA the following are prominent:

Hedera Etc, PO Box 461, Lionville, Pennsylvania 19353-0461. (A very extensive list published.)

Ivies of the World, PO Box 408, Weirsdale, Florida 32195.

Merry Gardens, PO Box 595, Mechanic St, Camden, Maine 04843.

Samia Rose Topiary, PO Box 23–1208, Encinitas, California 92023-1208

IVY SOCIETIES

Anyone with more than a casual interest in ivies should join the British Ivy Society. The Society produces a very readable and informative Journal three times a year, holds various ivy 'events' and is a ready source of information on how and where to purchase unusual ivies. It also has a useful and very economic arrangement whereby for an addition to the subscription members are enabled to receive the American Ivy Society Journal and Newsletter which are always rich in information. The Journal of the German Ivy Society contains information based very much on the collection at the Neuburg Monastery. Membership secretaries are:

British Ivy Society: Beryl Hutchin, 14 Holly Grove, Huyton, Merseyside, L36 4JA.

American Ivy Society: Daphne Pfaff, PO Box 2123, Naples, Florida FL 34106-2123

German Ivy Society: Ines Gretzchel, Deutsche Efeu-Gesellschaft, Weg 7, 16278 Welsow.

BIBLIOGRAPHY

American Ivy Society, *Preliminary Check-list of Cultivated Hedera* 1975.

American Ivy Society, Journals 1975–95.

Bates, Alfred, *The Elusive Ivy* Series of Articles in the American National Horticultural Magazine 1932–42.

Bean, W J, *Trees & Shrubs Hardy in the British Isles* 1st Ed 1914, 8th revised Ed 1973, Supplement 1988.

Bell, Leonnie, *The Beauty of Hardy Ivy* Morris Arboretum Bulletin Sept 1968.

British Ivy Society, Journals 1980–95.

Carrière, E A, *Une Importante Collection de Lierres* Revue Horticole 1890.

Cooper, J I, & Sweet, J B, *The Detection of Viruses with Nematode Vectors in Six Woody Hosts* Forestry 49 1976.

De Smet, P A G M, *Hedera Helix* in *Adverse Effects of Herbal Drugs*, Vol 2, Springer-Verlag, Heidelberg Germany 1993.

Fortgens, G, & Laar, H J van de, Hedera (winterharde bodembedekkers) Dendroflora 26:43–66 1989.

Graf, A B, *Exotica – Pictorial Cyclopedia of Exotic Plants* 1963.

Heieck, Ingobert, *Das Efeusortiment der Gebr Stauss* 1977 (privately printed); *Hedera Sorten* 1980.

Hibberd, Shirley, *Floral World* Vol 7, 1864; *The Ivy* 1872.

Jenny, Mathias, Jahrbuch Botanischer Garten Zurich 1964.

Koch, K, *Dendrologie*, Erlangen 1869; *Gartnerei und Pflanzenkunde* 1870.

Krüssman, G, *Handbuch der Laubgeholze* Bd II, 1977.

Laar, Harry van de, *Het Hedera helix Sortiment in de Bloemisterij*, Vakbladd voor de Bloemisterij May 1965.

Lawrence, G H M, *The Cultivated Ivies* Morris Arboretum Bulletin, Vol 7, No 2, 1956; & Schulze, A E, *The Cultivated Hederas* Gentes Herbarum, VI Fasc iii. The Bailey Hortorium of New York State College of Agriculture 1942.

McAllister, H, *Canary and Algerian Ivies* The Plantsman 1988.

Nannenga-Bremekamp, N E, *Notes on Hedera Species, Varieties and Cultivars Grown in the Netherlands* Misc Paper No 6, Landbouwhogeschool, Wageningen, Netherlands 1970.

Paul, William, *The Ivy* The Gardener's Chronicle & Agricultural Gazette 1867.

Petzold & Kirchner, *Arboretum Muscaviense* Gotha 1864.

Pierot, Suzanne Warner, *The Ivy Book* Macmillan 1974; 2nd ed Willow, New York 1995.

Rehder, Alfred, *Manual of Cultivated Trees and Shrubs* 1927.

Rose, Peter Q, *Ivies* 1981.

Rutherford, A, McAllister, H, & Mill, R, *New Ivies from the Mediterranean Area* The Plantsman 1993.

Seeman, Berthold, *Revision of the Natural Order Hederaceae* Journal of Botany 1864.

Shippy, Bess L, The Flower Grower, Articles 1950, 1951, 1955.

Simmons & Dimbleby, *The Possible Role of Ivy (Hedera helix) in the Mesolithic Economy of Eastern Europe* Journal of Archeological Science I, 1974.

Sowerby, *English Botany* 1804.

Sprenger, *Gartenwelt* VII, 1903.

Tobler, F, *Die Gattung Hedera* Jena, 1912; *Die Gartenformen der Gattung Hedera* Mitteilungen der Deutschen Dendrologischen 1927.

Weston, R, *Universal Botanist and Nurseryman* 1770.

GENERAL INDEX

PICTURE ACKNOWLEDGEMENTS

Karl Adamson 18-19, 26, 32-3, 46-7, 60-1, 74-5, 88-9, 102-3, 116-17, 130-31, 144-5; Victoria Gordon-Friis 6; Peter Rose 2, 3, 20, 21, 29, 48, 136, 138, 139, 148; Justyn Willsmore 1, 8, 10, 14, 16, 24, 31, 35, 42, 50, 51, 53, 56, 57, 58, 63, 66, 69, 71, 73, 76, 80, 82, 84, 86, 87, 91, 92, 93, 99, 106, 107, 112, 114, 120, 124, 133, 137, 140, 150, 151

The publishers would like to thank Fibrex Nurseries Ltd for their kind cooperation in supplying plant material for studio photography and the Benaki Museum, Athens, for permission to reproduce the photograph of the gold wreath which appears on page 12.